THE
UNINVITED

THE
UNINVITED
HOW I CRASHED MY WAY INTO FINDING MYSELF

CRAIG SCHMELL

AND ELLIS HENICAN

A POST HILL PRESS BOOK

The Uninvited:
How I Crashed My Way into Finding Myself
© 2017 by Craig Schmell
All Rights Reserved

ISBN: 978-1-68261-411-2
ISBN (eBook): 978-1-68261-412-9

Cover art by Ryan Truso
Interior Design and Composition by Greg Johnson/Textbook Perfect

Post Hill Press
New York • Nashville
posthillpress.com

Published in the United States of America

For my daughters Carly and Brittany,
who make it all worthwhile.

For Arthur Knauert,
the wisest and humblest man I have ever known.

CONTENTS

ACKNOWLEDGMENTS

I take full responsibility for the adventures and misadventures described here, the ones I am proud of and the ones I look back on in utter disbelief. A few fall into both categories. But as I scoured vivid memories and faced ancient demons on the road to writing this book, I was constantly reminded how blessed I am—blessed by opportunity, blessed by my amazing family and friends, and blessed by a higher power I finally came to discover in my life. This story couldn't be told, just as it couldn't have been lived, without loads of kindness and support along the way.

My parents, Herbert and Gloria Schmell, guided me with unwavering love and forbearance. They also found the courage to stand up to me when I needed it most. I hate to think where I'd have ended up if they hadn't finally said no to me. My brothers, Douglas and Eric, never judged me, never gave up on me and were there for me in bad times and in good.

Lynda Schmell, the mother of my beautiful daughters, showed me the meaning of kindness, sensitivity, and love. She displayed patience and grace that I did not deserve. She will always have a special place in my heart. My daughters, Brittany and Carly, inherited all my good characteristics and none of my bad. They bring me down to earth and hold me accountable every day. I love them more than I can ever love myself.

Some world-class friends—you know who you are—played a vital role in this journey. They shared my wonder and excitement. They saw the good in me. They occasionally pulled me back from the edge. It was Jennifer Hicks who, in the darkness, showed me the light and Laura Harrison who taught me about forgiveness and helped me to focus on a crucial question: "What is in the best interest of my children?"

Writing this book turned out to be an adventure in itself, which is why I needed such a top-notch team, enablers of the very best kind: Anthony Ziccardi, Michael Wilson, Billie Brownell, and Jon Ford at Post Hill Press; Peter McGuigan, Richie Kern and Claire Harris at Foundry Literary + Media, and media pros Leslie Sloane, Brian Muench, and Joanne Stevens. Big thanks to my cousins Lynne White and Joel Schnell for a key introduction. A special thank you to my co-author, Ellis Henican, who believed in the project from the beginning and somehow managed to pull out of me the book I always wanted to write. He says he'd be nothing without his own talented crew, James Gregorio, Janis Spidle, and Roberta Teer.

One of the great joys of sharing my story is the chance to spread the teachings of Dr. K. He helped me. He helped many others. He was able to articulate with utter clarity what is most important in life—then lay out a sober path for getting there. Years after his death, he is still saving lives. The many brave and generous souls in the recovery community—always open, always available, always here—powerfully reinforced what I learned from Dr. K. "Go easy," Bobby O constantly reminds me, and I try to. I pass it on to others. They pass it on to others still.

INTRODUCTION
RADIO CITY RECON

"I'm sorry to bother you, sir," I said to the guard outside Radio City Music Hall, as politely as I knew how. "I had to run out to my car for a minute. My asthma's killing me tonight."

Every part of that was a lie, but I had proof. In my left hand, I held up an orange, plastic inhaler like the ones I had to use when I was a kid.

"I'm working inside," I said. "I need to get back in."

The guard was large and menacing-looking. He was stationed, arms crossed, directly in front of a massive metal door. He had a black police radio, a square badge, and a scowl that seemed to say, "How can I *not* help you?"

My technique that night was a simple one—the respectful greeting, the handy inhaler, the phony claim to be working the event. But I knew from past experience: with the right self-assuredness and an appropriate prop, I could talk my way into almost anywhere. That plastic inhaler hadn't failed me yet.

The guard didn't utter a syllable. He didn't demand an ID. He didn't even ask for my name. He just stepped aside, pulled open the massive door, and motioned me inside.

||||||||||||||||

was one thing I had a talent for, it was bullshitting my way into places I didn't belong. I had a rule, a credo, a guiding principle that I had already road-tested at professional sports stadiums, major concert venues, even at the Kremlin in Moscow. *It's not who you are that matters. It's who they think you are.* That Radio City security guard *thought* I belonged inside.

The evening had begun like so many others before it, on the terrace of my high-rise, one-bedroom apartment, thirty-five floors above Manhattan's East Thirty-Ninth Street, with a few spirited rounds of a game we called bong golf. My friends Barry Zuckerman and Keith Wiley—Barry from childhood, Keith from college—were with me that night, as they so often were. Barry and Keith were rising young brokers in New York's commercial real-estate industry, leasing office space and bringing home some fairly sizable commissions. I was two years out of law school and pretty much just killing time. I had failed the bar exam—twice already. I wasn't working, I had no prospects, and I didn't give a crap. The three of us were fueling up for another night in the bars and clubs. The nighttime was my time to shine.

My terrace had wide-open, north-facing views. The city twinkled for miles below us—the United Nations, Midtown Manhattan, and the Upper East Side. The large, dark rectangle up and to the left was Central Park. But as we stood together on the terrace, Barry, Keith, and I hardly noticed the view. All our attention was transfixed on the game.

The concrete floor of the terrace was covered with green, indoor-outdoor carpet, a passable substitute for a putting green. I'd taken the grate off the drain in the corner, uncovering a perfectly sized hole. I had an entry-level Cleveland putter and three clean Titleist balls. The rules for bong golf came from H-O-R-S-E in basketball: If you made the putt, the other guy had to match it. If he missed, he had to step into the living room and take a hit off the water pipe. I missed an easy ten-footer that Barry had made. It wasn't the first putt I had missed.

As I went inside for my penalty hit, the channel 7 *Eyewitness News* was on. A skinny, blonde reporter was doing a live shot on busy Sixth Avenue in front of Radio City Music Hall. Talking excitedly to the camera, she said that the following night the Grammy Awards were coming to New York. The stars were inside at that moment, she said, gathered for sound checks and a final rehearsal.

From what I was hearing in the news report, it was going to be an awesome lineup: Billy Joel, Bruce Springsteen, Stevie Wonder, Michael Jackson, Whitney Houston, U2—so many stars I couldn't remember them all, maybe the greatest collection of musical talent ever assembled together on a single stage. "It's the thirtieth anniversary of the Grammys and the first time in six years the show is back in New York City," the reporter said. "Tomorrow night is going to be one for the ages."

By the time I got back out to the terrace, Barry and Keith were lining up fresh putts. But I had no interest in finishing the game. "We gotta go to the Grammys," I said. "It's tomorrow night at Radio City. No way I'm missing that."

Barry and Keith hardly looked up from the green carpet. They'd heard me talk like this before. They'd been around for plenty of my grandiose schemes. My friends always started out skeptical, but they had learned not to sell me short when I got an idea in my head. I had an uncanny ability for this sort of thing. Like the old friends they were, Barry and Keith were often shaking their heads at some of the places I had dragged them into. But the Grammys—even I knew that would be a reach. If I could pull this one off, it would be my greatest incursion yet. I just needed a plan.

I told the boys to sit tight—I was heading out, but I'd be back in an hour or so. "I need to scope out the situation for tomorrow," I said. "Let me see what we're dealing with."

|||||||||||||||||

Once past the guard and inside Radio City's art deco lobby, I was relieved to hear that the rehearsals were still underway. Whitney Houston's voice was the first one that I heard. Backed by the Grammy house band, she was belting out the chorus to a song I immediately recognized:

Oh, I wanna dance with somebody.
I wanna feeeel the heeeat with somebody.
Yeah! Wanna daaance with somebody,
With somebody who loves me.

Whitney was on fire. But much as I wanted to, I couldn't risk just standing there and listening to her. I knew I had to keep moving or someone would march over to me and demand to see my credentials or start asking who I was. I didn't want my exit to be in handcuffs.

I made my way quickly into the auditorium as Whitney was just leaving the stage. Musicians, sound people, roadies, and assorted other minions were milling around with headsets, clipboards, and various electronic gear. All these people seemed busy with whatever it was they were doing. They didn't seem to know each other or want to know me. Still, I didn't linger in the auditorium either. I made my way back out to the lobby and down a set of stairs to the lower level of the music hall. To stay invisible, I knew I had to keep moving until I could find what I was looking for.

But what was that? I wasn't sure. Something. A prop. A program. A ticket stub. Maybe I could yank a backstage pass off someone's bag. Anything that would help me scam my way back inside the following night, when the real show was happening and security would be really tight. I didn't know yet, but I would know what I was looking for when I saw it. I usually did.

The lower level of Radio City was, if anything, even busier than the main floor. There was a mob of assistants, publicists, stylists, technicians, carpenters, and others. They all seemed frantic, though it was hard to say exactly what they were doing down there. I was just reminded: musical superstars do not travel alone.

As I strolled around, trying to look like I belonged there, something on the floor caught my eye. It was a blue-and-white business card.

I leaned over and picked it up.

"MICHAEL HUDDLE, HAIR DESIGNER," the card read. "Features, TV, & Theatre."

My guess? Michael Huddle was prepping some of the artists for the show.

I still didn't have a plan. But I thought I might have found another prize on my treasure hunt. I walked up to an empty table as if I had business there. There was nothing on the table except for a busted dog-tag chain. It had no clip at the bottom. I grabbed the broken chain.

This could come in handy, I thought.

Really, I was just grabbing anything I could find. And if nothing came of it, I could always tell Barry and Keith, "Hey, I got into the rehearsals for the Grammys. Look at these."

I wandered for another twenty minutes. Down toward the stage and back to the other side. Nobody paid attention to me. As long as they didn't look too closely, I could be anybody. A caterer. A TV producer. An agent for one of the talent.

Stay cool, I said to myself.

Keep focused.

Don't give anyone a reason to approach.

I found an area where the stars had their dressing rooms. I certainly had no business being there. Billy Joel. Lou Reed. Bono. Whitney Houston's door was open, so I could see no one was inside.

On a table just to the left of the door was a giant bouquet of flowers and a card that read, "Whitney Houston: Welcome to Radio City Music Hall. We are proud to have the 1988 Grammy Awards here and proud to have you with us as part of the 1988 Grammys. Sincerely, James A. McManus, President and Chief Executive Officer."

I snatched the card, left the dressing room area, and returned to the auditorium, where Michael Jackson and his dancers were finishing their rehearsal. I was sorry to have missed that, but I had no time to linger. That's when I saw a man in an ill-fitting black blazer who seemed to be eyeing me suspiciously. Black Blazer Guy was definitely looking at me. Was he about to come over and confront me with some pointed questions? If he did, what would I say? I tried to look busy as I plotted where I should go next. This cat-burglar business is far more nerve-wracking than it looks. Right then, I heard a woman speaking to a man in jeans and a jeans jacket: "Go downstairs to the production area and find out about the hotel," she said.

I hadn't been to the production area yet. I wasn't even sure what the production area was, but it sounded like the next safe harbor to me. Maintaining a careful distance, I escaped the scrutiny of Black Blazer Guy and followed Blue Jeans Jacket underneath the stage, where a set of stairs went even further down beneath the theater. The stairs led to a large, open room with several folding tables identified with makeshift, balsa wood signs: "HOTELS," "LIMOUSINES," "AFTER PARTY," and "TICKET RESERVATIONS." Over in the corner was a table with a sign that said: "VIP PASSES."

Now, *that* was promising!

Finally, the cover story I was looking for began forming in my mind.

I took a deep breath and composed myself. I pulled the busted chain out of my pocket and put it around my neck. I tried to look concerned. With the hairdresser's business card in my hand, I walked up to the woman at the VIP PASSES table.

"Hi, how are you?" I said to her with just a hint of false panic in my voice.

"Fine," she said noncommittally.

"Listen," I continued. "I am so sorry to bother you." I spoke a little breathlessly, like I was in a hurry and important people might be waiting for me. "I work with Michael Huddle Hairdressers," I said, holding out the business card. "My chain must have broken. Somehow, my VIP pass slipped off. They're giving me a hard time upstairs. I've got so much to do. Please, could you do me a favor and just give me another pass?"

She looked at me, wanting to believe me but not knowing whether she could. I'm sure she wasn't supposed to hand out VIP passes to any idiot who happened to walk up with a broken chain.

She asked me, "What's your name?"

I wasn't sure how to answer. I hadn't thought about that. *Do I give her my real name? Should I tell her that I am Michael Huddle? That* second approach seemed too dangerous.

"Craig Schmell," I said, pulling my driver's license out of my wallet.

She didn't check some master list or summon a supervisor or phone upstairs. She was feeling my pain.

"Okay, Craig," she said. "Listen. This is totally against the rules. So when you find your pass, you have to bring this back to me."

"Absolutely," I assured her.

And suddenly, like magic, I had the keys to the kingdom in my hand, a light-blue, laminated plastic badge that said, "VIP Pass 2238, National Academy of Recording Arts and Sciences, Pierre Cossette Productions, Inc. CBS, 1988. All Access Staff."

All Access Staff.

Three of the most magical words I knew.

"Thank you," I said as resolutely as I could.

Then, I turned and got the hell out of there—up the stairs, into the lobby, and out a side door onto Fiftieth Street, then into a taxi and back to my apartment on East Thirty-Ninth Street, where Barry and Keith were off the green-carpet terrace now and slouching on the couch in my living room.

1

CENTER STAGE

That was me back then.

From my late teens through my late twenties, especially for half a dozen breakneck years in the late 1980s and early 1990s, I took a breathless joyride through the world of glamour, power, and fame. I pulled off a series of high-profile stunts that I don't believe anyone had ever achieved before or will ever match again. I would fortify myself with marijuana and alcohol, then head off in search of spectacular adventures that depended on nothing so much as my confidence, my cunning, and my utter willingness to stand in front of a perfectly nice person and flat-out lie. Yes, I did that and so much more. I was a semi-normal, fucked-up guy, just like a lot of semi-normal, fucked-up guys, except that I had a genius-level talent for inserting myself into places I most certainly did not belong.

Why did I choose to define myself this way? Well, that would take years—and more than a little prodding from a brilliant Manhattan psychiatrist—for me to unwind. Fully grasping that would be my biggest achievement of all. Just know for now that it all got started, like so many reckless adventures do, with an active mind, an excessive need for attention, and a bunch of people around me who were willing to tolerate far too much of my shit. But, oh, what a ride it was!

Have you ever used a bathroom in a random hotel lobby or slipped into a gallery opening just for the Chardonnay and hors d'oeuvres? Then you know what I'm talking about. I just took that concept to its absurd conclusion and rode it into the stratosphere.

That's where my ambitions led me. Soon enough, I wasn't only prancing behind the velvet ropes of flashy New York nightclubs or acting like somebody else's stadium box seats were mine. I was driving in the president's motorcade, high-fiving in the locker room with professional championship teams, celebrating Midnight Mass in Rome with the pope, and passing one lovely summer evening on the deck of Donald Trump's yacht.

This was pre-9/11, when America wasn't yet on total lockdown, when a wink and smile went a whole lot further than they ever could today. The social media age was just dawning. Old notions of fame and celebrity were collapsing around us, and the new ones hadn't yet taken hold. Facebook wasn't born yet. Neither was Twitter or Snapchat or Instagram. It was before selfies and paparazzi mobs. It was before TMZ and cell-phone cameras democratized the world of fame. Back then, there was a wall—it might as well have been a moat of hungry alligators—protecting the glitterati from the hoi polloi. You were on one side or the other—with the famous or with the nobodies—and almost no one crossed to the other side. Stars didn't tweet about what they ate for breakfast. No one became a YouTube sensation or a reality TV star because there was no YouTube and no reality TV. There were no Kardashians. You had to actually do something before you got to be famous, and that didn't include making a sex tape or getting butt implants—at least not only that. Anyway, that's what everyone believed back then, and they all acted accordingly.

Except for me.

I didn't see why the world had to be divided that way. Why should just a few beautiful people have all the fun? So I scaled that wall and spent my twenties romping on the other side with some of the best-known people on earth. I beat a path that no one had ever beaten, years before all this became utterly routine. I viewed these exotic creatures in their natural habitat and got many of them to open up to me. If you saw me then, you'd have said, "That guy's definitely famous," even if you weren't quite sure how. In fact, I was a nobody, just an upper-middle-class kid from the New York suburbs who refused to accept the usual boundaries, a natural confidence man whose own personal demons happened to coincide perfectly with the unique demands of the times.

I wasn't an overnight sensation. Far from it. My skills and my obsessions blossomed gradually, over the course of several years. But it turned out that some giant holes in my upbringing made me uniquely suited to this particular brand of oversized lies. I really was a savant at talking my way, scheming my way, ballsing my way into places I had no business being at all.

I wasn't a stalker or a deluded individual. I had no interest in invading anyone's privacy or ripping anyone off. I wasn't a publicist, a stylist, a manager, an agent, or some other industry professional. I had no ulterior motives beyond feeding my own insatiable ego and being where the action was. I was just a guy with some charm and moxie who liked to convince people that he was something that he wasn't and thereby hoped to build himself up. And damned if it didn't consume me!

If the quest for fame and attention is a near-universal affliction now—and we all know it is—so help me God, I was Patient Zero.

But I'm already getting ahead of myself. We'll get to that whole breathless ride. For now, let me just say that for much of a decade before it all crashed, I was there, wherever there was, just as a whole new world was being born. I was the rock-and-roll Forrest Gump. I was the Leonard Zelig of the New Media Age. I was *Catch Me If You Can* with celebrities instead of nurses and stewardesses. How I pulled this off will blow your fuckin' mind.

And the one who paid the price for it all was me.

||||||||||||||||||

The morning of the Grammy show, I took the precious all-access VIP pass to a quick-copy place near Grand Central Terminal and made half a dozen duplicates, which I offered to various of my friends.

"You want to go to the Grammys tonight?" I asked nonchalantly.

I got almost no takers. It wasn't that my friends hated music or that they all had plans that night. It was more that they didn't believe I could possibly have what I said I had—a handful of counterfeit all-access passes to one of the greatest music shows of all time—or that this latest scam of mine could possibly ever work. Even usually game Keith said, "No thanks." Only Barry agreed to come with me.

And so on that clear March evening, we both put on tuxedos and taxied to Radio City Music Hall in time to catch the red-carpet arrivals. But I didn't pay much attention to that. My first order of business: the five extra passes in my pocket, which I sold on the sidewalk to strangers for $100 each. The passes looked real enough to them. Then, Barry and I headed inside.

With our special passes, we really did have the run of the place. Thankfully, I remembered to bring a small camera. No smartphones yet. I got my picture taken with Billy Joel and Christie Brinkley, Herbie Hancock, Frank and Kathie Lee Gifford, even with Liza Minnelli, who seemed much nicer than gossip writers had been claiming and hardly crazy at all. None of these people had any idea who I was. But when I walked up in my tuxedo and asked politely, "Hey, Paul Simon, is it okay if I get a quick photo?" he and the others all said, "Sure." I talked Irish football with Bono and The Edge. Lou Reed was just as cool as I'd imagined. The legendary Paul Simon was gentle and nice, but a lot shorter than I'd imagined he'd be, and his hair looked funny. I made sure not to linger too long with any one celebrity. I didn't want to be a pest. I never spoke to Michael Huddle or even laid eyes on him.

"Kinda cool, huh?" I said to Barry.

He could hardly speak he was so excited to be there.

As the show was set to begin, Barry and I lined up with the fillers. The fillers were men and women in formal attire whose job it was to stand off to the side and be dispatched to any open seat. Whenever a seat was empty, a filler would rush over during a commercial break and sit down. The producers of the show didn't want any empty seats on the worldwide telecast.

No one said anything to either of us when Barry and I got in line.

We didn't have to stand for long. When the show began, I was dispatched to fill a seat in the third row, right behind an older man I recognized immediately as Atlantic Records founder Ahmet Ertegun. There I was, in a seat that wasn't for sale at any price, soaking up everything. Whitney was singing "I Wanna Dance with Somebody," now in full costume. With all the choreography, her performance was even more stunning than during the rehearsal. Billy Joel sang "New York State of Mind" with David Sanborn on a wailing sax. Los Lobos performed "La Bamba." A waifish Suzanne Vega sang "Luka." Terence Trent D'Arby let loose a plaintive "If You Let Me Stay." U2 won Album of the Year for *The Joshua Tree*. Paul Simon won Record of the Year for *Graceland*. Rock-'n'-roll legend Little Richard had the audience in stiches as he complained that co-presenter Buster Poindexter had stolen his pompadour.

"Everything I get, they take it from me," the flamboyant early rocker grumbled as the audience roared.

Lou Reed rasped his way through "Take a Walk on the Wild Side." I'd been hearing that song since I was in high school. I kept needing to remind myself that all this was real. I was at the Grammy Awards! In the third row! Watching Lou Reed perform live! When jazzman George Benson did his latest hit, "On Broadway," I felt like I could almost reach out and touch his hollow-body guitar. That's how close I was.

But the performance that really dazzled was Michael Jackson's. With a sensual resolve and an almost urgent pleading, he performed a breathtaking nine-minute rendition of "The Way You Make Me Feel/ Man in the Mirror" from his new album *Bad*. And then the King of Pop, right at the top of his game, proceeded not to win a single award.

As the evening wore on, I kept glancing over at Michael, who was sitting in the front row, two rows in front of me. During a commercial, I approached him and Stevie Wonder for their autographs. Stevie didn't answer, but Michael obliged. With each new category Michael didn't win, he looked more ashen faced as the winners were called up to the podium. The last time he'd come to the Grammys with a hit album, four years earlier with *Thriller*, he'd gone home with eight statuettes. Now, the most he could muster was a small smile when Smokey Robinson, one of his early heroes, beat him for Best R&B Song.

I watched it all from up close and loved every second of it. As bad as I felt for Michael Jackson, I still thought to myself: *Could this possibly get any better?*

It did.

During the last commercial break of the night, master of ceremonies Billy Crystal made an announcement. "Will all the stars come on stage for a grand finale," he said. The show was going to end with a special thirtieth-anniversary tribute to Dion and the Belmonts, the Bronx-based doo-wop pioneers, and three generations of music stars were going to join in. The performances had been spectacular. The TV camera booms were swinging frantically. No one seemed ready to call it a night.

My first thought was, *What a nice gesture.*

My second thought was, *What the fuck! Why not me?* I knew this was my moment to pounce.

I climbed out of my seat and followed the star-studded wave to the front. I didn't ask anyone's permission. I didn't wait to be told, "No." I just made my way forward and up the stairs.

The stars assembled behind the curtain. When the curtain lifted, Dion launched into the corny opening of "Runaround Sue" ("Here's my story, it's sad but true . . ."), and everyone moved toward the front of the Radio City stage to sing along. I was in the back of the pack next to Michael and Whitney, who were giggling with each other. They didn't seem to care where they stood. Despite their incredible voices, they were barely singing, I noticed.

I could hardly believe I was on stage at the Grammys, but I didn't like standing so far back. Slowly, I snaked my way forward, past a pale Roy Orbison, past Patrick Swayze (fresh off the enormous hit film *Dirty Dancing*), past the slouching Lou Reed. All of them were singing, and so was I. No one looked at me funny, though they certainly had no idea who I was. Buster Poindexter and Gloria Estefan were farther forward. I weaved my way past them too, 'til I was right up front with Dion's doo-wop backup singers.

And there I was, standing at center stage. Before a packed house and a worldwide television audience.

One of the backup singers leaned over and handed me a microphone. I moved my mouth closer and sang with everything I had. I couldn't believe it: my voice was coming out of the monitors. Right then, amid all that drama and excitement, a simple thought occurred to me:

Holy shit!

I am center stage at the Grammys!

The whole world is watching!

I am surrounded by this one-night-only music pantheon, broadcast live around the world and saved for posterity on videotape—and they were all singing backup for me!

I'd have proof forever and bragging rights!

For all I know, Stevie Wonder may still be wondering whose wobbly baritone kept throwing the harmonies off. But no one complained, then or later. Who cared if I was a total nobody or I wasn't invited or I couldn't carry a tune? The whole world was watching, and I was in the middle of everything.

Nothing could stop me now.

2

SHOWING UP

No one pops out of the womb fully formed, least of all someone as revved and needy as me. Whatever my God-given strengths and weaknesses, I'm also an undeniable product of geography, time, culture, and blood. It's hard to imagine my turning out like this if I didn't come of age in New York in the 1970s and 1980s, just as the modern media age was dawning and the world around me was careening into turmoil. I was also a Schmell. That last detail may not mean much to some people, but it was everything to us.

Both my parents were born in New York City to parents who fled Poland in the scary years after World War I. All four of my grandparents made the long trip to America for the same reason millions of other immigrants had. They wanted better lives for themselves and their families—and things back home were horribly bleak. They were the dreamers of a century ago, ready to take a giant leap of faith on a strange and distant land. And they were prepared to do damn near anything necessary to succeed in their newly adopted home.

The inscription on the Statue of Liberty in New York Harbor declares: "Give me your tired, your poor, your huddled masses

yearning to breathe free, the wretched refuse of your teeming shore."
My ancestors figured those beautiful words were calling out to them.

"Let's go," they answered.

Actually, what they said was *"lomir geyn,"* the rough Yiddish
equivalent. Everything sounded more urgent in Yiddish.

I grew up on endless stories about my family, especially my father's
side. I'm not sure that his people were any more interesting than my
mother's—but my father and his relatives certainly talked about themselves a whole lot more. I don't know much about my mother's family,
the Zinkins. I just know that many of them were wiped out in World
War I, the holocaust before the Holocaust. I never met my mother's
father. He died before I was born. My grandmother did remarry, to a
lovely man named Abe Brett who was always grandfatherly to me. But
it was the Schmells who really defined us.

The original family name was Trzmiel. They came from Ostrów
Mazowiecka, a *shtetl* in Łomża province, outside the Polish capital of
Warsaw at a time of grinding poverty and rising anti-Semitism. My
father's father, Samuel, eked out a living as a tailor and lived in constant
fear that he'd be drafted into the Polish army. He married my grandmother, Gussie Miller, in July 1913, and they had four children—my
aunts Fay and Dottie and my uncles Harry and Joseph. In 1921, when
my grandfather was thirty years old, he and my grandmother made a
bold decision: he would set sail for America. He'd find whatever work
he could and send for his wife and children as quickly as possible.
What my grandfather didn't know when he said goodbye—what
none of them did—was that Gussie was already pregnant with child
number five.

After the monthlong trip—first to Antwerp, Belgium, then steerage
class aboard the SS *Kroonland*—Samuel Trzmiel was processed
through the immigrant receiving center at Ellis Island on May 10,
1921. It was common back then for Ellis Island clerks to Americanize

the hard-to-pronounce names of new immigrants. Trzmiel became Schmell, still not all that New World to my modern ear. But that was suddenly my grandfather's new last name, and soon thereafter he landed on the teeming streets of Manhattan's Lower East Side. That part of the city wasn't remotely luxurious. But compared to where he had come from, Ludlow and Essex and Delancey Streets looked to my immigrant grandfather like the Champs-Élysées. He couldn't wait for his family to join him.

He rented a modest room at 47 Houston Street and looked for work as a tailor, but the heavily Jewish neighborhood already had plenty of those. Studying English at night, he spent long days selling pickles from a pushcart on First Avenue. The hours were brutal, and his hands were raw from pickle brine. On frigid days, he kept a fire in a metal bucket near his feet. But he earned enough to pay his bills, save some, and send a little extra home. On September 21, 1926, my grandfather—having sworn that he was neither an anarchist nor polygamist—became a naturalized citizen of the United States.

It took six years, but Gussie and the children finally made the trip from Poland, arriving in New York on March 1, 1927, aboard the SS *Pennland*. It was impossible to pick a single high point in the joyous family reunion, but nothing was any sweeter for my grandfather than meeting his six-year-old daughter, Blanche, for the very first time.

The Schmells never looked back. My grandfather moved everyone into a family-sized apartment—three bedrooms, a foldout couch in the living room, a small kitchen, and bath—on the ground floor of a six-story walk-up at 63 Avenue D between Fifth and Sixth Streets. Another son, Morris, was born a year later. My father, Herbert Schmell, the baby of seven children, came along six years after that, in 1934.

They were a loud, rambunctious family, in each other's business all the time. They soaked up all the promise that was mid-twentieth-century America. What they lacked in formal schooling and material goods, they made up for in family closeness and prodigious work habits. My grandmother, who was all of five feet tall and a hundred pounds, would trade shifts on the pickle cart with her husband, no matter how the weather was. Their Judaism was intertwined through everything. Every Thursday night, my grandmother washed the floors and cooked a Sabbath meal for Friday. On Saturday morning, they all walked together to a small synagogue on East Broadway. The girls were practical. The boys were wild. The older children looked after the younger ones. From all I've ever heard, not one of them ever felt deprived.

As the youngest in his immediate family, my father was the golden child. The whole family put an extra measure of hope in him. He was friendly, outgoing, and athletic. He wasn't much of a student. He often skipped classes at Seward Park High School. "In the front door and out the back," he liked to say. But he carried himself with an air of cockiness and passed his afternoons in one of several storefront social clubs. It was at one of those that he met the pretty neighborhood girl who would become my mother, Gloria Zinkin, when he was seventeen and she was fourteen.

None of the other Schmell children went past high school. But when it was time, my grandparents somehow scraped up the tuition for my father to attend New York University and then Brooklyn Law School. Not that my father held up his end of the bargain, which was to study hard and do well. For four years of college and one of law school, he rarely cracked a book, and he had the grades to show for it.

Then, he got an F on a second-year contracts exam. He also failed to turn in a couple of papers. My grandmother didn't seem too worried about the F. "You'll do better next time," she told him. But my father started to panic. He could see the cliff he was standing at the edge of. He thought he really might flunk out of law school and disappoint his family. Just as rattling, he hated the idea of getting a real job. He certainly didn't see his future standing beside a pickle cart. He and my mother were also starting to talk about getting married. All that taken together was enough to make him finally get a grip and buckle down. He graduated from law school. He and my mother stood beneath the *chuppah* at Clinton Plaza near the Williamsburg Bridge and exchanged traditional Jewish wedding vows, then joined with friends and family for a large Kosher reception with dancing, wine, and copious amounts of food.

My father took a job with a small, personal-injury firm and then a larger one, Kramer & Dillof, on the forty-third floor of the Woolworth Building. He represented people who'd been in car accidents, who slipped and fell on the sidewalk, or who'd been victims of medical malpractice. My father was a people person and a natural business magnet. Despite his slow start, this child of immigrants was on his way to what would become a lucrative legal career, one short generation after his parents followed their dream and landed on America's bountiful shore.

|||||||||||||||||

Thanks to the struggles of my parents and grandparents, I came into a world of relative privilege and affluence. The first of three boys, I was born November 25, 1961, just as my parents were moving from the Lower East Side and into a high-rise, three-bedroom, co-op apartment on Neptune Avenue in the Coney Island section of Brooklyn. Given where we started, that was big-time moving up. Eighteen months later, my younger brother, Douglas, was born. We were carrying on a great American tradition repeated millions of times before: The grandparents come with nothing. The parents establish themselves. The children accept all that progress as their unquestioned due.

My father was the one with a foot in two worlds, Old and New, tugged in both directions. Not wanting to disappoint his Jewish, immigrant parents, he took us to temple on Saturdays and sent his two sons to Yeshivah of Flatbush, a private religious school where we were taught in English and Hebrew. I hated that school. The days were longer and the curriculum tougher than in public school, where most of the other kids in the neighborhood went. I didn't understand why I had to learn two languages when I had no intention of speaking any more than one. But my father insisted, and off we went.

In 1968, when I was seven and Douglas was five and a half, our brother, Eric, was born. That year, we also moved from Brooklyn to a single-family house in the city's northern suburbs. By then, my father had opened his own law firm and was earning more money every year. Our new house was a two-story, five-bedroom Colonial on a cul-de-sac called Topaz Court, across the Hudson River and the Tappan Zee Bridge in the Rockland County hamlet of New City. It wasn't a huge house by today's standards, but it was large for back then, a giant leap from the apartment on Neptune Avenue. Each boy had his own bedroom, and we had a large backyard, perfect for having friends over and staying out of our parents' hair. For the first couple of years, Douglas and I were dragged to a nearby religious school, Hebrew Institute of Rockland County. It was just as strict as the other one.

By then, my brothers and I had developed distinct personalities. I was like my father—a naturally gregarious social animal. I had lots of friends. I was always talking and joking and playing sports. School was more a struggle for me. I'd rather be out playing. My mind was bouncing all over the place. Douglas was the brainier one. That's how he stood out. He read voraciously, had a lightning-quick mind, and, from the time he was little, he collected comic books. They were piled so high in his bedroom, my mother couldn't get in to clean. I can still hear her yelling, "Get these *facacta* comic books outta here!" Later, a psychologist friend told my mother, "Gloria, don't poo-poo the comic books. It's healthy for him to have a passion. He's reading. He loves the comic books. You should embrace that."

As Eric's personality developed, he had the benefits of being the much younger brother to Douglas and me. He got Douglas's intelligence and my social skills. Things just came easier to him. Since he was so much younger, he didn't have to compete with Douglas or me. He became the balanced Schmell child.

In his own unique way, my father presided over us all. He rose every morning before the sun came up to perform a prayer ritual that Jews call laying *tefillin*. The *tefillin* are two small, black leather straps inscribed with verses from the Torah. Like generations of Jewish men before him, my father wrapped the straps just so around his bicep, forearm, hand, and head, reciting blessings in Hebrew. Only then would he exercise and shower and make the hour-long drive to his law office in Lower Manhattan, arriving well before the rush-hour traffic at 7:00 a.m. He ate breakfast at his desk, read *The Wall Street Journal* and the *New York Law Journal*, then got busy with his med-mals and his slip-and-falls. Even as little boys, my brother and I sometimes rolled our eyes at his superhuman habits, as I swear our mother did.

My father didn't get embroiled in the psyches of his sons. He provided a comfortable lifestyle for the family. He seemed proud of us boys. But he certainly wasn't what I would call a hands-on dad. He came home at night exhausted. He had his dinner and went off to bed. He wasn't jumping into his sons' activities. He rarely came to my Little League games. Though we were all New York Mets fans, I can only recall one occasion when he took my brother Douglas and me to Shea Stadium to see a game. My mom was the one who came to school events. My father was busy with other things. I place no blame here. Some of this was just the times, I know. Some of it was also my father.

Still, he had an ironclad concept of how his family should present itself to the outside world. I'm sure this came from his own immigrant upbringing. But he considered it crucial that we always be seen as a happy, successful Jewish family. That the kids seem to be performing admirably. That he and my mother appear to get along. That none of us should want for anything. Any problems we might have—and even he understood that all families have some—well, why advertise the problems or even acknowledge them to ourselves?

The Golds were a family who lived near us on Topaz Court. They were friends of ours. One day, I overheard my mother telling my father that the Golds were seeing a family therapist. I didn't know what the issue was, but I was shocked.

Oh, my God! I thought. *The Golds are sick! They must be a really messed-up family.*

My family would never have done something like that. In our family, seeking professional help was a shameful, shameful thing. We just kept moving forward, presenting a successful front to the world.

We had a family credo. We might as well have printed it on matching T-shirts.

If it looks good, how broken can it be?

|||||||||||||||||

I never doubted that my parents loved my brothers and me, not for one minute. My father wasn't always patient with my mother. He had a volatile side and insisted that things revolve around him. He could be tough on my mother, yelling when he he thought she'd stepped out of line. My father was such a powerful presence, she never confronted him directly, though she had her own ways of getting under his skin. He could fly into rages when the boys frustrated him. Things were different then. If he could, I believe, he would take some of that back. But that was who my father was when we were little, a function of his upbringing, his temperament, and his times. He wanted to be something his whole family could be proud of, something no one else in his generation had managed to achieve. A professional. A financial success. A husband and a father who provided an upper-middle-class life for his family. I know he felt that pressure all the time.

Looking back now, I can see that my childhood was defined not just by my family history but also by a series of physical mishaps and risky behavior for which I paid a serious price. For such an athletic kid, I was truly injury-prone. Some of these were big things. Some of them might sound like small things when I bring them up today, but I can promise you they all had an impact on me.

When I was three, I ruptured my appendix. When my parents got me to the emergency room with a temperature of 104, the doctor told them I had "acute appendicitis with peritonitis in his system," adding glumly: "I'm not sure he is going to survive." I did, with a big scar on my tiny belly from where the surgeon sliced me open.

When I was four, I fell off a slide and broke my collarbone. When I was five, I jumped off my bed and cracked my eye socket against the corner of a chest of drawers. The wound went all the way to the optic nerve. When my parents brought me home from the hospital that time, my whole forehead was wrapped in bandages—"like a wild Indian," my father said. That injury left its own scar, of course. As if that weren't enough, I also made time as a child to have two hernia operations. But breaking my femur when I was seven was the mishap that affected me most of all.

My family spent summers at a bungalow colony in Monroe, New York, two hours north of New York City. They had some major trees up there. I loved climbing trees. The thrill of being up so high. The breeze rustling through my hair. The ever-present risk involved—that must have been part of it too. The older I got, the higher I wanted to climb. One summer morning, a couple of friends were at our bungalow playing with Douglas and me. We found our way to a certain red oak.

I was up the highest. Douglas was a few branches below me. Our friend Joel Goldstein was still on the ground, staring up at me, as I pulled my scrawny frame up through the narrowing branches.

"Go higher, Craig," he called up. "Go higher."

Of course, I did.

I was way up in the skinny branches taking in the mountain views and showing Joel what I could do, when I heard a sudden cracking sound. The branch beneath me snapped and gave way. Gravity took it from there.

I didn't fall directly to earth. I went tumbling, arms and legs flailing, through an elevated thicket of leaves, twigs, and branches—quite a body-banging journey through that beautiful tree. A little more than halfway down, I slammed into a fat, round branch, much harder and stronger than the one I'd fallen from. I heard what sounded like a bone crack. When I finally reached the ground, I was yowling at such a volume, my mother and father came running and so did the neighbors from half a dozen nearby bungalows.

Damn, that hurt! The worst was the big bone along my right thigh. I swear it felt like it had just been cracked and shattered.

No one dared to move me. I lay on the ground screaming, as everyone huddled around me and we waited for the ambulance to come. Joel Goldstein kept asking, "Man, are you okay?"

The paramedics put a funny-looking air bag around my whole leg, then carefully lifted me into the ambulance and hightailed it, lights and siren wailing, to Arden Hill Hospital, about fifteen minutes away. My parents grabbed my two younger brothers—Eric was just an infant—and followed in the family car.

After much frowning, poking, and X-raying in the emergency room, I was admitted to the hospital and wheeled up to a room, where my leg was suspended with a metal pulley device that everyone called "being in traction." What that meant to me was that I had to lie in bed without moving, especially my leg.

I stayed there just like that for three weeks, three days, seven hours, and twelve minutes—not that I was counting. I hated every second I was there.

I was in pain. I was immobilized. I was very, very bored. My mother visited when she could, but she had two little children back at the bungalow. My father came up from the city but only on weekends.

There wasn't much I could do but read and watch TV and eat when they brought me food. I made a little countdown clock to keep track of how long it would be until my father would come to visit again: five days . . . four days and twenty-three hours . . . four days and twenty-two hours . . . That clock hardly seemed to move at all. And even when I was finally released from the hospital, I still couldn't run outside and play for eight weeks longer because they kept me in a body cast.

Altogether, the broken leg cost me the rest of the summer and the first couple of months of the school year at Yeshivah of Flatbush. By the time I showed up for classes, I was hopelessly behind. I had no idea what the teachers were talking about. When they called on me in class, I never knew what the answer was. The best I could manage was to say something goofy or make a funny face—anything to get my classmates laughing and stop them from realizing how dumb I was.

Right there—first quarter of third grade—that's where the rest of the world kinda passed me by.

There was no discussion of holding me back and running me a second time through third grade. We didn't do that in my family. We pressed ahead. In my parents' eyes—and therefore, I guess, my own—that would be an outward admission of failure. Who knew what people might have thought? So I stayed with my classmates and learned to do whatever I had to in order to get by.

3

SCHOOL DAZE

When I returned to school after my long recuperation, I reconnected with my friends without too much trouble. I was happy to see them, and they seemed happy to see me. I entertained my classmates with harrowing stories of stabbing pain, lying in traction, and plastic trays of hospital mystery meat. "I swear," I said, "hospital food is even worse than what we get in the cafeteria!" They believed everything I told them except for that. By the time I finished with the accounts of my dramatic tumble, the oak outside our bungalow was 1,000 feet tall. Joel Goldstein, who still felt guilty, was happy to back me up.

But nice as it was to see my friends, I'd been away from my schoolwork for a solid two months. A disruption like that might not sound like much in the course of a long academic career. But to a third-grader like me, it felt like an eternity. Back in the classroom, they were already adding and subtracting fractions, diagramming run-on sentences, and mapping out the various regions of the Amazon. I didn't know my denominators from my numerators—or the difference between the Torah and the haftarah.

I tried to hide my ignorance. I didn't want people knowing how clueless I was. So I deflected. I avoided answering. I sat low in my seat and never raised my hand. When the teacher called on me, I made smart-ass comments—"It'd be fun to wrestle one of those crocodiles in the Amazon"—or, more often, responded with silence and a blank stare. "Who knows the answer?" the teacher would ask, scanning the room for someone who grasped the material. I never volunteered, but when I was called on, I did learn that if I just repeated what the teacher said, I wouldn't be too far off.

For the first time ever, I felt like I was dumb. The other kids in class seemed to understand what the teacher was talking about. They had answers. They were raising their hands. What was wrong with me? I did what generations of struggling students had done before me. I tried to hide my insecurity. I told myself I'd catch up later. I acted like I didn't care how well I was doing. I did whatever it took to survive.

My problem was that schoolwork, especially at that age, was not a collection of independent knowledge blocks. Today's lesson built on yesterday's, which built on the lesson from the day before. If you didn't know the difference between a noun and verb, diagraming really was like wrestling a crocodile in the Amazon. The teachers and the other students kept moving forward. The further they went, the more behind I got.

That's how it seemed, anyway. I needed to do something so I wouldn't fail my tests, get held back, flunk out of third grade, embarrass my parents, and stink up my permanent record, whatever that was. I could only imagine how my permanent record must've looked, covered with Fs and big fat Xs and warnings about the increasingly dim path that was my future. I couldn't seem to catch up with my classmates, no matter how hard I tried.

I was struggling in every subject area—in English *and* in Hebrew. Then I discovered cheating. It wasn't something I liked doing. It wasn't something I did all the time. But sometimes I'd ask a friend for the answers on a homework assignment. Or I would copy off someone's answer sheet on test day. I had excellent eyesight so this wasn't too hard. I knew that cheating wasn't right. I'd heard that all my life—from my parents, from our teachers, even on television shows and in comic books. But I felt like I had to cheat occasionally, just to get by.

The teachers probably should have been suspicious of my abrupt improvement. Maybe they were. But no one called me on it or asked any probing questions. I guess they didn't want to open a can of worms. By sixth grade, I was a pretty good cheater. No one forced me to take the cheater's way out. I could have buckled down. I could have gone home and studied in the afternoon instead of playing with my friends. I could have arranged extra help or had my parents hire a tutor. I am sure they would have if I or my teachers had asked. But I didn't worry about the learning I might be missing out on. I just did what I believed was necessary to get by. The truth was I didn't have the focus or the discipline to do what I was supposed to. I didn't have the confidence in my ability to perform. But I could cheat. So I did. And once I started cheating, it was hard to stop.

||||||||||||||||

After sixth grade, under relentless pressure from my brother Douglas and me and even our mother—"why, why, why?"—my father gave in. "You can go to public school," he announced. I felt like I'd been sprung from Sing Sing. I was done with Yeshivah but still reciting whole sections of the Talmud in Hebrew in preparation for my bar mitzvah. Afternoons, when my friends were out playing ball at the park, I was sitting for long, tedious sessions with the rabbi or cantor. When the big day came that November, I didn't exactly think I'd become a man but I did enjoy the huge kids-and-adults party my parents threw for me. One by one, the adult guests handed me sealed envelopes filled with checks in various multiples of eighteen dollars—and not just one or two times that. My father took all the checks and deposited them in an account for my future. I got a sore wrist from writing all those thank-you notes.

I did get a memorable flash of encouragement from an unexpected source. One Saturday, my dad took me and my brother Douglas to see the New York Mets play the Philadelphia Phillies, a rare father-son outing. As we reached the Shea Stadium parking lot, the game had already begun. The lot was packed solid, and attendants were turning cars away. After quickly assessing his options, my father pulled the car into the one open spot he could find, which was right outside the main entrance to the stadium. There was a reason the spot was open. A large blue-and-white sign said, "RESERVED PARKING. HANDI-CAPPED ONLY." And just so there would be no confusion, the sign also had a stick drawing of a person in a wheelchair.

Given what a stickler my dad usually was for doing things properly, I could hardly believe what I was seeing—or what happened next. My father climbed out of the car and shut the door behind him. After my brother and I joined him, we all walked together toward the stadium entrance, my father putting on a fake, exaggerated limp. Step, drag, step, drag—he looked like Ratso Rizzo, Dustin Hoffman's tormented character in *Midnight Cowboy,* the first R-rated movie my friends and I ever snuck into.

I didn't know what to say so I didn't say anything. The stadium personnel didn't say anything either. I guess they believed the Ratso limp. We had our tickets. We went inside and found our seats without any further limping. The car was right where he had left it when the game was over and it was time to leave.

That memory stuck with me because it was so unusual. It was unusual for my brother and I to spend several hours of quality time with my father and unusual to see him pull a stunt like that. To me, it hinted that maybe my father had been more of a scamster in his early years than I had realized.

But for my family and me, life in those years mostly just rolled along. People looked at us and, I'm sure, got the impression that things were going pretty well. My parents stayed together and raised their children. My dad's career stayed on an upward track. My mother seemed to enjoy her role as a stay-at-home mom. We fit in well. Our neighborhood was filled with growing families like our own—professional parents, enriched children, and a comfortable, suburban style of life. Whatever the issues were—and don't all families have some?—they stayed mostly below the surface, almost never addressed on the outside. Clearly, we weren't the only family on Topaz Court or in greater Rockland County who clung to the same unofficial motto: if it looks good on the outside, how broken can it be on the inside?

By the time I got to Clarkstown High School South, the patterns were mostly set. I had plenty of friends. I underachieved in the classroom. I cheated when I had to. I never felt confident that I was good enough. But I always assumed that whatever little fires broke out, my parents—my father, especially—had the resources and the inclination to extinguish quickly and quietly.

When I was fifteen, I discovered alcohol. What a glorious development that was! My friend Barry Zuckerman showed up at my house with a twelve-pack of Budweiser. We went into the woods behind my house. I think I had five, and he had seven. He had a little more experience than I had, so he could handle a little more. Drinking wasn't the only thing Barry and I shared, but it was one thing. He became my very best friend.

Our early drinking experiences mostly involved pinching beers from our friends' houses. A kid would show up with a six-pack or more. We'd go outside somewhere or into someone's basement and get lit. Sometimes, it would be just a couple of us, sometimes dozens. When my friends started getting their driver's licenses, we would DWI around in each other's family cars.

Drinking was social, an excuse for hanging out with my friends. But it did something for me that nothing else ever had: it eased my anxiety and made me feel better about myself. I loved the way that felt. Loved it. Positively loved it. It wasn't intoxication that I was seeking. It was confidence.

My friends and I never had trouble finding beer, wine, or something stronger. When we'd taken too much from home to go unnoticed, we'd enlist an older friend to buy for us. By junior year, we were all getting fake IDs. And they worked. Suddenly, we had no trouble buying whatever we felt like drinking. By then, to our great delight, we had also discovered marijuana.

The first time I smoked pot, Barry and I were in the woods behind my house, roughly the same location where he had introduced me to beer. In those ways, Barry was always a little ahead of me. He had a joint. I had heard of joints, but I had never held one or smoked one before. Barry lit it just like a cigarette and took a long, hard drag. I watched carefully. Then, he held his hand out and passed the joint to me. I inhaled just like he had, though the smoke made me cough the first couple of attempts. Quickly though, I got the hang of it and did not look back.

I loved everything about smoking marijuana. The taste. The ritual of sharing. The mellow high. Especially the way it boosted my confidence and my self-esteem in a smoother way than alcohol. Pot did the same thing alcohol did, only better—and it was even easier for a kid like me to procure. All I had to do was buy some from a friend. Everyone knew someone who had some. Suddenly, I was feeling better about everything. We'd get high before class in the morning. We'd slip out at lunch and get high. After school, we would drive around, listening to Pink Floyd and Led Zeppelin, getting high.

It was around that time that I met Debbie Glass. Debbie was a pretty, blonde-haired freshman, two years behind me in school. I still carried my lingering insecurities, but I was finally feeling at least a little more sure of myself. What anxieties still lingered inside me, the pot and the booze were helping to ease or at least to hide. When I drank or got high, I quickly felt better about myself and far more comfortable in the world. I had a group of friends now—Barry Zuckerman, Rob Freireich, Mitch Polay, and a few others. Physically, I had filled out a bit. Some of the girls even thought I was cute. Just being an upperclassman meant something at Clarkstown South. Wasn't it time I had my first real girlfriend?

Debbie and I were a perfect match. Everyone said so. Besides being smart and pretty, she was the youngest of four children in a Jewish family very much like mine. They lived in West Nyack, the next town over from New City. Her father, Sol, worked on Wall Street. My parents thought Debbie was terrific, and her family could not have been kinder to me. She was always fun company.

She had her own insecurities. What high-school freshman doesn't? When she was a little girl, she'd had a detached retina that left her with one lazy eye. She was self-conscious about that. She didn't really need to be, but she was. I know she liked having a boyfriend a couple of years older than her. That was a point of status for a freshman in our school. It made her feel part of the in-crowd. And with Debbie on my arm, I also fit in better and felt better about myself. We went out on weekends and talked in the hallway at school. She came with me to the junior prom and then to the senior prom. Whatever the event, I liked not having to worry if I would have a date.

||||||||||||||||

There were little eruptions along the way. Several of them.

Soon after I got my driver's license, my dad bought me a Pontiac Firebird. That was a pretty cool car for a sixteen-year-old. I was at a party one night, drinking, of course. We also smoked some pot. I was driving home with a friend in the car.

I came around a turn. I don't remember exactly what happened. Being sloshed behind the wheel will do that to you. But I hit the gas instead of the brake. I knew immediately I was losing control. I closed my eyes. That's all I remember except for the sound of breaking glass and smashing metal. I slammed into another car.

Nobody was hurt, thank God. But the police came, and I was taken to the Rockland County jail.

My dad came to get me in the morning. I knew he considered it embarrassing for my family. This was a line I wasn't supposed to cross. But dad agreed to act as my lawyer, and he came up with what turned out to be an effective defense.

He told the assistant district attorney that I had asthma. He said I'd taken some asthma medication and it had reacted badly with the small amount of alcohol I had consumed, causing me to black out behind the wheel.

I never even had to go back to court. Somehow, the case just went away. I did learn a lesson, though it wasn't the lesson I probably should have learned. What I learned was that there aren't many consequences to bad behavior. If something unfortunate happens, don't worry too much. It probably isn't as bad as you think. Chances are, nothing terrible will happen. And when needed, your parents can probably bail you out.

Early junior year, my classmates and I all signed up for the PSAT, the practice exam for the SAT college-admission test. I was pretty sure I wouldn't do well on the test. Why should I? I had hardly prepared. So I used one of my most reliable test-taking methods, a time-tested grade-raising technique that had bailed me out many times in the past: I copied off the answer sheet of someone sitting next to me. Someone at the College Board, the organization that administered the exam, discovered that my answer sheet bore a remarkable resemblance to the answer sheet of the student sitting to my left. It was pretty clear that I had cheated.

My parents got a call.

They were not happy.

This was beyond the pale of acceptable behavior, even for tolerant parents with a sometimes maddening son.

They confronted me.

"We are so disappointed," my father said. In his frustration and his anger, he even slapped at me with the back of his hand. He hadn't done that for years.

"This is serious business," my mother told me. "The stakes are getting higher now." She didn't mention my permanent record. But that was kind of what she was driving at.

I felt bad. I really did. I told my parents with as much sincerity as I could muster that I understood that what I had done was reckless and unacceptable. They seemed to warm up to my apologies and declarations of remorse. But soon enough, the somber tones and angry consequences just seemed to fade.

This was just the PSAT. I said the P stood for Practice—even though it actually meant Preliminary. It was, I said, just a practice exam, wasn't it? This wasn't the real SAT. It didn't have actual standing. We were practicing. We were learning. We had to move on.

"Don't let that happen again," my father said in one last stab at reaching me.

Life returned to normal, and so did I.

In all my growing-up years, hardly anything was asked of me. I had to stay out of serious trouble, and I had to get through school. I don't ever remember my lackluster grades being that much of an issue. The unwritten rule in our house was, "You just focus on school. Dad will pay for everything."

I actually did okay on the real SAT—not great but okay. Good enough to be considered a credible applicant at several decent colleges. I'm sure it didn't hurt that my father could afford the full tuition without student loans or financial aid. Thanks, Dad.

I didn't give much thought about where I should apply to college. I did make a couple of campus visits during my senior year, including a memorable trip to Boston University with three of my friends. We drove up together and checked into a hotel near campus. Then, we did what we presumed college kids were supposed to. We partied so hard we never even made it out to see the school. All four of us skipped our interviews.

I drove up to Syracuse. That time, I did glance around the campus, which seemed nice enough to me. Oh, and I met a girl. She was very friendly. She came back to my hotel room with me. That was all it took. I told my parents: "If I get accepted, I'm going to Syracuse."

When I got the "congratulations" letter, I just assumed that the skills and attitudes that had gotten me this far would continue to carry me on. I had no plans to study any harder than I had in high school. I was confident I could keep getting by on charm, cheating, and the occasional parental bailout. Back then, Syracuse University had a reputation as a big sports-and-party school. I loved sports. I loved partying. Syracuse and me. What could be better than that?

4

COLLEGE BOY

I got drunk on Southern Comfort my first day at Syracuse. I passed out in my dorm room and never made it down to the dining hall. But I had finally arrived at a place I knew I was born to be. What could be greater than going away to college?

Everything was paid for. No one was watching me. Socially, I adjusted perfectly well. Socially was never my problem. I had people to hang out with from my first day on campus. I made good friends right away, some I would keep forever. Our full roster of Division I sports teams—*Go, Orange!*—gave the students a sense of shared purpose and something to pull for. The relative isolation of Syracuse, New York, a four-hour drive from New York City, made school feel like a world unto itself, a world where partying of any variety was never frowned upon.

I met lots of girls at Syracuse. That was much easier than it had ever been in high school. For one thing, there were a whole lot more of them. For another, we were constantly running into one another—in class, in the dining hall, in the bars, and in the brand-new Carrier Dome. Most of us were from similar backgrounds, suburban kids from places like New York, Boston, and Philly. We were all at the same point in life and away from home for the very first time. Was this a purposeful petri dish for young-adult mating rituals? I don't know about the purposeful part, but it might as well have been. The administrators didn't mess in our business, and all our prying parents were too far away to pry. Going to lots of parties, meeting and greeting and drinking and getting high—it really was the perfect laboratory for hooking up with college girls. Excuse me, college women. Many of them would correct you if you called them girls.

Let it be said that I still definitely considered myself a boy.

Most days, I went to most of my classes. I paid enough attention that I could regurgitate at least some of the material on the test. I wouldn't use the term "excelled" about my academic performance, but I floated through all my first-year intro classes. They really weren't that hard. The English and history was nothing we hadn't done at Clarkstown High School South, the few parts I'd paid attention to. The math came easily to me. I picked up that material without breaking a sweat. Overall, I'd have to say that college was easier than high school. I declared a major, political science. It just seemed interesting to me. And Syracuse didn't have an official major called "Bullshitting the System." I had to pick something off the list. And I continued honing my cheating skills.

The university had something called the honor system. That meant no one would be looking out for cheaters the way the teachers did in high school. Students at Syracuse were trusted to behave honorably. Was that a gold-plated invitation or what? With the honor system in place, there wasn't much stopping me.

I was always good at chatting up the professors. I think they found me friendly and engaging. But many of the exams were open book. How could anyone fail one of those? Some classes demanded essays. That could have been an issue. But I found a guy who agreed to write a couple for me. Later, someone told me about a company that would crank out a college-level essay on any topic I could name—or dig an old one out of the file drawer—for $200, no questions asked. The charges showed up on my father's credit card as "RESEARCH."

I was attending a good private college. I seemed to be progressing nicely. As far as my dad was concerned, I was living up to my end of the deal. He kept writing the checks.

I might have done better if I'd been drinking and smoking less. But this was Syracuse. I wouldn't call my intake far from the norm. It seemed like everybody was drinking and getting high. Certainly, no one ever said to me: "Craig, do you think that smoking pot every day at college might be a problem? You're drinking a lot too." I wasn't doing heavy drugs. I felt like I had everything under control. I was sure I could manipulate the system straight to graduation day.

I would see Debbie when I went back home for long weekends or holidays. She had two more years of high school, but she was waiting for me. I think she really loved me. I told her how much I loved and missed her. I said nothing about the girls I was meeting and more at Syracuse. I liked the security of having a long-term girlfriend waiting for me, even if I didn't see her that much. Despite the social swirl on campus, I was still a little scared of being alone. I wasn't letting trusting young Debbie interfere with my full college experience. I just had to keep the two worlds apart.

We spent time together in the summer after freshman year. Honestly, it was fun reconnecting with her. I remembered why I thought she was so great. But I did get a brief scare during my sophomore year. Debbie was a high-school senior by then. She was looking seriously at college, far more seriously than I had. Syracuse was on her list. As much as I liked having a girlfriend waiting for me four hours away, that's how much I didn't want her living in a dorm room across the Quad. I breathed a huge sigh of relief when she decided to attend

Boston University, which I assured her with a totally straight face was definitely a far superior school.

IIIIIIIIIIIIIIII

When I came home from college for the summer following my sophomore year, I discovered something I hadn't paid sufficient attention to in the past: the true awesomeness of New York City nightlife. My friends and I weren't driving around in cars drinking beers anymore or getting stoned out in the woods—at least not *only* that. We were learning the many joys of the city's after-dark scene—it's long-after-dark scene. And that meant clubs in Manhattan. Sometimes, I'd get together with Debbie. But several nights a week, I'd meet up with my male friends, people I'd grown up with like Barry Zuckerman and guys from Syracuse like Mitchell Ansell. The early 1980s was a glorious era for Manhattan nightlife.

These places all had stories to tell and colorful pasts. Limelight was a deconsecrated Episcopal church from the 1840s that became a drug-rehab center and, by the time my friends and I turned up, a teeming den of late-night debauchery. Studio 54 was still going. A former opera house and CBS radio and television studio on West Fifty-Fourth Street, Studio, as the regulars liked to call it, had defined New York's coked-up late-1970s nightlife when the regulars included Andy Warhol, Bianca Jagger, and Grace Jones. It might have faded a little by the time we arrived on the scene. Andy and Bianca had moved on. But the club was under new ownership after founders Steve Rubell and Ian Schrager (both Syracuse grads) were convicted of tax fraud and sent to federal prison—and the party had roared on. When Rubell and Schrager got out, they hardly missed a beat at their new place, the Palladium, a converted, 1927 movie palace on East Fourteenth Street. Over time, those venues would be replaced by others—Tunnel in far-west Chelsea, Club A on the Upper East Side. The names came and went like slivers of light reflecting off a spinning disco ball. But the fun was always somewhere.

The challenging part was getting in.

All these places had intimidating doormen and strict entry policies. But as I kept learning, who you seemed to be was at least as important as who you were. If you were with three beautiful girls, you'd get right in. But two guys wanting to pick up girls? Good luck getting past the steroid-pumped doormen without a fat wad of cash or at least a recent mention on the *New York Post*'s Page 6. My friends and I weren't famous. Our names had never been printed anywhere in boldface type. And it wasn't like any of us could slip the doorman a fifty to pull back the red velvet rope. Twenty bucks for drinks inside was a stretch for us.

What was I going to do? I certainly didn't want to stand on line for ninety minutes while pretty girls and pro athletes and Wall Street doofuses were ushered inside. I needed to get creative. I needed a plan. If money and fame weren't at my ready disposal, something had to be.

How about cunning and charm?

Nobody was better at getting into nightclubs than Barry and me. We were not line-waiters. But beating the system took ingenuity. It also took a plan. We had several. Our plans started out ridiculously simple. But simple, we learned, could be quite effective.

No matter how long the line was, I'd walk up confidently to the doorman while Barry lingered off to the side. At these clubs, the doormen always had a clipboard with a guest list. It had the names of celebrities, models, athletes, gossip columnists, second-string royalty, super-rich club crawlers, friends of the owners—people who were supposed to be ushered right in. I would say with my best cocky friendliness, "Hi, I'm Craig Schmell," acting like my name was on the list. While the doorman was checking, I would glance over his shoulder and spot another name or two. When the doorman didn't find me there, I'd say, "It's probably under my friend's name, Peter Vastos," repeating a name I'd just spied on the doorman's own list. "He's on his way now."

Then, I'd wave Barry over and introduce him to the doorman, as if I were friends with both of them. We'd thank the doorman. Then Barry and I would march inside.

You'd think a maneuver like this one was too dumb to work. You'd think the street-smart doormen at New York nightclubs would be hip to this sort of thing. Then, you'd be overestimating the prowess of nightclub doormen. Either they didn't notice or they didn't care. That ruse worked at least 90 percent of the time. And when it didn't? When too many questions were asked? We'd politely excuse ourselves and pick another club.

The only real risk was picking out the famous friend of a famous person—which I was good at avoiding—or the name of someone the doorman actually knew. That was hard to protect against, but it hardly ever happened to us.

It was important to have a partner like Barry, someone who rolled with whatever happened and didn't lose his cool. What will trip you up is fear or nervousness. I didn't have much and neither did Barry. We were New York guys on the make, young and energetic. We knew that nothing really bad was going to happen to us. All they could do was stop us from entering or ask us to leave.

My parents didn't raise objections, but they definitely noticed the late hours I was keeping. How could they not? I was staying at their house—was it still my house?—and coming home night after night at four in the morning.

That was just about the time my father was getting up to start his day. I was stumbling home, bleary eyed and tired. He was shaving, showering, laying his *tefillin*, doing his sit-ups and push-ups, having a sensible breakfast, and heading off to work.

With his silence and his stares, he let me know he thought I was behaving like an idiot. But the closest he came to saying so was the way he shook his head.

|||||||||||||||||

Travel is broadening. Or so I'd always heard. And now was my chance to prove it.

During my junior year of college, I decided to spend a semester abroad, living and studying in London and getting full academic credit back at Syracuse. I'd been to Aruba and Puerto Rico on family vacations. But I'd never been to Europe before, and I'd heard nothing but good things. That part of the world wasn't warm, I knew. But it was filled with young people looking for adventure, and it had to be warmer than another winter in upstate New York.

Today, lots of American college students spend a semester or more abroad. I wouldn't say the idea was novel in 1982. But it was definitely far less common, and Syracuse was at the forefront. The university had programs in France, Spain, and Italy—in all kinds of cool-sounding places. Of all the many choices, London was my first choice. It was big, exciting, and I knew I could handle the language, once I got used to the blokes, lifts, and car boots.

I had no trouble getting accepted. I made a point of schmoozing the head guy at SU-DIPA, the Syracuse University Division of International Programs Abroad, telling him how eager I was to experience more of the world. "Being a political science major," I added, "I would hate to come to Syracuse and not take advantage of such an excellent opportunity."

He heartily agreed.

I wasn't worried about paying the extra fees. If Syracuse University saw the educational value of my spending spring semester in London, I had no doubt my father would gladly cover whatever the costs were. Who was he—or I—to second-guess?

I flew out of Kennedy Airport in mid-January, landing at London's Heathrow Airport, where the temps were just as low as they had been in New York. I shared a well-heated, three-bedroom flat (another Britishism!) in Kensington, just off Kensington Park Road, with six other Syracuse students.

The classes couldn't have been much easier. Theater Arts was my favorite. We went to plays at various theaters around the city. Then, we got together and talked about them. That was about it. No tests. No papers. Just another play the following week. The major requirement of the Syracuse study-abroad program seemed to be hanging out in some interesting places and having an awesome time.

Ah, my specialty!

All this easy coursework left me with plenty of free time. My friends and I found some excellent pubs to drink in. Among our cross-cultural experiences was learning to appreciate room-temperature beer. We managed. Quite well, actually. It starts tasting pretty good after a while. We met girls from England, France, Spain, Morocco, South Africa—so many countries I couldn't keep track of them all. Almost all these girls seemed open to meeting American guys, even lowly college students just settling into a brief semester. We went out a lot—that wasn't so different from the States—and discovered All Saints Road, where you could buy all the hashish you wanted right on the sidewalk. How great was that?

One of my Syracuse friends in London discovered a working phone in his rental flat with international long-distance service. I guess the owners had forgotten to disconnect the line. We'd all go over there to drink and make phone calls. Overseas phone calls were a whole lot more expensive back then. I called my parents in New York. I called friends in Syracuse. When I was lonely, I called Debbie at Boston University. She'd say how much she missed me. She was still there for me. Whatever was happening on my side of the Atlantic, I still liked knowing I had someone waiting for me. It made me feel loved and connected even if I had long since stopped deserving her generosity.

With one friend or another, I took wonderful weekend trips, often on the power of our thumbs. Hitchhiking wasn't dangerous back then, not in Europe anyway. We hitchhiked to Amsterdam. That trip was 540 kilometers, a longish 335 nonmetric miles, but definitely worth it. Two words: legal pot. We hitchhiked to Val d'Isère and Chamonix in the French Alps. We hitchhiked to Ireland for St. Patrick's Day, only to find out that, there, it's a religious holiday and nobody goes out drinking. We were relieved to discover an open pub on a side street in Dublin that was still pouring delicious pints of Guinness. We had our own American-style St. Paddy's, the falling-down drunk kind. We hadn't gone to Ireland just to pray.

Western Europe was tiny compared to where we had come from. Most places were no more than a few hours away. We took full advantage of the compact geography. Any extra expenses, I just slapped them on my dad's Amex.

In early April, two of our classmates, Buzz and Roger, spent a week in Russia. They came back to London swearing they'd had the time of their lives.

"You might have heard the Soviet Union is a terrible enemy of ours," Buzz said with a grin. "Well, they certainly seemed happy to see us."

In fact, 1982 was just about the apex of the Cold War, a time of sharp hostility on both sides. Ronald Reagan hadn't yet called the Soviet Union "the evil empire." That would come in a year. But the Cold War was growing hotter by the day. The Soviets dominated Eastern

Europe. The Russian military was muscular and well equipped. The United States had boycotted the 1980 Summer Olympics in Moscow to protest the Soviet invasion of Afghanistan. Russia was threatening to return the favor in 1984, when the games were moving to Los Angeles. You couldn't even go to Russia if you lived in the United States. From my political science courses, I already knew a lot of this.

"Don't worry about any of that," Buzz said. "Just go. You'll thank me."

All we had to do, he explained, was contact the Russian tourist agency in London. They would handle everything—the flights, the hotel, the visa, everything. "Just be sure to bring some blue jeans when you go," he added.

"Blue jeans?" I asked.

"To sell," he said. "They don't have denim blue jeans in Russia. The Russians love American blue jeans. They feel deprived. You can sell blue jeans for a lot of money on the black market in Moscow."

I learned later we could also have brought *Playboy* magazines or chewing gum, two other treasured Western products that were not easily available in Russia and would have fetched good money on the black market. But even a couple pairs of blue jeans, Buzz told us, could help to pay for the trip.

There was only one catch, he said. "When you sell your jeans, you will get paid in Russian rubles, and you have to spend them before you leave. Russian rubles are totally worthless outside Russia."

I didn't care. It all sounded like an unforgettable adventure to me.

5

COMRADE CRAIG

I recruited a classmate, Glenn Borden, to make the trip to Moscow with me. I didn't know him well, but he was a fellow political science major, and he was totally game to go. "The Cold War keeps getting hotter," he told me.

We went to the Russian tourist office, where a woman with a *Doctor Zhivago* accent explained the trip was leaving London the last week in April.

"We're ready," Glenn said to the woman.

"Let's do it," I agreed.

We signed up for a ten-day "education tour" of Moscow and Leningrad. "Your timing is perfect," she told us. "You will get to see our parade on the first of May. It is spectacular."

The day before we left, Glenn and I found a store in London that sold American-made Levi's blue jeans. They had a huge selection. We noticed one pile that was cheaper than the others, by a lot. "IRREGULARS," the sign read. They weren't used or from some knockoff brand. They were just in funky sizes. One had a 28-inch waist and a 42-inch length, which would have been perfect for someone who was, say, 6 foot 5 and 150 pounds. Maybe Jimmy "J. J." Walker from *Good Times*? Could he have Russian relatives? But the price was right, and from what Buzz had said, we didn't expect the Russians would mind too much.

I bought two pairs, and Glenn bought two pairs. I considered buying three, but I wanted to pack light, and I was worried the Russian customs agents might check our bags and wonder if we were intending to open a US Army-Navy store off Red Square.

Before we got the blue jeans, I had already taken care of another important trip detail: access to marijuana and alcohol. I couldn't see taking a ten-day vacation to a foreign country and remaining stone-cold sober the entire time. How much fun would that be? I knew Russia was the vodka capital of the world, so I didn't think we'd have much trouble procuring alcohol. But I didn't want to be without an ample supply of pot. I shared that concern with Barry Zuckerman in one of our calls on the magic phone. A few days later, I got a small, manila-wrapped package in the mail.

"Dear Rock 'n' Roll Animal," a two-page, handwritten letter began.

How's it going, buddy? Everything is great here in the states. School is cool and pussy is as plentiful as ever.

Enclosed you will find some necessary partying equipment for a Russian Roadie.

The letter was wrapped around a one-hit, dugout marijuana pipe, the kind that gives off hardly any smoke, perfect for imbibing discreetly. The chamber of the pipe was jammed with high-quality Colombian marijuana. The letter continued:

I know that your dugout is out of commission, and I figured that you would like to do a few hits behind the iron curtain. My buddies told me that there is plenty of good hash over in England, but that it is hard to find good pot. Well—I struck it rich here with some gold, and I'd like to share some of my good fortune with my best friend. Enjoy, and party hearty.

    P.S. Be careful and don't let my dugout fall into the hands of the KGB. Say hello to Brezhnev and give him a few one-hits for me. Have a really excellent trip and get psyched for a great summer!

    All my Love,

    B.Z.

In my youthful stupidity, I didn't even consider the possibility that it might be unwise for Barry to mail marijuana to me in London and even more unwise for me to smuggle illegal drugs into a nation famous for barbaric prisons and Siberian exile, a nation that also happened to be the number-one enemy of the United States. What was I thinking? I'd seen *Midnight Express*! I'd even been assigned to read *The Gulag Archipelago*, Aleksandr Solzhenitsyn's harrowing account of Soviet prison life. Of course, I didn't actually read the book. I just glanced at it, then paid $175 for a prewritten essay that I submitted to my War and Literature professor. I didn't read that either, but I was a little pissed when I only got a B.

None of this dissuaded me as I packed my bags. I slipped the dugout pipe and the pot into the back of my Nikon camera where the film would usually go. I'm sure the Russian customs agents had never encountered that trick before!

||||||||||||||||

Aeroflot covered the distance from Heathrow to Moscow's Sheremetyevo International Airport in less than four hours. There were about fifty other people on our tour. I didn't give the pot in my bag another thought until I got off the plane and was standing in the customs line. Then, it hit me. I could see the customs agents going through peoples' luggage. Oh, my God! Suddenly, I was scared shitless. What if the agent found my contraband, the pot *or* the jeans? What happens in Russia to people who import things they aren't supposed to? It can't be pretty. I hardly took a breath until my turn came and the agent rifled through my luggage. But he didn't open the camera, and he said nothing about jeans. He waved me through. Our visit could easily have ended—ended very badly—even before it began. I just got lucky, I suppose.

The tour company had set up a full itinerary of historic sites, cultural landmarks, and important buildings for us to visit. We ditched the tour immediately. After we checked into the hotel, Glenn and I headed out on a short walk around the neighborhood. We did not blend in. The moment we hit the sidewalk, young people were walking over to us.

"Jeans?" they asked.

"Jeans, jeans?"

It might have been the only words of English some of these people spoke, but I had to say their pronunciation was excellent. Somehow they knew we might be a source of treasured blue jeans.

We settled on an Asian guy whose English was slightly better than the others', though only slightly. He followed Glenn and me back to the hotel and up to our room. In a rare exercise of good judgment, I thought we shouldn't be conducting our black-market blue jean business right out in the street. It didn't cross my mind until later that if the Asian guy had been some sort of undercover KGB agent, there also would have been no witnesses to explain our disappearance.

We pulled out my two pair and Glenn's two pair.

Our buyer appeared interested. The sizing didn't seem to be an issue. "Four thousand rubles," he said. "One thousand for each."

I had no idea how much we should be charging or even how much money that was, though it sounded like a lot of rubles. I just figured that, since he was an experienced black market purchaser and we were a couple of inexperienced American college kids, he would naturally come in low.

I gave him a look that was meant to convey, *Are you fuckin' kidding me? That's not nearly enough.*

He raised his offer.

"Five thousand," he said.

I scrunched up my nose and my forehead. I tried to look disappointed. I let the silence hang dramatically in the air.

"Tell you what," I said finally. "My friend and I will take six thousand rubles for these four pair of brand-new American Levi blue jeans. That's a good price."

Now, he was the one shooting me a disappointed look. But he didn't counter my counter. With no further equivocation, he just said, "Okay."

I immediately felt like I had settled too cheaply. But I did feel better when our buyer started counting out the ruble notes on the hotel room bed. It was a huge stack. Now, all Glenn and I had to do was spend every last one of them before we boarded the Aeroflot jet back to Heathrow.

We got busy right away.

It turned out that six thousand rubles was a shitload of Russian money to spend in ten days, especially when our hotel and airfare were covered. I was already softening on the nefarious economic system of Communism. We could buy anything we wanted here!

There wasn't much in the stores. Just basic stuff like bath soap and clunky toasters. This much became clear in a hurry: if we were going to spend all this funny money, we'd have to spend it having a good time. A really good time.

||||||||||||||||||

A tour bus would have been too ordinary and confining for two flush-with-rubles college boys. We hired a chauffeur. Boris was his name. He had an immaculate stretch Mercedes-Benz. We hired a pretty translator. Her name was Svetlana. We bought a case of the highest-grade Stolichnaya vodka at a state-owned liquor store so we wouldn't get thirsty along the way. Boris picked us up at the hotel each morning. Svetlana was waiting in the car for us. They drove us around to all the top attractions in Moscow, including Lenin's Mausoleum (neat history lesson), the Tomb of the Unknown Soldier (just like at Arlington Cemetery outside Washington), the GUM department store (Bloomingdale's and Macy's have nothing to worry about), and the high-rise Seven Sisters (seven Stalin-era skyscrapers, all equal distance from the Kremlin, an odd thing to brag about, I thought). We walked along the Moskva River. We stopped at Moscow State University and rode up to the Sparrow Hills, gazing down on Luzhniki Stadium, Luzhnetskaya Bridge, and the Russian Academy of Sciences. We took a train trip to Leningrad, the past and future St. Petersburg, where our stops included the Hermitage Museum, St. Isaac's Cathedral, and another nice hotel.

We were capitalist kings in a socialist society, riding around in our stretch Mercedes limo, swigging Stoli from crystal glasses, taking turns with the one-hit pipe, taking advantage of this crazy exchange rate as only a couple of American college kids knew how.

We dined in the very nicest restaurants. We went to the Bolshoi Ballet—twice—because we could. We met two gorgeous young women in a nightclub who were more than happy to join us for a night of drinking, dancing, and riding around. Glenn might have slipped them a few rubles, I'm not sure. But none of this cost much at all. The Bolshoi tickets were thirty rubles. The fanciest dinner might have been fifty. We had thousands more where those came from.

One of the high points for me was St. Basil's Cathedral, but not because I was religious, which I wasn't remotely. It was because the architecture was so stunning and because Svetlana told us such a memorable story about how it was built. "The year was 1555," she said, "the time of Czar Ivan IV. Some people called him Ivan the Terrible. You might have heard that name." Oh, we'd heard of *him*.

"The czar wanted to commemorate the capture of Kazan and Astrakhan in the Russo-Mongol War," Svetlana said. "So he summoned two of the greatest architects in the world, Postnik Takovlev and Ivan Barma. The czar said to them, 'I want you to build the most beautiful building that has ever been constructed.'"

The architects got right to work. The result of their genius was truly spectacular. The cathedral had nine separate chapels, eight around the edge and one in the middle, each topped with a spectacular, onion-shaped dome. When seen from above, the cathedral resembled nothing less than a shimmering, eight-pointed star.

"When the cathedral was officially consecrated in 1561," Svetlana said, "Czar Ivan was thrilled. He summoned the brilliant architects and told them what a wonderful job they had done. Then, he ordered their eyes removed so they could never build such a masterpiece again."

I supposed his cruelty worked. I haven't seen too many buildings more beautiful than that one.

||||||||||||||||

I should probably mention that I got stoned inside the walls of the Kremlin.

Let me say that again, because even I can't believe I ever did something so reckless. *I got stoned inside the walls of the Kremlin,* the official seat of government of my nation's greatest enemy.

Glenn and I were standing beside the famous Tsar Bell, which is said to be the largest bell in the world. Made of bronze in 1735 with a twenty-foot diameter and a weight of nearly half a million pounds, the bell sits between the Ivan the Great Bell Tower and the Kremlin Wall, one of the must-see stops on any Kremlin tour. It was cracked during metal casting and has never been rung.

We walked around the back side of the bell, where the broken part was. I tried to look as casual as I could. I pulled the one-hit pipe out of my pocket. It was already loaded with pot. People were coming and going in all directions. They were *oohing* and *aahing*. Over the bell.

I pulled out a bright red disposable lighter and held it to the tip of the pipe. I fired up and gave the pipe a strong, smooth suck.

I could feel the smoke filling my lungs. I held my breath as long as I could, then let the smoke out gently. I managed not to cough. I didn't want to exhale too quickly and call attention to myself with any telltale odors.

It was only after I had exhaled that a man in a dark suit—KGB? A Kremlin staffer?—gave me the eye. Could he guess what I was doing in there? The pipe was hidden in my hand. Did he smell anything? Was I just being paranoid? All of those things were possible. He said nothing and walked on.

"You want a turn?" I said to Glenn.

"Not now," he said, shaking his head, before mumbling, "You're crazy."

I didn't think so. My head swirling with a familiar, warm, mellow feeling, we continued our self-guided tour.

Why was everyone else so uptight?

||||||||||||||||

Everywhere Glenn and I went around Moscow, we kept seeing gigantic pictures of Karl Marx, Friedrich Engels, and Vladimir Lenin, the original power trio of Communist Russia. One or another of them—often all three—were displayed prominently on the fronts of all the city's major government buildings. A two-story portrait of the threesome was even hung from the GUM department store. Many of the huge displays seemed new and even temporary—large billboard-sized posters and flags. This had to be something more than a random expression of honor and admiration. In fact, it was.

"The May Day parade is tomorrow," Svetlana explained. "The parade salutes the international workers. It's a socialist tradition going all the way back to 1918. The Moscow May Day has been called the greatest show on earth."

Entrance to Red Square was by ticket only, but Boris and Svetlana were able to score a pair for Glenn and me. When we got there early in the morning, the square was already packed with workers, children, and athletes, lined in neat ranks in front of Lenin's Mausoleum. Russian military music was playing over giant speakers on top of the Kremlin walls. The crowd erupted in regular chants of, "Hurrah! Hurrah!"

At one point, Leonid Brezhnev wandered onto the reviewing stand above the mausoleum, as a dozen other government officials walked gingerly behind him. He came out and waved, but he didn't say much, not that I could hear.

This was all a very dramatic spectacle—and, clearly, a carefully orchestrated one. But from our vantage point we hadn't seen most of it, not yet. As Glenn and I were standing on the sidewalk, watching the marchers go by, a man walked over to us and spoke in English.

"You like to march in the parade?" he asked. A boy was standing next to him, holding a small sign that read "MAR 1," which is Russian for May 1.

"Sure," Glenn and I both said, almost in unison.

The boy handed me the MAR 1 sign. The man opened up a spot in the metal barricade that separated the marchers from the spectators. Glenn and I stepped off the curb in our American blue jeans and joined the people marching in the street.

Everyone else seemed to be wearing a uniform or they were at least marching behind a banner of some sort. This wasn't Mardi Gras. It was the May Day parade. Order was the order of the day. We weren't part of any organized unit, company, or industrial group. But march we did, me waving my little sign, Glenn with his fists in the air.

There was a youth group from Minsk in front of us and, just behind us, a 1960s-era IS-3M heavy tank with its 12.7mm machine gun. I took a picture and looked it up later. That was the kind of thing I could never detail on my own.

We waved. We clapped. We smiled at the crowds. We had no idea what we were marching for other than the sheer improbability of it all. The people we passed had no idea who we were, but many of them waved and smiled back at us.

We passed many pictures of Marx, Engels, and Lenin. They were gazing proudly down on the citizens of America's single greatest enemy.

|||||||||||||||||||

I didn't want to leave Moscow with memories, photos, and nothing more. We'd done a fine job going through the big stack of rubles, but we hadn't found anything special to buy and bring home.

"We need a proper souvenir," I told Glenn on our last night in Moscow.

I needed some kind of evidence of all we had done. I had to impress my friends, desperate to convince others how big I was.

Glenn and I had taken some pictures, but that didn't seem like enough. A handful of ticket stubs from the Bolshoi wouldn't quite do it either.

I knew I had a great story to tell my friends back in London and back in Syracuse, and I wanted to tell it as vividly as I possibly could. But, I wondered, what was the right memento?

Then, I saw it.

Flapping on the front of our hotel, above the lobby and the main ballroom, was a large Soviet flag, protruding off of a third-floor ledge, out at the end of a long, metal flagpole. Bellmen, taxi drivers, and hotel guests were milling below outside the busy hotel entrance. The flag was lit by two powerful floodlights.

"Follow me," I said to Glenn. "I need you to help me with something."

We took a back staircase up to a service floor where we clearly didn't belong. That's where I found a window that led to a ledge that led to the flagpole.

"You're the lookout," I said to Glenn. "Make sure no one comes up behind me."

Glenn didn't like anything about this.

"You're nuts," he said.

"Just be a lookout," I snapped. "I'll do the difficult stuff."

And I did.

I climbed through the window and hoisted myself onto the ledge. I shimmied partway out the flagpole, three full stories above the people below.

No one looked up at me or said anything. I just tried to keep my cool. I pulled a cord and the flag slid toward me. I unsnapped the flag from the rigging and pulled it off the pole. I tucked it under my warm jacket until I was safely back on the ledge, where I folded the flag neatly into a triangle and then joined Glenn inside.

||||||||||||||||||

When I got back to London—and especially when I got back to America—I felt like a different person. I felt like I had seen the world. I felt, in a funny way, like I had made it into the big leagues.

When I told friends stories about our trip to Russia—especially when I pulled out the Russian flag and told them about my high-wire flagpole act—I have to say they were flabbergasted.

"You're crazy, man," more than one of them said.

Laugh if you want to, but that made me feel fabulous about myself. I had gone far from home. When I got there, I did things. I didn't just sit around. I didn't just blend in. I had made something out of my opportunities. Maybe I'd gone a little crazy. That was an undeniable possibility. But you can't say my trip overseas was boring. No one could say that.

And I was gaining confidence.

I can do anything, I thought to myself.

If I can think of it, I can do it.

If I can sell blue jeans on the black market, if I can get stoned at the Kremlin, if I can march in the May Day parade, if I can capture a Russian flag—what can't I do if I set my mind to it?

6

LAW AND DISORDER

College was everything I had hoped it would be and more. Friends. Girls. Drugs. Booze. Travel. Adventure. Distance from my folks. And time. At Syracuse, I was given the gift of time. Time to do whatever I wanted. Time to do nothing at all. With all that time on my hands, imagine how much I could have learned if I had only bothered to study.

In the course of four years, I got around to pretty much everything else except studying. Given how little time I'd spent with my nose in a textbook, my grades at Syracuse had been surprisingly respectable. Picking easy courses, schmoozing the professors, and hiring occasional outside help—that turned out to be a winning formula for me. I wasn't going to graduate magna cum laude. I wasn't going to graduate magna cum *anything*. But as I sailed through senior year and started to think about the future, I had a grade point average in the low 3s—Bs and C-pluses—and the full expectation that I'd soon be in possession of a bachelor's degree in political science from a respected, private university. And here was the best part as I saw it at the time: I'd done it without ever once buckling down. God gave me the gifts of avoidance, smooth talk, and manipulation for a reason, I figured. Wasn't I supposed to use them?

Thanks to my dad, I'd even be graduating without a dime of student debt. Whatever I did next, I wouldn't be saddled with monthly student-loan payments, the dreary fate many of my friends were about to face. That, in turn, freed me from the urgent need to seek immediate, gainful employment. As I weighed options for my future, I certainly had no thirst for that.

It wasn't self-confidence that I honed at Syracuse. It was, some people might say, something shallower and far less admirable than that. But to my eye, it was more like self-absorption, the constant, relentless focus on me. My whims. My needs. My pleasures. Avoiding my fears. It manifested itself in cockiness and ego and a knee-jerk tendency to ignore the needs of others. That sounds bad but the truth is I was just trying in my own way to survive. That was always my excuse. It wasn't that I was suddenly secure and comfortable in who I was and where I was going. It was that I had learned to shove aside my lingering inse-curities and self-doubt—the nagging belief I'd held since childhood that I was never quite good enough—and dull those anxious feelings with an ever-increasing intake of drugs and alcohol. Looking out for number one, that was my direction. Fast and furious, that was my speed. Intricately manipulative, that was my chosen methodology.

Look out, future! Here I come!

My semester in England, especially the side trip with Glenn to Russia, was definitely the high point of my college career. In a funny way, Russia launched me. Russia was the site of my first big-league incursion—the May Day parade, the Kremlin, the flag pole feat would all set a standard for many more adventures to come and pack my twenties with unimaginable surprise, excitement, and fun. On that trip to Russia, I realized I had an extraordinary talent for inserting myself in places I didn't belong. I was prepared—thrilled, actually—to do things nobody else would dare to in ways that nobody else had. And I loved telling the stories afterward.

When I got back to America and told my friends about Moscow, people lit up instantly. They were impressed. They were entertained. "Wow, that's amazing," they said. They could hardly believe that what I was saying was the truth.

"Every word of it is true," I swore. "You want to see the flag?"

I loved sharing what I had done. In the telling, I felt better about myself. For a few minutes at least. I wasn't an aimless slacker fucking off in college and heading nowhere in life. I was a man on a mission—a twisted mission perhaps but a mission nonetheless. If I could get in anywhere, I could achieve anything. I had the balls and the charm and the intelligence. I was the man. I didn't realize it yet, but the pleasure I felt was strangely addictive. I just didn't realize that this type of addiction could be so dangerous to me.

I came to realize one other thing as I neared the end of college, an insight that I eagerly embraced and acted on. What I realized was this. I could delay adulthood indefinitely. This life of pointless debauchery didn't have an expiration date, not one that was arriving anytime soon.

Why rush? I had nowhere I really had to be.

But even with nowhere to be, I couldn't stay in Syracuse, and I didn't really want to. Four years was long enough. My friends would all be leaving, heading off to jobs or graduate school, and I wasn't up for another frigid winter in central New York State. I was twenty-one years old. I'd be twenty-two in November. I would soon be a college graduate. It was time for me to find somewhere fresh to land.

Wasn't that why God invented law school?

|||||||||||||||||

There certainly wasn't anything I was burning to do after college. I knew I didn't want to follow my friends to Wall Street, real estate, or some other boring job. My father was a lawyer. He seemed to have a good career. And I figured law school wouldn't be all that different from college, if you could play it right. You picked easy classes, snowed a few professors, found some cool guys to hang with, and did the bare minimum to get through. I knew I was good at all of that. I'd been proving my system for years. Plus, law school *sounded* impressive. "Hi, I'm a law student" had to be a better pickup line than, "Hi, I'm a college graduate who's floundering around with no idea what to do next." My parents could tell their friends, "Oh, Craig's in law school now." And I could buy myself another three years, pushing genuine adulthood that much further into the future. Who knew? I might even decide to become a lawyer one day! I made up my mind: I'd take the LSAT.

Next, I had to get in somewhere. With my gentleman's Bs and C-pluses at Syracuse and a so-so score on the Law School Admissions Test, I knew it wasn't going to be Harvard or Yale. I applied to twenty law schools and received eighteen swift rejections. I was accepted by one and a half. The half was the Delaware College of Law at Widener University, a former military college in Wilmington, Delaware. I'd never heard of Widener before I applied. I wasn't exactly sure where Delaware was. But they agreed to take me if I'd be willing to delay my arrival until the following spring. That sounded tolerable, although I suspected my father would expect me to work during that time. Luckily, I didn't have to wait.

The only law school that agreed to take me was Touro College, a brand-new institution that had set up shop in the former Robert K. Toaz Junior High School building in Huntington, Long Island. When I applied, Touro was just about to graduate its first class and was still awaiting provisional accreditation from the American Bar Association. I suspect the admissions committee could not afford to be too picky, and I also had an in. My father's niece, Mona, who ran one of the largest kosher caterers in the Northeast, knew someone on the board of trustees, who put in a good word for me. Whatever combination of factors did the trick, I was admitted to Touro and promised to arrive on campus as a first-year law student in September 1983.

I attended my Syracuse University graduation. It could have been an interesting day. In the years before and after, the commencement addresses were delivered by Ted Koppel and Dan Rather. My year, we got Daniel Boorstin, the librarian of Congress. A very brilliant man, I am certain. But he was about as exciting as his job title sounds. Not quite inspired, I said goodbye to my college friends. I spent the summer at home, entertaining myself, achieving nothing, and resting up for law school.

I had no idea what to expect.

I was right about one thing: law school was the perfect stall for me. My father would be paying for everything—tuition, rent, car expenses, credit card bills, bar crawling in the city, and pocket money too. My job was to stay in school. I rented a two-bedroom house behind a bagel shop on Pine Tree Road in Huntington. To fill the other bedroom, Vic Shapiro, a fellow law student from Augusta, Georgia, agreed to move in with me.

Our house quickly became Touro Law Party Central. I connected with five or six other guys who liked getting stoned and hanging out between classes and into the night. On the weekends, we'd watch sports on TV and throw loud house parties. I went to class, as did most of the others. But none of us spent a lot of time in the library. I spent no time studying at home. We'd make comments about the hapless professors. We'd trade suggestions on which classes to take and avoid. Mostly though, we kept dreaming up fresh ways to duck schoolwork.

I had the usual first-year schedule. Torts. Contracts. Legal writing. Criminal law. Civil procedure. Constitutional law. That sounds intense,

I know. But the classes were large. You only got called on occasionally. If you could keep your cool standing there, the answers were usually pretty obvious. The professors repeated the basic concepts over and over again. If you were halfway paying attention—even one-third of the way—you didn't need to spend late nights studying. You could easily regurgitate the material on test day.

I'd always heard that school got tougher the higher you went. In my experience, the precise opposite was true. College was easier than high school. Law school was easier than college. With that nugget of realization, I probably should have thought of going for a couple of PhDs! I'm sure there are plenty of serious students who would disagree with me, but I don't think this pattern applied only at Clarkstown South, Syracuse, and Touro.

For one thing, the law school style of learning, I discovered, was a better fit for me. Law school wasn't so much about soaking up material and memorizing facts. It was all about reasoning and thinking critically. I grew up in a verbal, New York, Jewish family. Some days, all we did was think critically. That's a social skill as much as an intellectual one. Partly, that was just the way I was wired. Partly, it was my culture and background. And partly, it took less work. Put another way, there was far more room for bullshit, and no one could say I wasn't good at that.

There was a practical consideration too. The higher we went, it seemed, the more the teachers trusted us—totally unjustified in my case. Study groups were encouraged. More of the exams were open book. Cheating was definitely easier. I had no trouble finding prewritten law school papers the couple times I needed one. At Touro, the honor system was far looser than it had been at Syracuse. As far as I could tell, the written policies were based on what they said was honesty, fairness, respect, and an ability to trust one another. It never actually said "don't cheat." The professors certainly didn't think it was their job to monitor us.

There was one other thing. Touro, being a Jewish school, meant classes ended early on Friday for the Sabbath. The campus, even the law library, remained closed all day Saturday. Less time to study and more time to party. I can't say I was learning much, but law school was definitely for me!

As far as my parents were concerned, I was holding up my end of the free-ride bargain. I checked in with them on holidays. I was still progressing with my education. I cashed my dad's checks. I wasn't getting kicked out of school. Everything looked great on the outside. My mom and dad could keep telling their friends, "Craig's in law school," then nod appreciatively when someone would say, "You must be so proud of him."

||||||||||||||||

Approached my way, law school left plenty of free time for going out, and now I had a whole new set of running mates. I met a girl in my class named Stacy Burrell. We dated. Debbie Glass was safely off at Boston University. Though I stayed in touch with her, she wasn't nosing around. I had friends from law school, friends from college, and friends from childhood. There was always someone to hang out with.

Much like my undergraduate days of partying, I spent a lot of time in Manhattan trying to get into the trendiest bars and clubs. And like I'd learned in my Syracuse days—if you weren't rich, famous, or beautiful, the hottest bars were the hardest to get into. Unfortunately the new more sophisticated bouncers were a little less likely to fall for those old-school methods of charming my way in. I needed something smarter to outsmart the keepers of the list.

My campaign began long before the famous people arrived. I wouldn't wait until nighttime. I would call the club in the afternoon to seed the field.

"How are you today?" I'd say when someone answered.

"Fine. What can I do for you?"

"Hi," I'd continue, friendly as I could. "My name is Craig Schmell."

I always used my real name. It gave credibility. And why not? "Who's the manager on duty tonight?" I asked.

"May I ask what this is regarding?"

A little reluctance was normal. People in the nightlife business are used to being nudged and even scammed.

"I was in the club the other night," I'd explain. "I left my jacket there. I forgot the name of the manager I spoke with who held my jacket. He was very nice."

That almost always produced a name or two. My story was credible enough. I didn't sound deranged. I wasn't asking for anything outrageous. People leave their jackets in nightclubs all the time.

"Damian Smith?"

As soon as I got the name, I'd say: "Let me run. I've got to take another call. I'll call back."

Now, I had the manager's name.

I'd wait an hour or two. Then, I'd call back. I'd introduce myself and ask for the manager by name.

"What does this involve?" came the inevitable question.

"I was there the other night," I'd say, "and Mr. Smith gave me his card. He asked me to let him know when I'd be returning. We had a terrific time."

Incredibly, it was that simple. Usually I would get the manager on the phone.

"Hi, Damian," I'd say. "How are you today?"

"Fine. Who's this?"

"Damian, I don't know if you remember me. My name is Craig Schmell. I was there last weekend. I had such a wonderful time. You gave me your card and told me if I ever wanted to come back, you'd be more than happy to accommodate me."

Ninety-five times out of a hundred, a nightclub manager was not going to say, "I don't remember you." That would feel rude. The manager would be embarrassed for forgetting. A nightclub manager meets many, many people. He can't possibly remember them all. It's far easier for him to say, "Of course, I remember you."

"Great," I'd answer. "I'm coming in tonight with a friend or two. If there's something you could do—put us on the list or help with access to the VIP area—I'd certainly appreciate it. May I ask for you when we arrive?"

That rarely failed.

Even in the status-conscious world of New York nightlife, an exchange like that was nearly as valuable as money or fame. The manager almost never asked exactly who I was. He just assumed I was somebody. People in that business deal with self-important assholes all the time. They have to. It comes with the territory. I was being polite. I was carrying myself with confidence. I must be somebody. I'd made a point of mentioning what a fine club he ran and how much I appreciated his excellent hospitality.

You don't need to study Dale Carnegie to understand that people like being appreciated and admired and singled out by name. I might as well have said, "I'm Phil Collins" or "I'm Jack Nicholson." The way I called, people just assumed I was someone special. When I said, "I'm Craig Schmell," I really seemed to mean that name carried weight. I sounded legit.

This was something anyone could do, but almost nobody did. All it took was a nice manner, some self-confidence, and an idea. I was full of ideas.

The vast, vast majority of times, that one short call would get my name on the guest list of a popular club and, often, access to the VIP room for me and my friends. We'd hang out. We'd meet girls. They'd think we were somebody. We'd dance and talk and be where all the pathetic bridge-and-tunnel people from Jersey and the outer-boroughs could only dream of. At some point during the night, I would always go over and introduce myself to the manager I had spoken with. That way, he'd remember me next time. The occasional times that my approach failed or I could tell that the person I was dealing with wasn't buying my load of crap, I'd just say, "I'm sorry. Maybe I have the wrong Damian Smith," and I would hang up the phone. If I decided to go to the club anyway, at least I'd have the manager's name.

Even if Damian Smith had blown me off on the phone, I could tell the doorman, "Hi. Damian Smith said to come by." The doorman knew Damian Smith. Damian Smith was his boss. Just that name carried credibility. The doorman wasn't calling Damian Smith every time somebody claimed to be a friend. At least we wouldn't have to wait on line too long.

Looking back now, I can see what an empty prize this was, getting into some stupid nightclub with a bunch of other drunk and stoned idiots. Who cared about hanging around with all these status-conscious social climbers? Well, I did, and so did a lot of other people in those days—and not just then, I'll bet. I can tell you this much: it all seemed very glamorous to a first-year student at a no-name law school in the Long Island suburbs. If these were the prized locations, I knew I wanted in.

I never forgot how these forays into the city made me feel.

Driving back to Long Island one night at five o'clock in the morning, I was just leaving Manhattan in my car alone. There was no traffic heading east at that time of the morning, but the early commuters into the city were already clogging the entrance to the Midtown Tunnel.

What losers, I thought to myself as I flew through the tollbooth and onto the Long Island Expressway. *Those people are sick. Getting up every morning and driving into work. How empty! All of them are wasting their lives.*

I had it all upside down and backwards, of course. I can see that now. They were the ones who were supporting their families, doing something useful, getting up early and carrying on with a meaningful life. I was the one who was sick, and I didn't have a clue. I couldn't see it at all.

||||||||||||||||||

Early in the year, I had met a fellow first-year law student named Brad Blakeman. He wasn't one of my closest friends, but he was part of our regular crowd. He was from Long Island and knew the area really well. We hit the bars together a few times and he came by the house on Pine Tree Road.

Before arriving at Touro, Brad was active in Republican politics, volunteering on campaigns, getting to know other young politicos. He never said so exactly, but I had the distinct impression he was thinking about making his own run for office one day. At some point, he had worked for George Bush, the father, who'd been elected three years earlier as Ronald Reagan's vice president. I didn't know exactly what Brad had done for the vice president. But even if it was just a low-level volunteer position, he had clearly made some contacts and established some personal trust. Good for Brad!

On December 12, 1983, President Reagan was scheduled to visit New York. The president, I knew, always traveled with a large entourage—staff members, Secret Service agents, media people, and others. What I didn't know until Brad explained was that, this time, there was also a role for Brad's friends. As a trusted law student and rising young

Republican, he was helping to organize the local crew. I made sure to buddy up to Brad. He had several roles to fill, he told me one day at school. Among them, he needed a dozen responsible, local people to drive in the president's motorcade.

"Who better than me?" I asked Brad as soon as he mentioned that.

He shrugged and said, "Sure."

|||||||||||||||||

I had no idea if I'd even lay eyes on Ronald Reagan. But driving in a presidential motorcade sounded to me like a once-in-a-lifetime opportunity, a fitting follow-up to my adventures in and around the Kremlin. Frankly, I was surprised I'd be allowed in the president's motorcade without a formal interview or at least a thorough pat-down by the Secret Service.

But, hey. That was their problem, not mine.

On the morning of the big day, we all met near a special gate at Kennedy Airport. I recognized several other people from our law school class.

Brad briefed us on the rules, speaking far more commandingly than I was used to hearing him around school. "Keep your place in line," he instructed. "Don't try passing the vehicle in front of you even if it's going maddeningly slow. And no photographs. This is important. No photographs. You are here to assist with an official presidential visit to New York City. This is not a tourist trip."

Brad gave each of us a little pin to wear on our lapels, identifying us as members of the president's party. He held a sheet of paper with our specific assignments and began directing us to our vehicles. Most of the guys from law school got cars 14 through 25, which carried staff members, aides, and media people who were traveling with the president. Mine was car 19, camera 4, a family-style station wagon with room for five or six camera people, writers, and producers and their gear.

We lined our assigned cars in numerical order and were escorted into a special area of the airport, where we waited for Air Force One to land. Once the plane landed, people began walking toward their assigned vehicles. Some departed the plane on the tarmac and other people seemed to have already been waiting at the airport. Up toward the front of the line—not the very front—I could see a flurry of activity that I assumed was President Reagan getting into one of the armored black limousines. By then, the TV camera crew I was driving was in place and ready to roll.

Driving in a presidential motorcade into New York is the way commuting ought to be. All lanes were kept open for us. Traffic was held back at each intersection by NYPD officers to allow us through. We didn't stop at the tollbooth entering the Midtown Tunnel. We didn't stop for anything. We cruised along as if we owned the roads, which in a way I guess we did. The first thought that entered my mind was, *I could get used to this. How do I keep it like this when I drive into the city on my own?* I could see why presidents like to travel. Who wouldn't if traveling was like this?

Our first stop was the United Nations, and I promise you we didn't have to circle the block looking for a place to stop. All of First Avenue was held clear for us. I just rolled up and stopped. I waited with the car while the camera 4 crew chased the president around the UN.

As we waited, I wanted to get a closer look at one of the limousines that followed the president's. It was a convertible and seemed to be the prime security car. I could tell the limo was heavily armored. It had been carrying several Secret Service agents, two of whom had what looked like submachine guns.

I remembered what Brad had told us. But I really wanted to take a photo of that car and those guns.

Smartphones with built-in cameras hadn't been invented yet. Motorola had started selling a mobile phone, but it was $4,000. It weighed two pounds and was the size of a man's shoe. And the only thing you could do with it was make phone calls. It would be years before I'd have even a flip phone. But I did sneak in a small point-and-shoot camera with me that day. While the president was inside the UN, I walked by the armored car with the camera under my arm and got off a couple of quick snaps.

The whole day was like that. We raced through empty city streets as we delivered President Reagan to his various stops. I heard on 1010 WINS news radio that traffic was clogged almost everywhere, but it wasn't clogged for us. Police were stationed at every intersection, holding back the cars as we went from our first stop at the United Nations to the Waldorf Astoria Hotel, which was just five blocks away. Even the side street, midday, crosstown traffic between First and Park Avenues was no issue for us.

Several of us, me included, were allowed to go inside the Waldorf while President Reagan was there. I didn't see that coming, and I didn't know exactly what to expect. Turned out, that was my chance to meet the most powerful man on earth, the president.

It wasn't a long conversation. He just said "hello" and "thank you for all your help." We shook hands and had our picture taken together. I had a longer conversation with the president's acting press secretary, Larry Speakes, who told me how much he always loved visiting New York even though he came from tiny Cleveland, Mississippi. Speakes knew the danger of any public foray for an American president. He had the "acting" in his title because he became the president's spokesman when press secretary James Brady was shot in an assassination attempt on President Reagan on March 30, 1981. Though unable to return to work, Brady retained the title. I glanced over at some of the many Secret Service agents. I wondered if they were supposed to take a bullet for volunteer motorcade drivers. Either way, I felt grateful to have the armed agents nearby.

Our final motorcade destination was the Wall Street heliport. It was another glide through empty city streets. From there, President Reagan was being choppered to his next stop and my brush with greatness was over. For now.

It had been another magical day. Everything went off without a hitch. This wasn't a scam exactly, my driving in the president's motorcade. But it demonstrated my continuing interest in being where the action was, whatever the action might be. It gave me yet another story to tell. And the president seemed to appreciate my being there.

A couple of weeks later, a letter was waiting for me at school. The return address said 1600 Pennsylvania Avenue, Washington, DC.

"Dear Mr. Schmell," the letter began. "Thank you for your efforts on my visit to New York in December. I know a lot of time and energy were devoted to the visit and I am grateful for your supportive assistance. With best wishes, sincerely, Ronald Reagan."

7

GOLD MEDAL SUMMER

Though my first year of law school wasn't nearly as terrible as it could have been—not the way I did it—I was still relieved when June finally rolled around and I could forget all about contracts, civil procedure, and con-law. I didn't want my head to explode. Compared to some of my classmates, I supposed I wasn't all that stressed out. The drinking, pot smoking, and partying certainly helped. But ever since that third week in August when classes first met, I hadn't been able to fully relax.

By the time the professors were done with us in May, many of my fellow first-year students had lined up summer jobs for themselves, working at law firms, interning at the district attorney's office, or getting other firsthand experience in the legal profession. God bless 'em. I could see how that might be valuable. But frankly, it sounded a little dreary to me. After nine months of professional school, I was supposed to put on a jacket and tie and spend the next three months toiling in a stuffy office somewhere? No, that didn't sound like me!

What I needed instead was LA.

That wasn't a random choice of locales. This being 1984, the Summer Olympics were being held in Los Angeles, which everyone seemed to agree was a very big deal. No US city had hosted the Summer Games since Los Angeles in 1932. And this year's games were already swirling with drama. Four years earlier, the United States boycotted the Summer Olympics in Moscow to protest the Soviet Union's invasion of Afghanistan. In retaliation, the Soviets were boycotting the Los Angeles games. Since many of this year's prime venues were in Westwood, the neighborhood around UCLA, young people would be arriving from all over the world. I could only imagine the wild times to be had.

I have to be there, I decided.

One of my friends from Syracuse, Mark Weiss, had a childhood friend, Randy White, who was an undergraduate on the five-year plan at UCLA. I gave Randy a call and told him I was thinking about coming out for the summer. "When I get out there," I promised him in all my New York cockiness, "I'm gonna show you the summer of your life!"

Randy was a cocky New Yorker too, though he might have mellowed a bit from his years in sunny California. I'm sure he was shaking his head at my obnoxious attitude and thinking, *Who's this East Coast hotshot ready to show* me *LA?*

I didn't care. All I knew was that Olympic summer in Los Angeles sounded like an ideal sequel to my semester abroad. Living in London and roaming the European continent had turned out well. But in LA, the weather would be warmer and the girls would be wearing a whole lot less. Randy said he looked forward to hanging out and I was welcome to stay at his fraternity house for a few days while I got my bearings.

I discussed all this with my father. I explained to him that, after the exhausting year I'd just had, I could really use some downtime in the California sun. I had two more years of law school and didn't want to risk burning myself out prematurely. That sounded sensible, he said. He agreed to help with the expenses. I promised to pitch in as well as I could by looking for work once I got out there.

Randy was waiting for me at LAX when my flight arrived. In his car on the way to Westwood, he fired up a joint, which I interpreted as a welcoming gesture. I took a hit and reminded him that I was going to be the best guest ever. "You will never forget this summer," I promised, "the times we're going to have."

Judging from the grin on Randy's face, he half believed me and half thought I was totally full of shit. But it was summer. His schedule was light. He seemed up for whatever. He helped me haul my duffle bag into the Zeta Beta Tau house just off campus on Strathmore Drive—enough socks and T-shirts that I'd hardly need to do laundry at all—and up to the bedroom he shared with one of his fraternity brothers. Now, we were three.

And so the California party began.

Every night, Randy and I and various of his fraternity brothers and hangers-on would hit the bars and clubs around Westwood. Bistango. Dillon's. Baxter's. The Chart House. We'd sleep late, maybe go to the gym, sometimes shoot some baskets, and always go out at night. Given my many boasts, I felt almost duty-bound to out-party the LA frat boys, though I have to admit they gave me a pretty good run. On one of our first nights together, we drove to a rundown motel on the Pacific Coast Highway. The Sun Spot, it was called. Originally opened in 1938 as Carl's Sea Air, it had become a sprawling, open-air, disco-themed cocktail lounge. Guys and girls in beachwear—hardly anything, in other words—were dancing, drinking, and making new friends. The part of the night I remember most was when Randy and I were laughing so hard, we tumbled together into a giant popcorn machine. I wasn't sure we'd ever get out.

LA was everything I had imagined and more—with one key exception. The bars out there had to stop serving alcohol at 2:00 a.m., two hours earlier than I was used to in New York. One night, we were at Bistango on North La Cienega Boulevard, one of our favorite places. We'd had the thin-crust ratatouille pizza, the football-sized smoked-chicken calzones, and many rounds of vodka-grapefruit-tequila shots. We definitely weren't ready to call it a night. In the celebratory swirl of Bistango, 2:00 a.m. seemed absurdly arbitrary. So I did what seemed like the only sensible thing. I stood up, reached behind the bar, and grabbed a full bottle of Stolichnaya—cheers, comrades!—and carried the bottle back to our booth. As the waiters and waitresses bussed around us, I poured fresh rounds of Russian vodka for my many new friends.

"Gentlemen," I announced, raising my own glass in a toast at the stroke of 2:00 a.m., "do you realize we have the only open bar in all Los Angeles?"

I think I won some frat boy converts right there.

||||||||||||||||||

Randy could not have been a more gracious host, though after a week or so his roommate was becoming less keen on my extended residency. To him, the prospect that the three of us might remain jammed in this room all summer sounded downright claustrophobic. Randy finally said to me, "We love you, man, but you really can't stay here any longer. You have to get your own place. Keep coming though, okay?" I knew it was time, and thankfully an even better opportunity opened up. I rented a spare bedroom at the Delta Sigma Phi house around the corner on Landfair Avenue, $500 for the rest of the summer. Immediately, I called Barry Zuckerman in New York.

"BZ," I nearly shouted into the phone, "you gotta get out here. The Olympics are coming. The room is already paid for. This place is like paradise. Just bring money for your bar tab."

With Barry, that was almost too easy a sell. He promised to arrive by the weekend.

I did feel pressured to look for a job. I'd promised my dad I would. I was sure I could find something.

One of the hottest bars that summer was a place called Yesterday's. It was on Westwood Boulevard a few blocks south of campus. It had a carved-oak bar, a second-story balcony, a stage for live music, and lighting that made everyone, male and female, look great. That last one could also have been the alcohol. If I had to look for a job, why not try Yesterday's?

I walked in one afternoon and asked for the manager. A guy in his thirties came out. I introduced myself as a Syracuse University graduate and a first-year law student from New York, spending the summer in Los Angeles. "You'll be needing extra people because of the Olympics," I told the manager. "You should hire me."

He seemed to agree.

"Have you ever been a bartender before?" he asked me.

"Absolutely," I assured him. "Back in New York. Before I started law school."

That was a total lie. I'd never mixed anything more complicated than a gin and tonic. Ever. But how hard could bartending be? Serve a beer, pour a glass of wine, mix the occasional cocktail—I knew I could handle that.

He must have appreciated my confidence. He hired me on the spot.

I didn't last a single shift. About half an hour in, five people at once were ordering cocktails I'd never heard of. "What the fuck is Sex on the Beach?" I mumbled to myself, not a question I'd ever asked before.

"Did you say peach schnapps?" A guy in aviator shades was demanding to know where his change was and asking to see the manager. I was ignoring three or four other people who were waving at me. The one technique I picked up instantly was the vacant waiter stare. But the orders all sounded like chemistry experiments, and I wasn't hiding my incompetence from anyone, especially not the manager.

He called me over and said calmly: "Tell me the truth. Do you know how to bartend?"

"No," I answered.

"And you thought you could learn here?"

He never raised his voice. He didn't even sound angry. He also didn't sound like he was in a mood to negotiate.

"Get the fuck out of here," he said firmly.

"Now."

And I did.

The next day, I applied for a waiter's position at the Old World Restaurant, another spot I'd been to in Westwood. The Old World was owned by Barry Comden, who'd been Doris Day's fourth husband. They'd divorced by the time I showed up. According to Barry, his TV-star wife preferred the company of her dogs. She had fourteen of them and kicked Barry out of bed, he said, to make room for Tiger, a frisky poodle.

I was sure I could make this work. My extra-help-for-the-Olympics line worked just as well on Mr. Comden's manager as it had at Yesterday's. The manager hired me as a waiter and told me I would start with brunch. The brunch was legendary. It was the reason Doris Day had first come to Old World and met her future husband. I had four tables that Sunday morning. One of them was occupied by BZ, Randy, and two of my new LA friends. I was touched they had pulled themselves out of bed in a kind show of support.

I did no better as a waiter than I had as a bartender. I couldn't keep the orders straight. I couldn't remember who wanted a mimosa and who wanted a Bloody Mary. I couldn't communicate with the guys in the kitchen, who seemed to speak no English at all. I couldn't balance the plates on my arm. I couldn't add the bills right. In every way imaginable—other than welcoming the people to the table and announcing the daily specials—I sucked.

The Old World manager was just as calm as the Yesterday's manager had been but slightly more insistent. He physically escorted me out the door, and he watched for half a block as I walked up Sunset Boulevard. My friends were still at their table wondering why someone else was suddenly waiting on them.

That pretty much ended my food and beverage career. I fell back on the usual option: I called my dad. "The job thing hasn't gone as smoothly as I'd hoped," I said. "I was hired as a bartender and then as a waiter. I don't think I'm cut out for either of those. But everyone's getting excited about the Olympics, and I'd love to be part of that somehow."

My father sounded resigned.

"I'd like to stay out here for another four or five weeks," I said, "then get back to New York in time for school."

My father just sighed and said, "Okay." He sent me another thousand dollars, and he kept paying the credit card bills.

|||||||||||||||||

With my frat-boy posse and made-to-order nightlife, I was meeting new girls every night. Even Barry was getting lucky. I was meeting so many LA girls, in fact, I was having trouble giving all of them the attention they deserved. I'm not sure if it was my bravado or the fact that I was the new boy in town. But after one long night of laughing and drinking, I ended up in a beautiful mansion in the Hollywood Hills. The dark-haired woman from the bar didn't mention her age, but she seemed to be a few years older than I was. She certainly didn't lack vigor in the mansion's master bedroom. When I woke the next morning, she was still in bed.

I pulled on my pants and tiptoed to the bathroom. I didn't see or hear anyone, but the views from every window went on and on. There was something else I noticed in the light of day: hanging on the walls were a dozen gold and platinum records, all honoring top-selling releases by the Bee Gees.

Oh, my God, I thought. *This house must somehow be connecte to one of the singing brothers Gibb!*

And the woman still asleep in the master bedroom? Was she a Bee Gees' wife or ex-wife, a daughter, a boarder or a friend? My brain was filling up with snatches of Bee Gees songs, every one of which seemed written for me and this very moment.

"I started a joke . . ."

"To love somebody—the way I love youuuuuuu."

"Stayin' alive, stayin' alive, ah, ha, ha, ha, stayin' alive, stayin' alive . . ."

For all I knew, this kind of thing might happen every night in Hollywood, meeting someone in a bar and ending up in a pop star's mansion, not quite sure who anybody is. But until I came to California, nothing like that had ever happened to me. I wasn't sure exactly how to behave. I certainly didn't want some jealous, shaggy-haired singer coming in the front door and taking a swing at me. I was pretty sure I should just get out of there. But I wanted to be certain where *there* was, and I wanted some proof for my friends I'd been there.

I thought about taking one of the gold records off the wall, but that seemed too risky. Instead, I made my way into the kitchen, looking for something else. No one else seemed to be around. On a counter, I saw an opened envelope with a piece of paper right next to it.

"Mr. Andy Gibb," the envelope read. "1710 Crisler Way, Los Angeles, CA 90069."

Beside the envelope was a bill from a company called Business Jet Airlines for $32,795.83.

All I could think at that point was, *I hope Mr. Gibb is off on a very long trip.*

I snuck back into the bedroom, grabbed my clothes, and left without saying goodbye.

||||||||||||||||

I was pretty certain that none of my law school friends could match my summer. They were probably trotting over to the clerk's office or sucking up to the hiring partner in hopes of being invited back the following summer. What a grind all that sounded like! I guess you could say I hadn't accomplished too much, depending on your meaning of "accomplish." To me, I was accumulating experiences that would last me a lifetime. My classmates were the ones wasting their time.

By the time the Olympic torch reached Los Angeles on July 28, I considered myself a full-fledged young man about Hollywood. I had my entourage. I had my credit cards. I had no reason to get up in the morning before ten. We got tickets to a few Olympic events—a day of track and field competition and the women's gymnastics. They were interesting, but not as interesting as our own gold-medal events.

On August 9, the night before we were flying back to New York, Randy and I finagled tickets to the boxing semifinals. The big heavyweight fight was American Tyrell Biggs against Aziz Salihu of Yugoslavia. Until we sat down, I didn't realize how good our seats were, two rows back from the ring. But proximity to the action wasn't the best thing about our seats. Not even close. The best thing was the man a few seats to my right, eating popcorn. I recognized him immediately. It was Muhammad Ali. To me, that was far more thrilling than anything that could possibly happen in the ring. Before he became the heavyweight champion of the world, when he was still Cassius Clay, Ali had won the light heavyweight Gold Medal for team USA at the 1960 Olympics in Rome. I was transfixed. Instead of watching the fight, I watched Ali watch the fight. It was the best night of boxing I had ever seen.

After the match, which Biggs won in a 5-0 decision, Randy and I met a bunch of our friends at the Hard Rock Cafe. Since this was going to be my last night in Los Angeles, they offered to take us out for one last night of West Coast debauchery. Turns out, they had a special goodbye in mind.

Maybe they were getting me back for my New York attitude, I don't know. Maybe it was my repeated boasts that I could outdrink any of these California college boys. Maybe they wanted to teach me a lesson. Maybe they were just having a little frat-boy fun. One thing for sure, the model/actor/whatever behind the bar at the Hard Rock was in on it. The bartender's name was Stewie, and they knew him from somewhere. Stewie kept pouring rounds and rounds of shots. Unbeknownst to us, they were all downing shots of water, while Randy and I got full vodka pours. I was getting totally hammered but these guys all seemed fine. On my last night in California, I wasn't about to be left in the dust by these amateurs.

"Pour me another, Stewie," I said.

I went outside to pee. I'm not sure why I decided to do that. They must have had a bathroom at the Hard Rock. But as I was walking Beverly Boulevard looking for a good spot, two uniformed officers drove up in an LAPD radio car.

"You all right?" the cop in the passenger seat said out the window.

He might as well have been speaking Mandarin. Given the shape I was in, the question utterly stumped me. The next thing I remember I was waking up in a holding cell at the LA County jail. That's when the officer explained that I'd been charged with violation of section 647f of the California Penal Code. It said that a person is guilty of public drunkenness if "he or she is unable to exercise care for his or her own safety or the safety of others." Yep, that sounded about like me.

I called Randy White to come and get me. It must have been four or five in the morning by then. When Randy answered the phone, I could hear that people were still up in the fraternity house. I heard Barry's voice calling, "Craaaaig!" I was still suffering mightily, but somehow Randy had managed to get back home. "Damn," I said to Randy, "you guys are still partying?" Stamina: that's one of the differences between vodka shots and water shots. It took them a long time to get downtown. I had a lot of time to sober up and a chance to wonder why no one had noticed that I'd left the bar and that I'd never come back. But mostly I wondered why they were taking their sweet time coming to spring me. They knew I had a flight to catch. Randy told me later that Barry wasn't ready to break up the party, although Barry denied that. By the time they got there, I had been given a desk ticket and released on my own recognizance. When they finally pulled up, I'd given up waiting and was walking toward Chinatown on North Vignes Street, a block and a half from the LA County jail. Randy was driving. Barry was riding shotgun.

"Look at you, man," Barry said. "Get in."

I missed my flight and a couple of flights after that. I didn't get out of LAX until the next day.

||||||||||||||||||||

Despite the last-minute hiccup, I considered the summer a smashing success. I got to know Los Angeles. True, I saw three big Olympic events. And not only that, I ran my own marathon and jumped a few hurdles. I was still standing when the final bell rang. I wasn't a champion employee, but that was not a high priority. I consumed a lot of alcohol, left a lot of money on bar tops, and I met a lot of great-looking girls. What no one told me—and I didn't yet have the insight to recognize—I also acted like an unrepentant, obnoxious, self-absorbed jerk.

By the time I was safely back in New York, I'd already forgotten many of the women I had spent time with. But one of them, at least, had not forgotten about me.

I'm not quite sure how she did it. This was pre-Google. She obviously went to some trouble, tracking down my parents' address in New City and sending a carefully crafted letter to me. My parents sent it, unopened, to my apartment on Long Island.

I was back in law school. Second year had begun. My LA summer was already fading from my mind.

It was not a nice letter. In fact it was the angriest letter I had ever gotten in my life. I can't say it wasn't deserved.

"Craig Smell," it began. The misspelling wasn't accidental. I am sure of that. I jumped to the end of the note, but the letter wasn't signed, not in any normal way. I went back to read it from the top. Try as I might I couldn't figure out—or I couldn't remember—who the author was. But it was obviously one of the women I had met that summer, and boy was she steamed.

"First and foremost, you make me want to throw up," the letter began on a less than promising note. It went downhill from there.

After all the shit you dished out, it's about time you took some back. You tried to force yourself on a girl who really found you repulsive and who was only trying to blow off a deadly boring night or two. And believe me, it wasn't worth a pot to piss in. You were shitty in bed. The crust on your mouth was so unattractive and I can't believe I let you come near me. Sleeping with you is like being humped by an epileptic rhinoceros. I must have been so bored to even look at your gold chains dripping off of your repulsive olive-colored neck. Your constant complaints embarrassed me in public and only reinforced my repulsion for Jewish mothers. Anyway, I think you're better off a homosexual because you and your John Travolta hair can only attract the most desperate effeminate male. Good luck, baby, you'll need it.

Yes, there had been some drunken, stoned nights. Too many to remember them all. Try as I did to remember, I had no idea who my letter-writing critic was. There was an initial down at the bottom. It looked like a G or a J. I couldn't be sure which. There was no return address and no way for me to write back.

8

COOL AID

Second year of law school was no more strenuous than first year had been. If anything, it was slightly easier. Ducking classes, doing the bare minimum, going out at night. Debbie and I got together when she was back home from Boston University. I still enjoyed the security of knowing I had a girlfriend, but all my assurances of faithfulness did nothing to cramp my style. I also kept dating Stacy Burrell. And I kept hitting the clubs with my friends and meeting more young women there. But as easy and fun as that year was, I knew that eventually I would have to try my hand at the law.

As second year was winding down, I swallowed hard and applied for a summer position in what was supposedly my chosen field. I was hired as a summer associate with a small Long Island law firm. Before I got there, I had dark visions of barking partners, endless billable hours, and early-morning client conferences. But the reality wasn't bad at all. For a law firm, the place was fairly laid back. I'd get there when I got there in the morning. Everyone was friendly to me. No one asked me to do very much. When someone did, I usually had a reason why I couldn't. It wasn't the sort of thing I had agreed to do. It wasn't an area of law I knew about. I was too busy with some other assignment. It was easy to spend a whole day doing almost nothing. This was my kind of job! And best of all, it gave me plenty of time for the business I really cared about—hanging out with my friends, hitting the clubs in the city, and sitting around the house in Huntington. In other words, living. I still had another year of law school and, just as I'd told my father on the phone from California after first year, I didn't want to risk burning myself out.

Then came the morning of Saturday, July 13, 1985. I woke up at my parents' house and turned the TV on before I even pulled myself out of bed. Through the haze of another hangover and for the first time ever, I heard the words "live aid." Like Kool-Aid, but Live Aid. Clearly, this was going to be an unforgettable global event.

Live Aid was a fundraiser for the famine in Ethiopia. You can imagine how concerned I was about that. But this was not just any do-good music festival. Organized by Irish rocker Bob Geldof, Live Aid was a dual-venue, satellite-linked extravaganza unfolding that day and night at Wembley Stadium in London (where 72,000 fans had already gathered) and at John F. Kennedy Stadium in Philadelphia (90,000 tickets sold), with side concerts in Japan, the Soviet Union, Austria, West Germany, and other far-flung locales. In all, the world-wide TV audience, including MTV's live broadcast in America, was predicted to top 1.8 billion in 150 nations around the globe. Those were McDonald's numbers, live music on a scale that had never been attempted before!

What a show it was going to be. As I sat in my parents' living room in New City, watching my MTV, the band Queen already had the London crowd in a frenzy with a twenty-minute rendition of "Bohemian Rhapsody." Now, singer Freddie Mercury was leading everyone in unison refrains on "We Are the Champions." Damn, that looked like fun! I knew it was great, but even I couldn't have imagined that twenty years later the BBC would vote this Queen performance the greatest rock gig of all time. The London lineup also included U2, David Bowie, Elvis Costello, Paul McCartney, and The Who. Not too shabby, I thought. If anything, the bill at JFK Stadium was even stronger: Tom Petty, Bob Dylan, the Rolling Stones, Tina Turner, Madonna, a reunion of Crosby, Stills, Nash & Young, the original Black Sabbath with Ozzy Osbourne, the surviving members of Led Zeppelin, and Teddy Pendergrass's first public appearance since a near-fatal car accident had left him paralyzed. That last one was a nice touch, I thought. Phil Collins was vowing to appear on both stages, thanks to a mad dash to Heathrow and a nonstop, transatlantic flight to Philadelphia. I'd never heard of someone playing England and America in a single day!

How could I not be part of that? I called Barry Zuckerman immediately.

"BZ, wake up!" Under normal circumstances, this was way too early on a Saturday for a phone call. But I was excited, and I needed him to be too. "We gotta do this!"

After Moscow and Los Angeles, I was really feeling like the Batman of sneaking into places I didn't belong. Barry was my Robin, the only guy I knew who could sorta keep up with me. He wasn't quite as good as I was, but almost, and he never flaked out on me in a pressured moment. He could keep up with me as well as anyone I had ever met. That was true. And he was always ready to go. It was good to have a partner, I was discovering. And all these adventures were more fun with an audience.

As usual, Barry said, "Sure."

And that was that. We were going to Live Aid.

The time in London was five hours ahead of us. That gave us time to leave New York and drive the two hours down to Philadelphia without missing too much. We had no tickets. We had no plan. All we knew was that some of rock-'n'-roll's greatest all-time acts were going to be there, and so would we.

"Any idea how we're getting in?" Barry finally asked me as we pointed my Pontiac J-car down I-95 on what was already turning out to be a broiling hot day.

"The usual," I said. "We'll wing it once we get there."

||||||||||||||||

I was pretty sure that Barry and I would be able to make something out of nothing. And nothing is what we had—the concert's $35 tickets were totally sold out. We'd scope out the situation. We'd rely on our God-given gifts. We'd slip in somehow. The goal was the same as it always was: getting inside and as close to the action as we possibly could. I'd had plenty of experience at the velvet ropes of New York. This was three years before the Grammy Awards, but I'd been honing my craft for longer than that. I knew nothing yet about all-access passes or stage entrances or how to blend in with performers at major, once-in-a-lifetime music shows. But my boldness was rising. My ego was large. And I was about to learn the special nuances of crashing one-time-only events. I'd found a way into the president's motorcade, hadn't I? How hard could a rock concert be?

We picked up as much of the concert as we could on the car radio. From New York to somewhere in New Jersey, the live feed from London was on our local powerhouse rock station, WAPP/103.5 FM, which was amazing. After every band, an announcer reminded us to call 1-800-LIVEAID and make a donation to the cause. But this was way before cell phones, and we weren't stopping to find a phone booth. When the New York radio signal finally faded, we threw in a couple of cassettes until we were just outside Philadelphia and able to hear a rock station from there.

By then, the Philly show had already started. We tuned in just as Bette Midler, with her usual winking bravado, was introducing the next performer. "I want you to know I have no idea why I was asked to introduce this next act—because you all know, I am the soul of good taste and decorum. However"—she paused for effect there—"we are thrilled to be able to introduce to you today a woman whose name has been on everyone's lips for the last six months. A woman who pulled herself up by her bra straps and has been known to let them down occasionally."

Who else could that be but Madonna?

The always provocative singer, whose pre-fame nude photos had just been published by *Playboy* and *Penthouse*, grumbled into the mic, "I ain't taking off shit today," which wasn't bleeped. Then, Material Girl, as the world had known her for six months by then, flew into a rousing version of "Holiday," which was finishing just as we pulled up to JFK Stadium and found a place to park.

We were both so psyched. From outside the stadium, I could hear Tom Petty blasting out his heartland anthem, "American Girl." Barry and I still had no plan. But it turned out we didn't need one to get inside. As we walked up to the main stadium entrance, I could hear Tom Petty's soaring vocals: "The way-ay-ting is the hardest part." But oddly, there wasn't any waiting for Barry and me. No one was guarding the entrance. All the ticket takers seemed to have left their posts. I guess they figured if 90,000 people were already inside rocking to Tom Petty, they might as well do the same. All I know is that no one stopped us, asked to see our tickets, or even seemed to notice as Barry and I strolled in.

The first thing we saw when we got up the ramp was the *Saturday Night Live* star "I'm Chevy Chase and You're Not" introducing the cheerful folkie Kenny Loggins, who got most of the crowd on its feet with "Footloose." As we worked our way through the packed stands,

The Cars got on and off the stage quickly, and then I recognized the voice of another *SNL* cast member, Joe Piscopo, introducing Neil Young.

Football stadiums are not perfect venues for rock concerts, and JFK was no exception. Seating was general admission. A huge throng of people—the ones who'd gotten there early, I presumed—were on the field, looking up at the mammoth, elevated stage. The vast majority of others were in the stadium seats, looking down at the performances from a variety of weird angles. As far as I could tell, no one seemed to mind. Thousands were dancing in the aisles. They were singing along and roaring their approval after every song. The musicians were clearly feeding off the good vibes.

This was all great to see. But Barry and I didn't travel from New York to stand with tens of thousands of people five hundred feet from the stage, even if the bands were famous and the music was spectacular. We'd come to be *part* of Live Aid. The game from here, both of us understood, was improving our situation inside the stadium. Get up front. Grab choice seats. Insert ourselves as close to the action as we possibly could.

As I plotted our next move, I knew we had one factor on our side—the special vulnerabilities of one-day events. Live Aid was only happening once. It wasn't a long-running show or a city-by-city tour where the same production would be staged over and over again. This was a total one-shot. Tomorrow, as far as anyone knew, there would be no more Live Aid, only a gauzy memory. So no one involved in the current event—from Bob Geldof to the Philadelphia ticket takers who had abandoned their posts—had the luxury of learning from experience. Everyone was brought in fresh and for just this once. The vendors, the roadies, the sound engineers, the PR people, the catering staff, the managers, the artists, the security crew, the groundskeepers, everyone—they'd all be back at their day jobs tomorrow, doing whatever it was they were doing for the rest of their lives. The simple fact was that many of them—most of them—didn't know each other any more than they knew me. That gave someone like me an advantage. At an event like Live Aid, everything was being done on the fly. Believe me, the ticket takers at Philadelphia Eagles games don't disappear after the opening kickoff. If they tried that once, someone would notice and it would never, ever happen again.

That recognition set the environment for Barry and me at Live Aid. Now, all we needed to do was to maneuver inside it. We had to make someone believe we were somebody. *It's not who you are, it's who they think you are.* Not somebody famous, necessarily. Not somebody important. Just somebody who should be invited where we wanted to go. Then and only then, I knew, would we get the access and proximity we so patently did not deserve.

||||||||||||||||

Since no one told us not to and no one stopped us when we tried, Barry and I made our way down onto the field. This wasn't all that special. I'd guess 10,000 other people were also there, the early birds. But it did provide one key advantage. Once we were on the field, I got a better view of access to the stage. I noticed a set of gates to the left of the stage and another set to the right. We were on the left side. A large security guard—brick-house build, arms folded, somber expression—was standing at the stage-left gate. No way were Barry and I just breezing past him. He seemed to be taking considerable care as he checked credentials and allowed only certain people into the backstage area.

Damn.

Even without my saying, Barry knew exactly what was on my mind. "How are we getting backstage," he asked, "with *him* standing there?"

"I don't know," I said. "I'm working on that."

By this point, Eric Clapton was on stage backed by 90,000 voices wailing the chorus to "Layla." This was simply an incredible concert, and if we hadn't been so focused on our mission, we might have relaxed and just enjoyed it. We had so much more music ahead of us, I knew. But I also knew that Barry and I were still on the wrong side of Mr. Arms Folded while a veritable horde of rock-'n'-roll legends were lounging—and doing God knows what else—just out of my view backstage. Make that *our* view. Since I was with Barry, I had to think for the two of us. If I made it backstage, how would I slip Barry in too? Even with all those celebrities, it wouldn't be nearly as exciting being backstage at Live Aid alone. The whole idea was to do it together. We came together. We were good friends. We were a team. This wasn't necessarily a disadvantage, but it was a consideration.

Then, I got an idea, a brilliant idea if I do say so myself, though the brilliant part revealed itself only gradually. In front of the left gate, probably thirty yards out, was a beer and hot dog stand, a brightly painted wooden construction that looked like it had been nailed together the night before. I walked over, not quite sure what I was looking for. I hoped to get inspired. I wasn't yet the experienced expert at creative incursions that I would become. But I had good instincts and thankfully they kicked in here. I knew I needed something to give me credibility.

Concertgoers were standing in line. They were walking away with their beers and their hot dogs. As I lingered next to the stand, just soaking everything in, I noticed a clipboard with a piece of paper on it, sitting unattended at the edge of the stand. I walked to where the clipboard was. No one seemed to be paying attention. I casually picked up the clipboard and walked away. I made sure to hold it against my hip to shield it from view by the people at the stand. If one of them glanced over, all they would have seen was a guy in baggy shorts and a light-blue T-shirt melting into the crowd on the field.

Grab and go. That's all it was, a simple grab and go.

I hate to say this, but I was good at being sneaky. I kept my cool. I didn't hang around too long. I tried not to look furtive or sheepish. I just walked away with that clipboard in my hand.

I still had no idea what I was going to do with the damn thing. But I knew that a clipboard can make you look official, and looking official could be valuable in a situation like this. One step at a time I was making progress toward our goal. I just wasn't sure how exactly my progress was going to get me there. Route uncertain, destination clear.

The clipboard alone wasn't enough to get me backstage. I was sure of that. I needed something else, something confirming, something that would help convince people—that stage-left guard, especially—that I was legitimately working the Live Aid event and really did belong backstage.

I slipped the clipboard into the back of my shirt, anchoring the bottom at my belt. With the clipboard out of sight, I walked back to the hot dog and beer stand. I thought I needed a pen or a pencil to put in my ear. I saw a pencil right where the clipboard had been. I couldn't believe I'd missed it before. I slipped the pencil behind my right ear. I wasn't wearing a uniform, just my shorts and T-shirt. But together, the clipboard and the pencil props did seem to say "working," I thought. At least I felt legit.

Now properly outfitted and prepared, I walked up to the large man guarding the backstage entrance.

"How are you today?" I asked.

When it came to talking your way into places, a little politeness goes a long way. It's a respectful, human gesture. It breaks the ice. It gets the other person relating in a cheerful, conversational way.

From the guard, I got exactly the answer I expected: "Fine. How are you?"

Only his affect was a whole lot flatter than the words alone suggest.

"I'm so sorry," I continued. "I work with the concession stand." I nodded in the general direction of the stand, gripping the clipboard and making sure he saw the pencil in my ear. "Unfortunately, we're running low on hot dogs now. Can you do me a favor? I've got to go back there and get them to bring more stuff to the front."

I'm not even sure the story made much sense. Running low on hot dogs? Get *them* to bring more *stuff*? Who was *them*? What *stuff*? Jack Nicholson was on the stage now, and Bette Midler was back. They had an incredible announcement to make.

"Miracle," Jack declared.

"If I didn't know, I would say that was impossible," Bette continued.

But there they were on the Live Aid stage in Philadelphia, introducing Phil Collins who had indeed flown via British Airways' supersonic Concorde from London to become the only performer to appear at both concerts.

The gate guy with the folded arms didn't seem to notice the stage at all. His eyes were on me. And I wasn't at all sure he'd buy my ridiculous story. Was the multitasking Phil Collins also keeping an eye on the concert's hot dogs? Why would hot dogs be backstage, anyway? I had no answers, and, thankfully, the guard didn't ask. I was gripping my clipboard in an authoritative way. The concession stand was right over my shoulder. The pencil wasn't going anywhere. I was friendly and polite. Though my tone was slightly urgent, I didn't think I sounded totally nuts. Would someone really go to that much trouble just to get backstage at a music festival? Yes. Someone might. Someone with sufficient energy and something to prove.

"Of course," the security guard said, stepping aside to let me pass.

||||||||||||||||

It wasn't until I walked past the guard and through the backstage gate that I realized what was printed on the sheet in the clipboard. It was a minute-by-minute, act-by-act schedule of everyone who was performing in Philadelphia at Live Aid. It must have belonged to one of the general managers, who I could only assume left it at the wrong place at the wrong time, allowing me to scoop it up from the hot dog stand.

I made a quick loop through the backstage while I figured out how I was going to get Barry back too. I saw Jack Nicholson wearing those sunglasses that had for decades been his singular style statement. I saw Robert Plant from Led Zeppelin right away. Then, I saw Neil Young, who looked even skinnier than he did in his photos. I wanted to say hello, but I didn't have the nerve at first. That would come later.

For an outdoor concert, the backstage area was very well appointed. There was a catering area with a whole lot more than hot dogs. Plates of shrimp, bowls of salad, healthy-looking sandwich wraps. There was beer and soda, and camping tables so people could sit and eat comfortably. Everyone seemed very relaxed.

Phil was singing "Against All Odds" while I made my way back to the gate where I assumed Barry was still waiting. The same guard was standing there. With an extra shot of command in my voice, I gestured to Barry and told the guard, "I need him back here working with me."

The guard agreed again without any fuss.

And why shouldn't he have? This wasn't so different from a trick Barry and I had pulled dozens of times in any number of New York City nightclubs. I'd get inside first, then come back out to the door and confidently assert, "He's with me." It was amazing how often the doormen believed that I, a certified nobody, had the authority to wave him in.

"Can you believe this?" I said to Barry as soon as the two of us were safely inside.

"I can't believe we didn't bring a camera," he said, another pre–cell phone opportunity missed.

"Partners in crime," I agreed.

"It's like we've been planning this since we were sixteen," he said.

That was exactly how it felt.

The both of us were backstage at Live Aid. No one was challenging our right to be there. We seemed free to walk around. But I couldn't help noticing that everyone else backstage seemed to have the same security credential, a laminated card hanging on a neck chain. I had the clipboard. I had the pencil. I had my "concession assistant" Barry. He and I found a place to sit on a set of risers at the side of the stage, where we had a perfect view of the performances, half a level up from the action. We'd gotten this far. But still I couldn't help worrying that someone might come over and demand to know who we were. I held the clipboard close to my chest. Maybe no one would notice that I had no backstage credential like everyone else seemed to.

Then, something shiny caught my eye.

A woman was sitting just in front of us and slightly to the left. She had a purse in the seat beside her. She was watching the show a whole lot more than she was watching her handbag. Phil Collins, who looked perfectly rested despite his swift trip across the ocean, was sitting back at his drum set, this time backing up one of the most anticipated musical reunions of all time. He was pounding away, duplicating the drum parts made instantly recognizable by the late John Bonham, while Robert Plant, Jimmy Page, and John Paul Jones, together again as Led Zeppelin, commanded the stage. The woman in front of me was giving them her rapt attention. I wasn't. What I noticed was this: clipped to her purse was a laminated-plastic card, pale blue.

I didn't recognize the woman. She might have been a band member or a backup singer or someone's girlfriend. I had no idea, though I'm pretty sure she wasn't Madonna or Tina Turner or some other big star I would have easily recognized. But as I leaned in for a closer look at the plastic pass clipped to her bag, I could see it had a large S on the front and the word "PERFORMER."

That seemed promising.

Very gently, I shifted my body so I was sitting even closer to her purse. Looking in the opposite direction and making no abrupt movements, I slid my right hand closer.

The woman was still watching the stage, transfixed by Plant and the band, as the first, unmistakable notes of "Stairway to Heaven" paralyzed the rest of the stadium. In one swift snatch, one and a half seconds tops, I loosened the clip from her handbag and slipped the blue pass into the right pocket of my shorts.

I glanced at Barry, who'd been watching what I was doing and hadn't uttered a syllable. I nodded. He nodded back. We both stood and walked away—from the woman and her now clipless bag. I wanted to get away from her. I didn't want her noticing the pass was gone, then looking up and seeing me.

I clipped the PERFORMER pass onto my T-shirt.

I was nervous for a minute or two, as Barry and I strolled to the other side of the backstage area. But after we grabbed a couple of sandwich wraps off the food table and had a chance to catch our breath, I wasn't even worried anymore. We were just soaking it all in. Barry and I were backstage at Live Aid. No one was challenging us. We were surrounded by half the rock stars we'd loved since we were kids. And clipped to my T-shirt was a full-access, VIP, backstage pass. For all I knew, with that blue plastic card, I could wander onto the massive stage and start belting out a song. Look out, Mick! It said PERFORMER, didn't it?

I handed Barry the clipboard so he'd have some cover of his own. As far as anyone else was concerned we were as good to be back there as Mick Jagger or Roger Daltrey. Okay, not Daltrey. He was in London, but you get my point.

Soon though, I asked Barry for the clipboard back. I wanted an excuse to mix and mingle with some of these rock stars. Now, that sheet of paper with the Live Aid lineup became my autograph pad.

In this elite, backstage world, where everyone was someone, no one was too big to approach. "Hey, Jack," I said, seeing Nicholson walk away from the food table with, I swear, a small plate of salad. "What a great show, huh?" He nodded. "Do you mind signing for me?"

"Not at all," he said cheerfully.

Jack signed.

So did Chevy Chase. So did Robert Plant, Jimmy Page, and Don Johnson, the *Miami Vice* actor who was a big star at the time. So did Tom Petty, Phil Collins, and Neil Young—all of them scribbled their names on my Live Aid schedule.

I asked. They signed. We exchanged little pleasantries. It was just as simple as that. Nobody asked who I was, ever. Part of my gift, I was learning, was that I was comfortable talking with anyone like a regular person—no matter how famous, rich, or important they were. Didn't we put our pants on the same way?

We hung out at Live Aid, Barry and I, until nearly midnight, chatting up the artists, watching the show, grabbing autographs. The Stones had been amazing. Though Crosby, Stills, Nash & Young seemed to have some trouble with the sound system that affected their harmonies, Petty, Duran Duran, Patti LaBelle, Philly's own Hall and Oates, and Madonna all put on memorable performances. Talk about an embarrassment of riches! The epic "We Are the World" finale was not to be missed. I had to figure they were spurred on by one another's presence and the chance to help such a worthy cause.

For me, the very best memories were backstage, not on stage. Maybe because they figured I was one of them—or at least I sort of belonged there—these megastars couldn't have been more down-to-earth. Some were friendlier than others, but I really didn't encounter a jerk in the entire group.

All in all, it was one of the epic days and nights of my life. It reminded me again: it's not who you are, it's who they think you are.

That was also the day I learned how powerful a rectangular piece of plastic can be.

9

HIGH BAR

We had a side deal with Otto.

Otto was a bartender at America, a popular restaurant and bar on East Eighteenth Street in Manhattan's Flatiron District. America was one of our regular city haunts. I'd drag along some law school buddies. Or I'd meet up with friends from Syracuse or from high school. BZ and I logged plenty of stool time at America. And it wasn't only because of all the attractive young female office workers who stopped there after work. As I said, we had a side deal with Otto.

Right when we arrived, each of us would hand our man a $20 bill. If it was four of us, Otto would pocket $80. If it was five, his take would be $100. That was the last dollar that changed hands all night. Otto would make sure our whole group—however many people—drank for free the rest of the night. When he could, he'd also slip us a plate of chicken wings or some mini-pizzas or other treats from the kitchen. We loved Otto.

We never thought of this as stealing. We didn't care that Otto was ripping off his employer. All we cared about was that we could spend the whole night partying at America, and it would cost us twenty bucks.

One night, I met a young woman at the bar. Her name was Doreen McNally. She was pretty and dark haired and lived in Queens. She and I drank and talked for a couple of hours. She seemed really into me. Slowly, her friends and mine drifted off.

"Come back to my house on Long Island," I told her. "I'll drive you home later." She agreed, and we rode together to Huntington, giggling and flirting and talking all the way.

It was after three by the time we got into the house. Suddenly, she didn't seem so into me anymore. I didn't know if I'd said something wrong in the car or if she was too wasted or what. But she deflected my attempt to make out with her, and I was getting the distinct impression that the evening wasn't going to end the way I had hoped it would.

"Maybe you should take me home," she said curtly.

"Now?" I answered. "I'm not driving to Queens at four o'clock in the morning. Let's just go to bed. I'll drive you in the morning."

That really pissed her off. It was true I had told her I would drive her home "later." I didn't say "but only in the morning." Even with some law school under my belt, I wasn't trying to craft a legal argument. But the trip from the city to my house had taken an hour and we'd just barely gotten out of the car. I was trying to get this girl to come to bed with me. Now, she was getting angry, and I was getting angry, and the whole thing was going downhill fast. After being so bubbly in the bar and the car, she wouldn't fool around with me at all.

She insisted. This was a fight I wasn't going to win. Not if I wanted to get some sleep, which at that point was all I wanted. I finally said okay. I wasn't going to hold her against her will. I was being a jerk, just not *that* big a jerk. So we got back in my car but instead of driving her back to Queens, I headed toward the Long Island Rail Road station in

Huntington and told her, "Just get the next train." It was a little after four by then.

"When's the next train?" she demanded as we pulled into the train station parking lot. "You don't even know!"

That was correct. I didn't. "It'll be soon, I'm sure," I said dismissively. "Now get the hell out of my car." She opened the passenger-side door and I gave her a little shove.

This was not my finest hour. It reflected the kind of person I was becoming, someone even I couldn't feel proud of. That story makes me cringe now, and it wasn't over yet. As I screeched out of the parking lot, I caught one last glimpse of the young lady as she walked away from my car and toward the train platform. She seemed very angry but otherwise okay. I drove home and went to sleep.

I heard nothing from her for the next several weeks. But as I got home from school one day, a legal document was taped to my front door. It was a legal complaint and a summons, naming me as the defendant in a personal-injury lawsuit. She had sued me. She claimed in the lawsuit that I had struck her leg as I drove recklessly out of the Huntington train station parking lot.

I was pretty sure I hadn't run over her leg. True, I'd been anything but a gentleman to her. There was no denying that. I'd been a total dick. But as far as I knew, I had not run over or into her leg with my car. As she stormed away that morning, she appeared to be walking fine. Should I have stopped? Rushed her to Huntington Hospital? How was I supposed to know? I eventually learned that she hadn't sought any medical attention or gone to any hospital that day. Only later had she complained about any injury. Whatever. My guess was that if anything was injured, it was her pride more than her leg. Understandably.

But even as I read the legal papers, my biggest concern wasn't about Doreen McNally and her injuries. *Oh, my God*, I thought selfishly, *I'm a law student, and now I'm being sued. My life is over.*

I gave the papers to my father, whose first piece of advice was to please calm down. I told him about the woman I'd met in a bar who had come back to my house on Long Island and now was trying to get back at me. My father gave me a look that said, *Maybe you shouldn't be taking so many women back to your house after long nights of drinking.* But he said he'd try to get the lawsuit taken care of somehow.

||||||||||||||||||

With that unpleasantness being taken care of, I continued my legal education without much further disruption. Third year was even easier than first and second. I was through with most of my required courses. I took Entertainment Law, which was taught by Bruce Springsteen's attorney, and other fun classes. I had my system down cold. The only really hard course I had left was an advanced version of something called Remedies. It was way over my head. The hypotheticals were hugely complicated. The rules all seemed irrational. The concepts had grown more and more arcane. I sat through most of the classes, but my mind was anywhere but on the subject of law.

The night before the final exam, we had a party at my house. I'd meant to study—no, that wasn't true. I didn't mean to study. I meant to go in the next morning and wing it like I usually did. I knew nothing about the material. To me, it all seemed boring and dense. I had mostly daydreamed while this professor had tried to mold us into next-generation attorneys. Given how unprepared I was, I had no right even to be in the class, much less to be taking the test. Still, I wasn't worried. Sometimes, I reminded myself, you just have to believe in yourself.

The professor handed out the test sheet. This was no open-book exam. There were questions about various contracts issues, and we were all expected to know the answers.

I stared at the questions. I stared at the paper I was supposed to write my answers on. I stared at the pen in my hand. Lightning did not strike. My mind did not magically fill up with answers I had not previously known.

Then, I began to write.

I had no idea what the answers were. I hardly understood the questions. But I just started answering them. With words, sentences, and paragraphs—somewhere between gibberish and total nonsense. I wrote really fast. I wrote with confidence. I wrote the way I would have written if I had any clue what the answers were. My answers were really just a jumble of nonsensical assertions and facts. I kept writing—if you can call it that—until the professor said, "Time," and collected the answer sheets.

There is no way the teacher can even read this, much less understand it, I thought as I got up to leave the classroom with the other students. Had I just put a final period on my three-year law school career?

I have no idea how it happened. I can only assume the professor didn't bother to read the words on the page—or gave up quickly after being unable to decipher them. I got a B-minus on the test. As I kept discovering, law school wasn't nearly as hard as everybody said.

To me, that just proved my strategy was right. I'd earned reliable Bs and Cs by bullshitting, lying, charming the professors, leaning on my classmates, hiring people to write my papers, and, when I had nothing else, scribbling really, really fast. The way I looked at it, I was doing whatever I had to do to survive—everything other than buckling down and studying hard, which was both unthinkable and impossible for me. That option, if I'm being honest, never crossed my mind.

||||||||||||||||||

All along I still had Debbie waiting patiently for me. After graduating from Boston University, she moved to Long Island to attend law school at Hofstra University. My brother Douglas was in her class. After six years of long-distance dating, Debbie and I were thrilled to be living just a short drive apart. That was the idea, anyway. Her idea. The truth was that her proximity made me nervous. It turned out I liked the idea of having a long-term, steady girlfriend a whole lot more than I liked the flesh-and-blood kind. Luckily, Debbie was busy with the usual pressures of first-year law school, the kind felt by students who chose to study. And I kept making up excuses about how busy I was.

What I was really busy doing was meeting other women—and not just meeting them. I was hooking up with so many women in the city, it was nearly impossible to remember all of them. I was single, sort of, if you didn't count Debbie. I was voracious in my appetites and focused in my pursuit—very. AIDS was just a rumor at the fringes of the gay community. No one I knew was worried about it. I'm not proud of this. But over time, the number of women really did add up. If I was going to remember all or most or even some of them, I knew I needed some kind of memory aid. The one I chose to use was a yellow legal pad where I kept a running list. Yes, I finally found a use for those yellow legal pads, and it was not taking notes in Trusts and Estates class. By third year, there were a couple of hundred names and numbers on that list—and just enough detail to spark a memory about each of them.

"Jessica, rose tattoo, fucked in the bathroom at Club A."

"Alyssa J, sex in car after movie on Third Ave. Invited me to sail next summer on her family's yacht."

"Cyndi, redhead, met at America, just broke up with boyfriend. Careful! Wild but totally nuts."

That pad lived in a safe place, a drawer in the table at the side of my bed. The drawer wasn't locked, but who would find it there? I needed the pad accessible to add new names as they came up. And once in a while, I liked to check the list and dredge up happy, sleazy memories.

I got home late one night after a long evening out. I didn't know it at first, but Debbie must have come by the house looking for me. She'd been in my house many times before. Usually with me, but not always. Somehow, on this particular occasion, she'd ended up in my bedroom, where the worst imaginable catastrophe occurred. It was terrible. Just horrible. She'd found my precious, yellow legal pad.

I knew immediately it was her.

She'd torn the pad into thousands of tiny pieces, ripped up every page. It must have taken her an hour. Or longer. All that remained of the legal pad was a pile of yellow confetti on my bedspread—but she definitely wasn't throwing me a parade. The pieces were so small, I couldn't possibly read what was written on them. I suppose that was part of Debbie's point. Each tiny piece contained just a couple of letters, adding up to nothing but pain.

On one, full sheet of paper, Debbie left a note for me. All it said was "HOPE YOU ARE HAPPY NOW."

A wave of panic rushed through me, a feeling I hadn't experienced in years. My heart was pounding. Sweat was beading on my forehead. I didn't know what to do.

I called Debbie's apartment. She answered the phone. She sounded as cold as ice cubes. I didn't wait for her to rip into me. I tried to jump in front of that. I told her she had jumped to the wrong conclusion. This wasn't what it looked like. I told her she should really calm down. I told her I would come over to her apartment and explain everything.

"I don't think I need any further explanation," she answered. Even worse than the words was the flat, quiet voice that delivered them. She sounded done with me. To everything I suggested, she answered with a "no." Who could blame her? It was the night Debbie finally had enough.

You'd think, given how I had been behaving, I could have just shrugged and moved on. Had I been unconsciously setting up this night for years? Clearly, I had no idea what honesty and commitment meant in an intimate relationship and zero ability to live up to anything like that. I certainly didn't deserve Debbie. Every ounce of my behavior said I didn't want a serious girlfriend. I wanted to chase Jessica, Alyssa, redheaded Cyndi, and all the other girls whose names I needed a yellow pad to remember, our encounters had been so fleeting and repetitive.

This stung more than I ever could have imagined, given how I took Debbie for granted all those years. What was I going to do? I hadn't been without a girlfriend since junior year in high school. Now, Debbie was gone. When I lost her, I suddenly was that eight-year-old boy in the hospital bed, alone in traction with no one visiting him. I had never been so scared in my life. For almost a decade, whatever else I did, whoever else I might have been screwing, I always knew that Debbie was waiting patiently for me.

Now, she wasn't anymore.

It didn't take long for her to start dating another guy. I heard people talk about it. He was a student in her law school—not my brother, thank God. The new guy loved her, I heard, and treated her respectfully. It all made me feel like yesterday's news.

Being replaced like that was excruciating. I needed Debbie. I was jealous. I was mad. I called her and begged her to come back to me. "I don't think so," she said, not yielding an inch. I told her I had learned my lesson. I swore I had grown up. I would never make the mistake of not appreciating her. I had to have her back. I begged and begged some more. No one ever accused me of not being persuasive. Debbie finally relented. She said we could get back together on one condition—if we got engaged to marry.

I agreed immediately.

I would have agreed to anything. I felt that desperate and alone. She was my security. Despite how I had treated her, I didn't think I could live without her. Without her, I was sure I couldn't go on.

I bought a ring, which I charged on my father's credit card. She told her friends and family that we'd gotten back together and we were now engaged. I don't know what they really thought of that. I don't know if she'd ever told any of them how I'd betrayed her so completely. Debbie began planning a wedding.

But I was the worst fiancé ever. My heart wasn't in it, and I'm not sure hers was anymore. Both of us were just going through the motions. After all we'd been through, after all I had done, the trust and the ease just weren't there anymore. A couple of months later, as law school graduation approached, both of us finally recognized that the two of us getting married was just ridiculous. We called it off for good.

This time, Debbie really was gone.

|||||||||||||||||

We had a lovely graduation ceremony at Lincoln Center's Alice Tully Hall. My parents came. They understood I didn't make law review. I wasn't the class valedictorian. They knew I'd had some bumps along the way. But no one was obsessing on the crinkly edges. I was graduating from law school, just like my father had. Like him and all my classmates, I was earning the Juris Doctor degree. It looked good. It sounded good. My parents would be able to tell all of their friends. And they really did seem proud of me.

Just before I walked on stage to collect my diploma, I allowed myself one brief moment to take it all in: I'd done it my way. I had gotten through law school hardly studying at all. I had also wasted a great opportunity. Somewhere deep inside, I knew that. To anyone else—including my future self—it would be obvious: I had skipped a precious chance to learn. But at that point in my life, I was still immature enough to feel proud that I had so effectively conned the system and gotten through. In one final act of law school defiance, I left the ceremony that day with my cap and gown. I didn't return the graduation outfit like we were all supposed to. I removed the cap. I climbed out of my robe. I tucked them both beneath my arm—like so many other souvenirs of my deceptions—and marched out of Lincoln Center in my street clothes, carrying with me literal proof that law wasn't nearly as hard as everyone said.

Just look at me, Craig Schmell, JD.

Now, all that stood between me and being a full-fledged, practicing attorney was passing the New York State Bar Exam.

How hard could that be?

⁞⁞⁞⁞⁞⁞⁞⁞⁞⁞⁞⁞⁞⁞

Ah, yes, the bar exam.

I'd heard stories, and some of them were a little frightening. A two-day, standardized test administered every July and February by the New York State Board of Law Examiners. Hundreds of multiple-choice questions. Essay questions too. A comprehensive appraisal of the applicant's understanding of the fundamental principles and rules of law. The bar exam was serious business, and, no, serious business was not exactly my specialty. How was I going to talk my way around, through, under, or over *this*?

"Imagine how failing must feel," I said to Barry one day. "You've just slogged through three years of law school, and they still won't let you be a lawyer." I'd never heard of a law school refunding the tuition money in a case like that. Passing that test was an especially delicate topic around a law school as new and untested as Touro. The faculty and administrators all had their fingers crossed. Now, it was in our hands.

All my Touro classmates seemed to have signed up for bar exam prep courses. These courses weren't cheap. But test-prep companies promised a vast improvement in your chances of passing the daunting exam. Given all the scare talk, who was going to skip the prep course? Not anyone with a father, a credit card, or both! I signed up for the Piper Bar Review, which met at a Holiday Inn on Route 59 in Rockland County, not far from my parents' house in New City.

I moved out of the house in Huntington and into Manhattan. A guy I'd met in California, Brad Ruderman, was moving to New York City to take a job with the Wall Street firm Lehman Brothers. We found a two-bedroom apartment in New York Tower, a modern high-rise on East Thirty-Ninth Street between First and Second Avenues. Apartment 33P had endless views from a south-facing terrace. It was a fitting city pad, I thought, for a recent law school graduate and a rising young Wall Streeter. My dad agreed to pay my share of the rent until I got through the exam and started working as a lawyer. For now, my job was to pass the bar.

I managed to attend a few sessions of the prep course. But I missed a lot more of them. Never once did I study on my own, which the instructors emphasized was vital for anyone who hoped to pass. I understood how important the exam was. I really did. But I had trouble paying attention, and the whole thing just seemed so overwhelmingly tedious after four years of college and three years of law school. I desperately didn't want the party to end, and I wasn't convinced it had to. I'd been hearing dire talk to the contrary ever since I went away to college, but somehow I'd always gotten through.

I knew what I should have been doing, but I was far more interested in getting stoned and meeting girls and going out drinking with my friends. I'd just graduated from law school. Didn't I deserve a break? There was always another special night at another Manhattan nightclub. By this point, I actually knew a lot of the doormen and managers. I didn't even have to scam my way in. No one who saw me in those days would have thought I had a bar exam in my near future. But those who knew must have wondered what I was thinking. Even Barry was concerned. He tried to warn me about the risk I was taking, being so cavalier about the bar exam. He had what I now think of as one of the greatest double-meaning quotes of all time.

"Craig," he said after yet another night of drinking instead of studying, "in order to pass the bar, you're going to have to pass the bar."

Somewhere in the back of my mind, I probably knew he was right.

But I had an answer for that little voice in my head.

It's too late anyway. I couldn't go to law school again. What was I supposed to do about it? Would it really matter how hard I studied in the prep course after how I had spent the past three years? I was totally unprepared for the bar exam, and I knew it. It wasn't just that I didn't know the material. It wasn't just that I had slithered through all my courses without mastering any of the basic concepts. I didn't even know *how* to learn. I lacked the focus. I lacked the study skills. I lacked the patience and the drive to get this done. I wasn't unintelligent. If I'd have devoted half the effort to studying that I did to managing my social life—hell, I could have made law review or earned a prestigious clerkship. I simply didn't have what it took. I couldn't pay attention long enough to learn, even if my mind hadn't been clouded by so much ego, pot, and alcohol.

Someone might as well have told me: "Flap your arms and fly." It wasn't going to happen, and I secretly knew it.

I went through the motions. I took the test on one of the West Side piers with hundreds of other wannabe lawyers. I hoped, without any evidence, that my wits would somehow save me again. During the multiple-choice section, I tried glancing at the answer sheets of the two test-takers who shared my table. But we were so well spaced out, I could only glimpse a few of their answers, not nearly enough to put me over the top. I tried the trick I'd used in law school, scribbling really fast and crazy and hoping whoever was grading the exam would pass me in pity or exasperation.

What happened instead was the inevitable.

I failed.

Ultimately, everyone who took the exam would get a letter with the results, but people who take the bar exam don't sit around waiting for the mail. Weeks later, after all the answer sheets were tabulated and pass-fail lists were drawn up, the bar examiners published the names of all those who had passed.

My name was nowhere to be found.

10

RINSE AND REPEAT

Failing the New York State Bar Exam didn't have to be a life-altering tragedy. Ed Koch and Franklin Delano Roosevelt both flunked on their first tries and still had fairly productive careers—as mayor of New York City and president of the United States. The brilliant Benjamin Cardozo failed the bar exam five times before he passed on the sixth. He went on to become a legendary justice on the US Supreme Court. They even named a law school after him. I'd been collecting names like those. Too bad they couldn't soothe my wounded ego.

For me, failing the bar exam in the summer of 1986 was far from a trivial event. Quite the opposite. It launched me into a severe downward spiral, one that would take a life-changing turnaround to recover from. Failing the bar was truly the beginning of the end of the old Craig Schmell. Let me try to explain why that single disappointment mattered so much.

The immediate consequences could hardly be noticed from the outside. I wasn't fired from the job I'd recently talked my way into at Solomon & Weissman, a small law firm in the Lincoln Building across from Grand Central Terminal. As a fresh law school graduate, I couldn't practice law. But I was allowed to make minor court appearances and draft simple documents. You didn't need to be a licensed attorney to do that. The partners in my new firm were quite understanding when I told them my bar news. "You'll take it again, and you'll pass," the kindly Stanley Solomon said.

But inside my head, my bar news was a far bigger deal. It hit me like a blindside tackle. Failing the bar, it turned out, was almost impossible to hide. I was certain that everybody knew. Not just knew. I had the distinct impression that they were feeling sorry for me. I had never had that feeling before. I started to feel sorry for myself. Up until that point, I had never failed publicly at anything. I'd progressed appropriately through high school, college, and law school. I was a friendly, athletic, nice-looking young man whose cheerful façade had just been cracked.

My parents remained supportive.

"We believe in you," my father said.

"You'll pass next time," my mother agreed.

Was that a vote of confidence? Or was she laying down a challenge? A little bit of both, I am sure. I was willing to take the test again, but she had no clue just how ill prepared I was.

||||||||||||||||||

At least I had the Mets.

Nineteen eighty-six was the season of the Amazins. Keith Hernandez. Gary Carter. Dwight Gooden. Darryl Strawberry. Lenny Dykstra. Mookie Wilson. Against all odds, this scrappy team of misfits just kept winning. As I tried to find my bearings after the bar news, I clung to the Mets. They were impossible not to love. And this year, they were winners. Who doesn't love a winner?

We rode the No. 7 train out to Shea Stadium for quite a few games. Others we caught in sports bars or on the TV in my living room. When the team kept winning, cheering them on became something more than a hobby. It was almost a full-time job. Once the Mets won the National League pennant and were ready to face the Boston Red Sox in the 1986 World Series—what? We were supposed to watch on TV?

I probably could have found some so-so seats through a scalper. But even those would have cost a fortune, and I wasn't eager to watch from the nosebleed balcony or the right-field bleachers. It was scam time again. Luckily, I had been at Giants Stadium in the New Jersey Meadowlands for a Bruce Springsteen concert. On my way off the field, where I was sitting, I slipped past a police barricade and found myself in the bowels of the stadium in an area I clearly didn't belong. Off to the side, I noticed a vendor's locker room. Out of curiosity, I stuck my head in. On a table was a stack of light-blue T-shirts with black letters on the front.

"Harry M. Stevens," the T-shirts said.

There was also a pile of matching blue caps.

I knew that the Harry M. Stevens Co. was the beer vendor at Giants Stadium. I'd seen those light blue shirts before. I also knew that the company had vending contracts at almost all the major sports facilities in the New York area. I grabbed a T-shirt and a cap, not quite sure how they might come in handy but guessing that they probably would. Someday, somehow. Petty theft? Nah, I was just being prepared. As the World Series approached, I was so glad I had my uniform.

Game 1 of the Series was at Shea Stadium on Saturday, October 18, 1986. Barry and I took the train to Shea, arriving about an hour before the 8:30 p.m. first pitch. The night was cold. The wind was whipping, but we showed up without jackets. I had a Mets jersey over the Harry M. Stevens T-shirt. The parking lot was teeming with Mets fans. As we got close to the gate, I slipped off the jersey so the Harry M. Stevens T-shirt would be visible. I put the Harry M. Stevens cap on my head. With Barry standing back, all I had to do was nod at a security guard as I walked unquestioned into the stadium. Once inside, I slipped off the T shirt, pulled the jersey back on, and called Barry over to a spot in the fence, where I tossed the cap and shirt to him. Now, he could get in exactly as I had. Once inside, all we had to do was find some open seats and sit in them. It has always amazed me how some people with high-priced, sought-after tickets simply didn't use them. That's true at any large event. It was true for Game 1 of the World Series.

The first game didn't turn out so well. Boston pitcher Bruce Hurst had a curve ball that held the Mets to four hits in eight innings. Ron Darling pitched just as well for the Mets, but the one unearned run he allowed in the seventh was enough to give Boston a 1-0 win.

We couldn't help that. But we'd been in the stadium to watch it happen and in the good seats, and even a loss couldn't take away that high. All we could do was plan for games 2, 6, and 7, which were also scheduled for Shea. When our friends heard we had been just behind the dugout for the first two games, they wanted in. Sure, we said. That was easy. We just threw the shirt and hat over the fence a few more times.

We saw everything, including Mookie's easy grounder that rolled through the legs of Red Sox first baseman Bill Bruckner in the tenth inning of game 6 and the comeback victory in game 7 that handed the series to its rightful owners, our beloved New York Mets. We even talked ourselves into believing we needed to be there. We were the Mets' good luck charm. Imagine if we'd skipped a game.

|||||||||||||||||

I signed up to take the bar exam a second time the following February. I cut my hours at Solomon & Weissman so I could study full-time. As if! This was the perfect opportunity, I figured, to ask my father for my bar mitzvah money. Since I was thirteen, he'd been holding the $30,000 under the theory that one day I'd use those funds for something important. "It's your money," my father shrugged when handing me the check. What someone else might have used to help finance a wedding or for the down payment on a home, I spent on rent, pot, cocktails, and pizza slices. I couldn't believe I hadn't asked for it sooner.

With my financial pressures temporarily at bay, I may have even convinced myself I'd really buckle down this time. That minute didn't last. I'd been given a nearly unlimited amount of free time to study. If anything, I prepped even less than I had the first time around.

Though I had no set schedule anymore, I did have a daily routine. I would get up in the morning around ten, trying to remember the night before. I would go downstairs and buy a slice of pizza and take a long walk. I liked to stop at the Sam Goody music store at Second Avenue and Forty-Second Street. Whenever I did, I would steal a new CD. I'd get back home by one or two. I'd get stoned. I'd watch TV. I'd stare out the window, where workers constructed a new apartment building called the Corinthian. And wait for the night to come.

The night was my time. The night was when I shined. The night was the reason I waited through the day. As for the bar exam retake, I judged my chances as slim.

By test time, round 2, I was nine months—not two months—out of law school. The little I had learned in class was that much more of a distant memory. My study habits certainly hadn't improved. The only thing that was different was that I was having a harder time scamming myself. The second time around, even I didn't believe I'd be lucky enough to pass.

But I took the test. I tried my best. Then I bided my time like a convicted man waiting for his sentence to be handed down. It was coming. I could feel it. The feeling was dread.

Then, the results arrived.

I failed for the second time.

Damn!

I had finally met my match, it seemed, a challenge that my charm, my family, and my flexible sense of ethics were no match for. The bar exam was the bar exam. I'd been bested by the best. I simply didn't have what it took to pass.

BZ offered up another of his prosaic insights, this one playing off the famous Abraham Lincoln line. "You can fool all the people some of the time, and some of the people all the time. But you can't fool the New York State Board of Law Examiners."

No, you can't fool them.

||||||||||||||||

Thank God for Oliver North. He helped me fill my days.

By the summer of 1987, I wasn't working. I had nothing but time to kill. Thankfully, Congress was holding televised hearings about the Iran-Contra affair, and I was totally transfixed. I could hardly pull myself away as Colonel Oliver North and other Reagan administration officials were quizzed about an illegal arms-for-hostages deal, their scheme to sell weapons to Iran and thereby secure the release of several US hostages and fund the Contras who were trying to overthrow Nicaragua's Sandinista government. North bobbed, weaved, wiggled, and flat-out lied when he had to. It all seemed so familiar. He was a world-class self-justifier, just like me. I'd always heard that misery loves company. Watching other people in trouble, I discovered, made me think my problems weren't so bad.

The hearings were a godsend. After my slice, my walk, and my sticky-fingered visit to the CD store, I still had three or four hours to kill every day. I couldn't wait until five o'clock. All my friends were working. They were getting on with grown-up lives. Building careers. Getting married and having children. I was doing nothing and going nowhere.

By five, my friends were getting off work and the evening's activities could begin. Once the sun went down, I was in my element. My depression lifted. My confidence returned. I didn't feel so alone anymore.

The late 1980s New York nightlife was a neverending whirlwind. Sunday nights, we went to Club A on East Sixtieth Street, where any given week Madonna or David Bowie might show up. Monday night, it was the China Club on Upper Broadway. Tuesday nights were for the Surf Club on East Ninety-First Street. People would line up outside waving hundred-dollar bills at the doormen. BZ and I already had them wired. We'd nod, smile, and walk right in.

|||||||||||||||||

It was partly out of boredom and partly to feign interest in having a career. I got a new job at a law firm in Brooklyn, performing entry-level legal tasks like the ones at Solomon & Weissman. I was going through the motions again. The best thing about my first job in law was also the best thing about my new one: it left plenty of time to plot my next adventures.

I also met a girl that fall. Her name was Jane Lewis. I can't remember exactly where we met. I was meeting lots girls at the time, and I wasn't keeping my yellow-pad rundown anymore. Goddamn it, Debbie! I really missed that! I could have met Jane in a bar. Or it could have been at the Vertical Club, the flashy gym on East Sixty-First Street where I'd started working out. She was a buxom girl with dark wavy hair and some obvious intelligence. She had an apartment on Seventy-Fifth Street and Second Avenue. She drove a Porsche 924 and had a house-share in the Hamptons. She came from a prominent New Jersey family and worked as a buyer for Century 21 department stores. She radiated success. This girl had a lot more on the ball than many of the women I was meeting in those days. We clicked immediately.

Jane was savvy enough to know that I was floundering, but she also saw something in me. I think it was the confidence I exuded, even when I didn't feel it.

"You have something beneath all the other stuff," Jane told me one day.

"Thanks for recognizing that," I responded with a smile and some sense of relief.

Everyone, I kept discovering, had something to feel insecure about. For Jane, it was a small mole above her upper lip. It didn't matter how many times I told her how beautiful she was. When she looked in the mirror, she always saw that mole.

We'd get together three or four nights a week, anytime I wasn't going out with my friends. We'd catch a movie, have dinner, or just sit in her apartment on Second Avenue and watch movies on TV.

It really might have been a healthy relationship if I weren't such a mess.

||||||||||||||||

As far as I could tell, there was one and only one good thing about me and the bar exam. As long as I could say I *was* taking the exam—even retaking or re-retaking it—I had something to say when people asked what I was up to: "I'm studying for the bar right now." That was a whole lot better than, "Not much. Just hanging around. Letting my parents cover my bills." The only question was how much longer I could string this out.

I got one piece of good news while I was trying to predict that. My father informed me that he'd been able to settle the lawsuit from the woman who claimed I'd crashed my car into her leg.

The process wasn't totally painless. I had to sit through a deposition where the woman's attorney questioned me about what happened that night. I admitted I had some cocktails and added, "So had she." I said that the young lady and I had gotten into a small disagreement back at my house. But I hadn't held anyone hostage or made any moves on her without consent. When she had asked to go, I'd driven her to the train station and as far as I knew she was perfectly fine when she walked away from my car.

I wasn't privy to the negotiations. I never heard exactly what happened between my father, the woman's lawyer, and our auto insurance company. But I assume the company paid the woman something because I never heard about her or that lawsuit again. The settlement may have affected our insurance rates; I can't say since I wasn't paying them and my father didn't complain. I convinced myself the case was a good experience since I got to see firsthand how the legal system operated. Maybe it would even help someday on a future bar exam try. But there were no real consequences for me, not this time or any time, no matter what I did. That was one lesson I kept learning, maybe the only one.

With that out of the way, I continued my jerking, downward spiral. Ever since I'd failed the bar for the second time, I'd had a suspicion that people were catching glimpses of the real me, even people who pretended otherwise. It felt to me that of all the people in my law school class, I was the only one who hadn't passed the bar exam. That couldn't have been true, but that was how I felt. Were other people beginning to see me as I had secretly seen myself? As not quite good enough? Were the public Craig and the private Craig morphing into one? I was getting tense. I needed an answer, and I came up with one.

I thought I should relax a little more before I took the bar exam again.

|||||||||||||||||

At least I had my fun to feel good about! I had lots of going-out friends. Jane and I were spending time together. I was still meeting other girls in the clubs. And I kept getting better at scamming my way into the most exclusive events, often dragging a fun-loving entourage along.

On January 26, 1988, I read an item in the *New York Post* about a new show opening that night on Broadway. It was a musical by Andrew Lloyd Webber, who'd already had megahits with *Cats, Evita*, and *Jesus Christ Superstar*. For more than a year, the new one had been burning up the stage at Her Majesty's Theatre in London's West End. The story, first told in an early 1900s French novel, was inspired by historic events at the Paris Opera decades before and rumors about the use of a former ballet pupil's skeleton.

"It's called *The Phantom of the Opera*," I told Barry on the phone that afternoon. "It's got crazy costumes and over-the-top characters—they're saying it's better than *Cats*."

Though we had no tickets, Barry and I showed up at the Majestic Theatre on West Forty-Fourth Street a few minutes before eight. We were dressed nicely, in jackets and ties. No one said anything. The opening-night crowd was a massive, high-class mob scene. We floated in with the pretty people. In the opening-night excitement, no one asked for our tickets. We lingered in the lobby until almost everyone else had sat down, then grabbed two empty seats in the orchestra section, twelfth row on the aisle. The opening was a sold-out event. Many theatergoers would have paid a fortune for the chance to be there. But incredibly, whoever had those in-demand seats was a no-show. No one ever asked us to leave. The show was a tour de force, as the critics like to say, Broadway at its best. You couldn't help but love it. Barry and I bravo'ed our way through multiple standing ovations with all the other swells. As we left the theater that night, I couldn't get the songs out of my head. "The Music of the Night." "All I Ask of You." "Masquerade." Now, that was Broadway!

I loved the show so much, in fact, that the very next afternoon, I went to Sam Goody's music store on East Forty-Second Street and took a five-finger discount on the *Phantom* soundtrack CD. For the next five nights, when I got home, usually drunk, stoned, or both, I blared the songs at peak volume, which made me happy and helped me drift off to sleep.

Unfortunately, the reviews for my nightly concerts weren't total raves. On the morning after the sixth night, I woke to find a note taped to my apartment door. "We are fans of the Phantom," the note read in perfect, cursive script. "But at 3 in the morning we are not." And then this: "The Phantom will get you if you don't stop playing loud music in the middle of the night."

Through a fog of alcohol and ego, even I could see that this was a nice note, given how obnoxious my late-night music must have been. It sure beat, "Shut the fuck up, asshole," which is probably what I'd have said if the roles had been reversed. I kept my music lower after that.

||||||||||||||||||

Phantom was like a run-through for the Thirtieth Annual Grammy Awards, which came five weeks later (March 2, 1988). Broadway was big time, but I knew that security at Radio City Music Hall would be far tighter for a worldwide, televised extravaganza with so many huge stars in the house. Yes, I had already talked my way into the dress rehearsal on an asthma inhaler and a couple of white lies.

I'd interrupted an important game of bong golf on the terrace of my apartment for a preshow reconnaissance mission the night before. I thought I had to. I knew from my nightclub entries that seeding the field beforehand could make things far easier when show time finally arrived.

Without a doubt, that night at the Grammys was my greatest incursion ever.

Barry and I didn't only get inside. We didn't only have to-die-for seats. We didn't only have one-on-one, personal contact with the gods of rock, soul, folk, and jazz.

I performed.

Live.

On stage.

To a packed house at Radio City.

For that once-in-a-lifetime moment, when I took my solo, Michael Jackson, Whitney Houston, Paul Simon, Bono, Lou Reed, and just about anyone else you could name—they were my backup singers.

And a worldwide television audience of millions was watching.

As soon as I told Barry good night and got back home to my apartment, my phone was already ringing. The first call was from a friend who lived in LA.

"This is gonna sound crazy," he began tentatively. "But I was just watching the Grammys."

"Yeah?" I said, pretending not to know where he was heading.

"I could swear . . ." He was having genuine trouble getting the words out.

"I could swear I saw you in the finale, singing on stage. It definitely looked like you."

"Yeah, it was me," I said nonchalantly, as if singing at the Grammys was something I did every other night.

"It was a special night," I added, mimicking an answer I had heard from thousands of stars in interviews over the years. "A very special night."

"I knew it, I knew it!" my friend shouted into the phone. "Oh my God! How did you do that?"

I answered honestly. "I was there. Billy Crystal called the stars up for the finale. And I went." Then, I pushed it a little: "You can say the music overtook me."

For months, for years, I would hear from people about that evening. I told that story many times. I knew I'd have to find a video of the broadcast, in case I needed proof.

It turned out there were lots of people who taped the Thirtieth Annual Grammy Awards on their home VCRs. Plenty of them saved the VHS cassettes, the state of the art of recording in 1988.

Near the end, as the credits were beginning to roll, all those tapes show me singing the Dion doo-wop medley with all my latest acquaintances and friends.

II

GOING DOWN

A strange thing happened after the Grammys. My scams got better and better while my life got worse and worse.

From my experiences at the Grammys and Live Aid, I knew the true power of a backstage pass and also the strategic advantages of scoping out a venue ahead of time. I used both to fine advantage on May 14, 1988, at Madison Square Garden. Atlantic Records was celebrating its 40th anniversary with an endless-seeming lineup of current and past acts. The morning of the show, I was prowling the halls of the Garden, where I snagged a song-by-song rundown of the evening's Led Zeppelin finale and then, dangling unattended from a woman's pocketbook, a round, green pass that said, "STAFF, STAFF, STAFF." Shades of Live Aid! There was a big 40 in the middle of the laminated pass. The zero was a record album.

The show, a tribute to my Grammy-seat neighbor, Atlantic founder Ahmet Ertegun, was a twelve-hour, multigenerational marathon of R&B, soul, and rock-'n'-roll. Featured acts included Genesis, Yes, Foreigner, Crosby, Stills & Nash, Live Aid's Bob Geldof, Booker T. Jones, Wilson Pickett, the Coasters, the Spinners, the Blues

Brothers (featuring Dan Aykroyd and Sam Moore, minus the late John Belushi), Roberta Flack, The Manhattan Transfer, and my old California friends, the Bee Gees. No way was I going to say anything to Andy or Barry! The battered ex-members of Led Zeppelin, with John Bonham's son Jason on drums, closed the show with "Stairway to Heaven," a song Robert Plant had vowed he would never perform again. Thanks to my advanced reconnaissance, I watched it all from the edge of The Garden stage.

I had no opportunity for a morning walk-through on Donald Trump's yacht. I got a last-minute tip from my favorite source for New York celebrity gossip, the local TV news. The brash real-estate scion and his wife, Ivana, were hosting a series of parties on a yacht they had just purchased, a celebration of Independence Day weekend. The 281-foot vessel—a superyacht, the reporter called it—was moored at the most prominent berth imaginable, just outside the Water Club on the Manhattan bank of the East River. This was not a boat anyone was trying to hide. And when we got out of the taxi, I could see immediately that there was only one way aboard the *Trump Princess*: up a gangplank guarded by three walkie-talkie–wielding security men in dark wool suits, all sweating profusely on this midsummer night. There wasn't much breeze blowing off the river.

The boat had been built for the billionaire Saudi arms dealer Adnan Khashoggi, who named it the *Nabila*. The $100-million play-toy was outfitted with every imaginable bell, whistle, and heliport: five decks, eleven luxury bedroom suites, three elevators, a private hospital, and 210 telephones. The yacht was so large and lavish, it was featured as the villain's floating headquarters in the James Bond movie *Never Say Never Again*. When Khashoggi hit rough financial waters, he unloaded the *Nabila* at a steep discount to the Sultan of Brunei, who then unloaded it at a steeper discount to the boy developer from New York.

Barry and I were dressed in crisp, blue blazers and light-colored slacks, our best approximation of summer-in-the-Hamptons wear. What else are you supposed to wear on Donald Trump's new yacht? But wardrobe alone was not going to get us aboard.

That took some coordination and some experience, but it really wasn't that hard. We repeated a tag-team trick the two of us had perfected on the rope lines of New York nightclubs. Barry walked up to one of the security men, the one gripping the clipboard with the guest list. That's always somebody's job. I held back a pace or two, saying nothing at first.

"Bill Stern," Barry announced.

As the perspiring security man squinted down the list for the name Barry had just invented, I peered discreetly over Barry's shoulder. My job was to pluck an actual name off the list.

When the security man couldn't find Barry's Bill Stern, I stepped forward with a name I had just spied.

"Maybe it's under my name," I said helpfully. "Steven Steinberg," knowing full well that Steinberg, whoever he was, was definitely on the guest list for Donald Trump's floating bash. "Yes, here you are," the security man said. "Welcome. Enjoy your evening"

We spent the evening drinking, nibbling, and making vacuous small talk with rich people I had never heard of, the ones who weren't already off to their summer estates. The only celebrities I recognized were Jacqueline Onassis and the actress Barbara Eden from *I Dream of Jeannie*, a show I loved watching in reruns when I was a kid. I swear, Barbara still looked fit enough to come out of a bottle. That was a thrill. Mostly, Barry and I occupied ourselves by sneaking around the yacht and taking photos of extravagant rooms: The movie screening room with three rows of plush couches. The disco, with huge photos of Donald and Ivana flashing on the ceiling, was beautifully lit. Everyone looked marvelous in there. The master stateroom, its king-sized bed wrapped in sheer, red curtains. That room also had Mr. Trump's private barber chair!

I'm not sure where Donald and Ivana were hiding. We never saw them. None of the other guests seem to have either. But their hospitality certainly was grand. As we left long after midnight, we stopped at a table in the main salon. On the table was a leather-bound guest book. I thought it only appropriate to express my appreciation in a personal note. I got an extra thrill when I noticed my note would be just beneath Barbara Eden's.

"Dear Donald and Ivana," I wrote. "Thanks for having me. Love always, Craig Schmell."

I thought about signing Steven Steinberg, but that wouldn't have been nearly as much fun.

||||||||||||||||

Playboy had Playmates. *Penthouse* had Pets. I knew that much. Five months after Donald and Ivana's yacht party, I was back at the Water Club—in the restaurant this time, not at the dock—for the *Penthouse* Pet of the Year Christmas Party. I wasn't invited, of course. I just went. Alone. Anyone could have. That's how loose security was. It was mostly just a big New York media industry party—advertisers, sales reps, PR people, editors, the men and women who do the actual work inside the gritty business of glamour and fame. But since this was a *Penthouse* party, there were also some incredibly sexy women in the mix, including quite a few who had been prominently featured in the magazine photo spreads. I had one goal for the evening: I wanted to meet one of them.

I approached a shapely blonde woman who I recognized from the party invitation. She was wearing the same tight, blue-sequined dress.

Her name was Ginger Miller, and she had just been announced as the 1989 *Penthouse* Pet of the Year. She was far friendlier than I expected.

We chatted a bit. I asked Ginger for her phone number. She gave it me. Maybe I should have called her.

||||||||||||||||

When it came to party crashing, I felt like I couldn't miss. A week after the *Penthouse* party, on December 12, 1988, Barry, Barry's girlfriend, and I were elbow-to-elbow with the New York–Hollywood crowd to celebrate the premiere of the movie *Rain Man* starring Dustin Hoffman and Tom Cruise. Cruise had been on quite a five-year tear with *Risky Business, Top Gun, The Color of Money,* and *Cocktail.* Dustin Hoffman was Dustin Hoffman. Again, I had seen a report on the news about the stars leaving the premiere at the Loews Astor Plaza theater and heading to a dinner-dance after-party at the New York State Armory on Lexington Avenue. It was a fundraiser for the Robert K. Steel Family Foundation.

Barry and I threw on tuxedos. His girlfriend quickly slipped on a shimmery black dress. The three of us met on Lexington Avenue, across the street from the New York State Armory. We found a staff entrance and marched right in, mistaken for very well-dressed servers, I assume. No one knew anyone. It was another one-night event. We met Sean Connery, Mimi Rogers, and Faye Dunaway. I had my picture taken with the model Cheryl Tiegs. I was getting bolder at grabbing photos. "Hi, Cheryl," I said. "I've got to get a picture with you." Barry was already standing there with the point-and-shoot. She smiled and I instantly had proof we'd been there. But Hoffman was the high point of the party—and not because he was so charming and upbeat. Quite the opposite. He had worked so hard getting into character as

Raymond, an autistic savant, it seemed like he was having real trouble shaking the role.

He signed my program, short and sweet: "To Craig, Dustin Hoffman." When we posed for a photo, I was smiling straight at the camera. He was looking down at his shoes.

Whatever works! *Rain Man* would be the highest-grossing film of 1988 and win four Academy Awards.

|||||||||||||||||

Nighttime was still my time. Unfortunately, the sun still came up every morning. For me, the daylight hours were getting harder and harder to fill.

I couldn't hack it at the law firm in Brooklyn. I was supposed to go to court for a motion one morning. I was two hours late. The client was calling my boss every ten minutes, screaming and cursing. No one could find me. I was so hungover, I couldn't get out of bed.

There was no way I could stay there. There was no way they'd let me stay there. There went my latest stab at a fledgling legal career. I got a job as a business broker, connecting people who wanted to buy and sell businesses. That was the idea, anyway. That didn't work out either. They gave me a small draw against the promise of the commissions I would make once I started making deals. But it turned out you had to work hard to get deals, and I wasn't willing to put in the effort or the time. I hung around there for a while. It was some place to go. But I never did any business or made any real effort to, and after a while, they told me I wasn't welcome to come in anymore. I went back to doing nothing all day, which actually wasn't so different from what I was doing before I was shown the door. It was back to my natural rhythm of being an unproductive bum. Taking walks. Watching ESPN. Smoking more pot and earlier in the day. Having dinner at Jane

Lewis's house, then spending the night and raiding her refrigerator the next morning after she went off to work. Living off my parents' subsidies. Constantly lying to them.

I didn't tell my parents when I left the business broker's job. I just told them more lies about my imaginary job. I made excuses about the held-up checks, irresponsible bosses, and a company comptroller who was under suspicion for the theft. It was all to keep the checks flowing from home. Eventually, even my father said, "Maybe that's not a good place." Finally, I told him I had left, months after I actually had.

My nightlife was starting to feel like my fake life, though it was the only part of the day I was in any way alive. I just kept falling lower and lower, and even the highs were losing their edge.

I was really starting to feel sick. Not my body. My soul. It was a soul sickness. And all I knew to do about it was to bury my pain in more drugs and alcohol and keep going out at night.

|||||||||||||||||

To make things even worse—or was it a last gasp of self-delusion?—I'd signed up to take the bar exam again. The test was being offered in February, I was oh for two so far. Maybe three would be my lucky number! I had no reason to think so. But there was no limit to the number of times an applicant could take the New York State Bar Exam. Some gluttons for punishment, I'd heard, went back and back more than a dozen times. As long as you kept coming and you paid the application fee, they'd always find a seat for you. By some miracle, if you passed and made it through the fitness and character committee, you'd be a member of the New York Bar, fully licensed by the state Appellate Division in the practice of law.

Big ifs!

Even I knew that taking the exam at this point was a joke. Whatever little I'd learned in law school was ancient history now. My drinking and drugging were that much more out of control. My life made practically no sense. I couldn't afford my lifestyle. I was still living off my parents. I had no idea what I would do if—when—I had to give up the ghost of a law career. I was racing for thrills. I had no study skills. Why had I even signed up? I had already proven, twice, that I didn't have what it took to pass the bar exam. Sure, I liked being able to tell people, "Oh, yeah, I'm taking the bar exam." My father, I assumed, still expected me to take and pass the exam. But as the big day approached, the obvious was getting harder to ignore: there was no way I was going to pass this sucker, not without divine intervention or some very clever ruse. Of the two, I had far more experience with the latter.

I had an idea.

It was a horrible idea. Looking back now, I can see that. But it seemed quite ingenious at the time.

I would get my brainy brother Douglas to take the bar exam for me.

That past June, Douglas had graduated near the top of his class from the Hofstra law school, which was a step or three up the law school status ladder from Touro. He took the bar exam one month later in July and got the results in early November. He aced it.

There was no doubt in my mind he could pass it again.

"I need you to help with something," I told him one Saturday in late December at my parents' house.

"Sure," he said reflexively. Douglas was a sweet person and a loving brother. Whatever I needed, he would want to help.

I had it all thought out. Having taken the exam twice already, I was familiar with all the logistics.

I knew that security would be tight. The seats were assigned. You had to sign in before entering the exam room. The proctors checked everyone's ID. There was no voluntary honor code on exam day. They watched everyone like hawks—or in my case, like a buzzard, I'm sure, sensing the smell of proximate doom. I had already discovered how hard it was to shoulder surf off my neighbors. But for this last-gasp scam, I called on my most creative deception skills, the gift that had always bailed me out before. I swallowed hard and popped the question.

"I want you to take the bar exam for me," I told Douglas.

"What?" he answered, as if he couldn't possibly have heard me correctly.

I launched my explanation, talking as quickly as I could with as much confidence as I could muster.

"I will check in for the exam, everything normal," I explained. "I'll show my ID. I'll sign the paper. I will handle all that."

Douglas said nothing. He was just staring at me.

"Then, I will go to the men's room. You'll be waiting there. I will give you all my paperwork. Then, you'll come out of the bathroom. You'll sit at my table, and you'll take the test. Simple as that."

It took him a moment to answer. I filled the uncomfortable silence with words that must have sounded like they were uttered by a madman. "I know you can pass it again," I said. "You just passed it. You don't even have to prepare."

I could tell that Douglas was blown away that I would ask him to do such a thing, totally blown away. He loved me. On some level, he wanted to help me. He realized this was ridiculous. Why would he risk his own promising career to rescue his slacker brother, who couldn't even deliver his sorry butt to the prep course?

"I can't do that," he told me. "No. No. That's crazy. I just can't."

I didn't push him. In all my self-delusion, even I could see he had a point.

But that didn't mean I saw the plan as hopeless. On any scale of decency or family trust, it was ridiculous and indefensible. But I swear it had some simple brilliance too. It could have worked. It could have been the latest in a long line of my unauthorized incursions. And this scam, unlike almost all the others, actually had a purpose. An important one. It was easier than sneaking into the Grammys. The surroundings were different. The people were different. But at the end of the day, nothing was really all that different. The techniques remained the same: Find the vulnerabilities in the system. Run full-speed through them. Don't look back. The only real difference was that I was putting my brother and his entire future at risk.

This was the most horrible thing I had ever tried to do, an act of utter selfishness. When I snuck into Live Aid or some nightclub, who got hurt? No one. No one but me and my sense of honor and decency. But asking my brother to take the bar exam for me—my smart, decent, loving brother—right at the beginning of his own promising legal career?

Thank God he had the good sense to say no.

||||||||||||||||

As soon as the holidays were over, after thoroughly embarrassing myself with my brother, I was scheming up grand new incursions. The higher the profile, the better. My life was increasingly indefensible. But after sundown and especially after midnight, I was still the man.

Even random acquaintances were hearing about places I had gone and asking to come along. People actually started using the expression, "Pulling a Craig." Pulling a Craig, as in using ingenuity to get in somewhere you didn't belong. "We don't have tickets, but we could always Pull a Craig."

The first time I heard that, it was no substitute for passing the bar exam, but it did give me a thrill, which I promptly toasted with tequila shots.

I had heard that my old Grammys buddy Dion was being inducted into the Rock & Roll Hall of Fame. He was in typically excellent company. Slated to be inducted with him were the Rolling Stones, Stevie Wonder, the Temptations, and Otis Redding. The black-tie dinner and show was being held January 18, 1989, in the Grand Ballroom of New York's Waldorf Astoria Hotel.

Barry and I showed up early this time, dressed in our special-event tuxedos. I asked someone where the Grand Ballroom was. But as soon as we reached the check-in area, we saw that it was crawling with security people. I could tell there was no way we were getting in there. Not this way. We retreated immediately.

I asked someone else where the hotel's banquet kitchen was. No one was guarding the doors of the industrial-sized kitchen, the door from the hotel hallway, or the one from the kitchen into the ballroom. Without saying anything to anyone, we marched right through that massive kitchen and straight into the heavily secured ballroom. Once we got inside though, we faced another challenge. Since the show was being preceded by a formal, sit-down dinner, the ballroom was filled with large, round tables and chairs, every one of them assigned to someone.

I wasn't hungry, but we couldn't just stand around while everyone else was eating. We found an out-of-the-way table on the ballroom's second level that had several empty seats and just sat down. That was fine through the salad course. That's when the couple who were really sitting there arrived.

"Excuse me," the man said quite abruptly. "I think you are in our seats." He caused enough of a ruckus that an official-looking woman came over and asked: "May I see your tickets."

When we couldn't produce them, she said to us quite firmly: "You'll have to leave now."

We didn't argue. We didn't complain. We got up and left the ball-room, through the main entrance this time. Then, we turned around and went back inside through the kitchen.

We didn't even get to sit down this time. As we stood in the back scoping the room for empty chairs, a man came over and asked where we were sitting. "Over there," I motioned vaguely. "We're waiting for a friend." But he didn't buy it. "May I see your tickets, please?" he asked. When we had nothing to show, he tossed us out a second time.

Our plan wasn't working perfectly, but I still believed it was sound. We tried it one more time. The chefs must have been wondering who these AWOL waiters were as we came back through the kitchen for a third attempt.

This time, we didn't stand still. We prowled the ballroom until we noticed a more-than-half-empty table right up front. "Let's grab 'em," I said to BZ as we slid into two of the six vacant seats. By then, the Scottish salmon and British potpie—hail to the UK!—had already been served. We were maybe fifteen feet from the ballroom's giant stage. After the chocolate cake dessert was served, the show was about to begin. That's how close we were for the rest of the night to some of the real pioneers of rock-'n'-roll.

|||||||||||||||

Too bad that life kept interrupting my last, lingering talent.

Five weeks after the Rock Hall induction, on February 21, I was sitting at a familiar wooden table in a quiet, somber room with a couple hundred other nervous-looking law school graduates, taking my last, pathetic stab at the bar exam. Douglas having wisely declined to participate, I was fully on my own. Having failed twice already, I wasn't even sure what I was doing there. I was failing again, I knew. I could feel it. There was no doubt. And the same would happen again, I was certain, if I was enough of a masochist to sign up for a fourth, fifth, sixth, or seventh attempt.

I wasn't. I was done.

|||||||||||||||||

The hits kept coming, and I never really lost my touch. But the thrill of it all was fading fast. I still appreciated the craftsmanship required to get past all those velvet ropes. But once I was there, even with an appreciative entourage, I was starting to wonder, *What's the point?*

Still, on adrenaline and a lack of anything else to do, I pressed on. On May 11, 1989, it was the Songwriters Hall of Fame at Radio City Music Hall.

Like at the Grammys, I snuck in the night before. I found a yellow all-access pass. "STAFF," it said. Now, I was so confident in my technique, I brought a full entourage along. This time, I brought Jane, my brother Douglas and his girlfriend, and four other friends. I got pictures with Eddie Money, Paula Abdul, Patti LaBelle, and Liza Minnelli. We even went to the post-performance buffet supper in the Grand Ballroom at the New York Hilton.

On October 8, 1989, it was the Rolling Stones at Shea Stadium, the first of six sold-out shows. For access, I dug out the old Harry M. Stevens uniform. Once inside, I talked a well-connected Stones groupie out of an all-access VIP pass she happened to have.

"Knock yourself out," she said. And I did, with vodka tonics.

On December 12, 1989, it was the Paul McCartney World Tour at Madison Square Garden, his second of four nights there. For that show, I snuck into The Garden the night before and snagged a "Paul McCartney World Tour Handbook," an internal, not-for-public-consumption, stop-by-stop tour guide for the musicians and crew. I cut out the picture of Paul on the front and the cool tour logo. I copied that onto a pass-sized piece of paper and added, "ALL ACCESS, ALL AREAS." As an added touch, before getting it laminated, I put my picture on there too.

Imagine what I could have done if Photoshop had been invented in 1989!

On New Year's Eve, it was Billy Joel's Stormfront Tour at Long Island's Nassau Coliseum. I was still dating the very forgiving Jane Lewis. Her father somehow knew the concert promoter, Ron Delsener. I phoned Delsener's assistant, saying, "I'm calling from Mr. Lewis's office. Can we get a pair of tickets to the Billy Joel show New Year's Eve?" The promoter's secretary left two VIP tickets at the coliseum box office along with two backstage passes. That one was almost too easy.

It was right after the New Year that Jane asked me something that caught me off guard. "What would you think about us seeing a couples' therapist? It might be interesting. Maybe we could learn some things."

What was she getting at? Was something wrong? With me? With us? With her? Jane did seem to notice I was drinking a lot and my career really wasn't progressing. But she hadn't made a big deal out of any of that. I wasn't sure if one of those things was an issue or maybe this was just New Age-y girl talk. I didn't believe I needed therapy. But she asked so nicely—no hint of accusation—that I thought I should probably just go along.

"Okay," I said. "If you think we should."

We went to see a woman named Marilyn Minor, who had an office on the twenty-sixth floor of 280 Park Avenue South in the Gramercy Park neighborhood. I liked her immediately.

She asked a lot of questions. She wasn't judgmental. She seemed to care about us and wanted to be helpful if she could. We talked about the importance of two people communicating and listening to each other, which all couples could benefit from, right? The only uncomfortable topic that came up was my drinking.

"Do you drink too much?" Marilyn asked me quite matter-of-factly during our second or third session with her.

"I don't think so," I said. "Most people drink. I like to drink. I don't think it interferes with my life."

Jane didn't press the point, and neither did Marilyn. We went one or two more times and then we stopped. I was just happy to get out of there without both women finding something major to blame me for.

|||||||||||||||||

Meanwhile, my life was heading toward a terrible crash. Even I could tell.

I was totally despondent. My daytime walks around the east side of Manhattan were more like zombie marches. Old friends, it seemed, wanted nothing to do with me anymore.

One day when Jane and I were out, we stopped at the bank so she could get some cash. I watched over her shoulder as she dipped her ATM card in the slot and typed in her PIN.

3-4-1-9.

I made sure to remember the number she typed in.

The next night we were together, I waited until she was dressed for bed. Then, I said, "I'm gonna go out for Yodels. You want anything?"

Before I left the apartment, I slipped into her wallet and took her ATM card. After a quick stop in the junk food aisle at the deli, I also stopped at the bank, where I withdrew $300 from Jane's checking account. Three hundred was the maximum. With her good salary and her generous family trust fund, I figured, as long I didn't do this *too often*, she would never even notice.

By this point, my parents had grown quite weary about my constant pleas for cash. I wasn't working. There were no job prospects in sight. My illicit withdrawals from the First National Bank of Jane were my running-around funds. Sometimes, I'd spend the cash on her. Mostly, not. I bought pot. I paid bar tabs. I kept myself going in a life that was going nowhere.

IIIIIIIIIIIIIIIIII

I was twenty-four when I graduated from law school. Now, I was twenty-eight. Four years had come and gone, and what did I have to show for it? A giant pile of photos, VIP passes, hangovers, and a weird kind of fame. But no job. I couldn't really make a living sneaking into nightclubs and concerts. That wasn't going to support the lifestyle I wanted to live.

I woke up one morning in my one-bedroom apartment to an urgent knocking at my door. It was a man in a New York City sheriff's uniform and three moving men. They had come to evict me—now! This shouldn't have been a surprise. I hadn't been paying my rent, and I'd been ignoring increasingly hostile notices from the landlord saying I really did have to pay. Immediately.

The sheriff and the moving guys were actually fairly polite. They said I could call the management company and try to work something out in the next ten minutes. I called. I spoke to the woman who answered the phone. She sounded familiar with my case. She told me the only way I could stay in the apartment was to hand-deliver a check for $7,700—$2,200 a month for the past three months plus assorted interest penalties and fees. I told her I would try and then I put the sheriff on the phone. He told me he hoped he wouldn't see me tomorrow.

I called my father. I told him I was in a major jam. He sounded disappointed. But after my sufficient begging, he wrote a check which

I picked up at his office and delivered to the property management company.

I could stay. For now.

There I was, as the weeks and months crept by, trapped in this perpetual Groundhog Day. Dating Jane Lewis. Making regular withdrawals with her ATM card. Waking up with no job to go to, day after day. Drinking, ducking creditors, begging my parents for more help. Nothing ever seemed to change.

There were some memorable high points, but fewer and fewer, and even they rarely ended well. My father insisted I downsize to a lower-priced, studio loft at Turtle Bay Towers on Forty-sixth Street between First and Second Avenues. One night, I was calling some girl—not Jane—trashed out of my mind at four in the morning. I hit speed dial and a woman answered. In my best drunk-sexy mumble, I started telling the girl she should come over to my apartment, though I don't remember all the vivid details. Certainly, the "come over" came through the line loud and clear.

I heard a gasp that I recognized immediately as my mother. My mother! A shot of adrenaline raced through my booze-soaked brain. I grunted. I paused. I hung up the phone. But never, for the rest of my life, would I forget the sound of my mother's 4:00 a.m. gasp.

12

DOOR KNOCKERS

Bang!

Bang!

The horrible racket that crashed into my soggy, half-sleeping, hungover brain that fateful Saturday morning—that wasn't knocking. It was something louder and more persistent. *Banging* didn't even capture it. *Pounding, pummeling*—that was more like it. Whoever was outside the door of my loft apartment on East Forty-Sixth Street really wanted to come inside. Compared to what I was hearing, the sheriff and his moving crew from a few months earlier might as well have been the Welcome Wagon.

I'd been out late the night before. Of course I had. I'd consumed prodigious amounts of alcohol. Of course. Vodka stingers, to be precise. I returned home late, sometime after 4:00 a.m. All I wanted to do at 9:10 in the morning was keep the pillow over my head and fall back asleep.

But I couldn't.

Now, I was agitated and confused. Whoever it was, how did they get past the doorman and up to the eighth floor? The doormen at

Turtle Bay Towers wouldn't let *anyone* up without announcing them. But the pounding wouldn't stop. No way was I getting back to sleep again. So I yanked the sheets off and pulled myself out of bed. As I stood, I felt a little woozy. My mouth tasted like a gerbil might have died in there, dry and fuzzy. I could only imagine how my breath must have smelled. I climbed unsteadily down the stairs from the sleeping loft into the open living room. In dank, grey Jockey shorts and a faded red T-shirt, I opened the door a crack.

My mother and my father were standing there, and they did not look well. My mother was crying. My father looked like he was ready to kill someone, the way he used to look when he came home from a tough day at work to discover that one of the boys had broken something he cared about in the house or done something else that really pissed him off. I absorbed that initial impression, opened the door a little wider, and said the first thing that fell into my head.

"What are you doing here? Did somebody die?"

I had no idea that the real answer was "me."

"Nobody died," my father fumed. "But we need to talk to you. Right now."

"Okay," I said. "Come in."

I threw on some sweatpants and told the two of them to take a seat, motioning toward the two chairs across the coffee table from the couch. I plopped down on the beige, L-shaped, pee-stained couch. Pee-stained because of all those nights I'd come home drunk, in this apartment and previous ones, only to pass out on the couch and wake up after I'd had an accident in my pants. Sorry about the grossness of that, but the multiple stains on the couch were proof that's what happened on more nights than I could count.

That was the end of the pleasantries. As soon as everyone was seated, my parents got down to business. My mother dabbed her eyes with a Kleenex. She took one deep breath, and she spoke first.

"I love you very, very much," she said, her voice aching with a dire intensity I had never heard from her before. Still, I could hear a *but* coming. And after she took another long breath, it came.

"But I don't like you," my mother said. "I can't stand what you have become. I will always love you. But the person you are now, I want nothing to do with him. That person is repulsive to me."

Well, where the fuck did *that* come from?

Five minutes earlier, I was sleeping in my bed. Now, my own mother was telling me I was repulsive? This little visit was getting off to a highly unpromising start.

Then, my father began to talk.

"I have more respect for the bum on the street corner wiping windshields for a quarter at the red light," he announced. "At least he's making something of his life. In the pinkie on your left hand, you have more talent than most people have in their entire body."

I hadn't said a word yet. I was too stunned.

"I have spent hundreds of thousands of dollars," my father continued. "Putting you through college. Putting you through law school. Supporting you ever since you got out. What do I have to show for that? You have become nothing. My efforts have been a total waste. A waste of money. A waste of talent. A waste of time. All of that—*all of it*—stops today."

He glanced over at my mother, seeing if she was ready to pick it up from there. She shook her head. "Go on," she said softly. She was sniffling again.

"We know you are full of shit," my father said. "We know you are lying about working. You haven't even been trying to work. We know that. We know you stole Jane Lewis's bank card. How could you do something like that?"

Not her card, I thought to myself. Her PIN. How did they know about that, anyway?

"Jane called," my mother said, answering my puzzled look.

"We know everything," my father said. "You are lucky she didn't call the police. She should have. What the hell has happened to you?"

"Who are you?" my mother added. "We don't even know who you are."

For a moment, I thought about mounting a defense. I wanted to. This verbal beat-down from my parents seemed to come out of nowhere. Could I get a little warning next time? A simple heads-up so I could prepare myself? Was I really that deplorable? These reactions were off-the-chart extreme, were they not? All those thoughts were bouncing around in my head as I sat there on the stinky couch. But I didn't utter any of them. I still needed to hear where all this was going.

"You have two choices," my father said. "There are only two choices. It is very simple."

I was really starting to feel claustrophobic, like the walls of the loft were closing in. But there was no stopping my father now.

"You can continue on your destructive path," he said. "You can continue to live life the way you are living. Your mother and I will leave here right now, and we never want to hear from you again. Don't call. Don't write. Don't leave us messages. Don't have your brothers call on your behalf. You will be out of our will and out of our lives forever. We never want to hear from you ever again. Continue on this self-destructive path you are on, you are dead to us."

I shuddered at the sound of that. I could not believe my father was talking that way to me. But, he wasn't done.

"However," he continued, "if you choose to change your life and seek help, we will support you any way we can. You can come home with us right now. Figure out what the hell is going on here and figure out what to do about it. What you have become is disgusting. It is not you. We know you. Who you are. Your potential. Let's get you the help that you need."

141

That was a lot to absorb. As I sat there in silence and my mother started sniffling again, my mind went where it always did when faced with a challenge. I started searching for an escape. Those were awfully stark choices. There had to be some middle ground, some grey area, some one-time exception we could apply here. Life was never just black and white. So where was the wiggle room? I was famous for my creative strategizing and my verbal dexterity. If there was an angle, I could usually find it. But I heard nothing equivocal in my father's voice. He was talking about this choice as if I were driving my car on the interstate and the exit was flying toward me. Did I want to take it or not? I had no time to weigh the decision. I had no chance to seek other options. Yes or no? Left or right? I had to turn or not—now!

I felt cornered.

I felt panicked.

I needed more time to decide.

But the world's greatest talker had just been struck dumb.

My mind was racing faster than any car I had ever driven, drunk or sober. I knew if I didn't go with them, I would be homeless. There was so much that needed saying. But nothing was coming out of my mouth.

"All right," I said finally. "Let's go."

It would be nice to say that, right then and there, slouched on the pee-stained couch, I made a solemn vow to turn my life around. That I saw my breakneck existence with a new set of eyes. That in the shock of this parental beat-down, I recognized how much I needed the guidance and the motivation this intervention delivered to me. It would be nice to say that I stood up, looked in the mirror, recognized how right my parents were, made the necessary changes, and never looked back again. Yes, it would be nice. Unfortunately, that isn't what happened, not as cleanly or as quickly or as easily as that. Not even close. What happened was that I got up off the couch and found a pair of sneakers.

I traded my sweatpants for some jeans and pulled a sweatshirt over my T-shirt. And I walked out of my apartment with my parents, one step at a time.

We rode the elevator down to the lobby. We climbed into my father's car. My father drove us home to Rockland County. My parents sat stone-faced in the front seat. I sat in the back seat by myself and sulked.

I'll think of something, I thought to myself as my father headed north on FDR Drive. *This is just a holding pattern. If there is one thing I am good at, it is slipping past barriers that I am not supposed to breach. Not an incursion this time, a breakout.* The techniques, I suspected, were pretty much the same. I might have been in a temporary jam here. I just needed some calm and quiet to make a plan.

By the time we arrived at 10 Topaz Court in New City, still nothing else was said. I got out of the car, went up to my childhood bedroom, shut the door, flopped on the bed, and began to cry.

|||||||||||||||

Who do you call when you need to save your life? I had no idea. Actually, my current predicament was worse than that. I didn't even think I needed to save my life. Sure, I had issues. Didn't everyone? I was sequestered in my childhood bedroom at twenty-eight years of age— not as a launch pad to my reform and recovery but as a temporary stopgap, a chance to catch my breath, placate my parents, go through whatever motions I had to while I plotted my next moves.

I might give a little lip service to calm the immediate crisis, I told myself. *But I have no intention of dramatic changes here. If my parents or anyone else think I have a problem, that's their problem, not mine.*

It was true, as I lay on my bed trying to get a grip on all this, that another voice was also calling out to me. Not a voice I wanted to hear.

I was able to beat it down to a whisper, but I couldn't entirely silence it. The words were not so different from the ones my parents had spoken, but the tone and the timbre were undeniably me. Even in its softness, that voice cut through the fog of my self-delusion and denial. *You know your life is all fucked up*, this voice was telling me. *You aren't working. You have no prospects. You have no career. You are nothing but a faker, a brilliant faker maybe, but a faker nonetheless. Your father was right. You have talent, and you have squandered every ounce of it. What gives you the right to treat people like garbage? Who gives a shit about your silly scams? Who cares if you buddy up to vapid celebrities? That's no life.*

I wasn't able to make that voice stop talking. And believe me, I tried. But I still had enough pride and resistance to suppress those thoughts to the point that I could mostly ignore them. For the time being, that was good enough.

I spent the rest of the weekend in the house with my parents. It was uncomfortable, but I survived. They watched TV and went to their bedroom. I mostly stayed in mine. We saw each other in the kitchen. The tension was thick. Everything was weird. But until Sunday night, no one said much of anything.

"You're gonna deal with this in the morning?" my father asked me then.

I told him I would.

"Let us know how we can help," he said. "We are there for you."

When I woke up on Monday, I really didn't feel like I had much choice. I didn't think I had a problem, except for the fact that my parents had had a crazy meltdown. But I couldn't stay in my old bedroom forever. My father would want to know what was happening. My mother too. I had to take some kind of step.

But what?

The only person I could think of to call was Marilyn Minor, the couples' therapist Jane Lewis had dragged me to. I didn't know if this was her area or if she could help me or what. But people's fucked-up lives was more or less her field, wasn't it? She seemed like a decent person at least.

I left a message on her answering machine. She called back within an hour. "How can I help you, Craig?" she asked.

She sounded just as cheerful as I remembered her. I was pleased she remembered me. I told her a little about my current situation, though I wasn't quite sure how to explain it.

"You were so helpful when Jane and I came to see you," I said. "I was hoping you might be able to point me the right way. You have such a knack for this sort of thing."

I was still selling, even in my current predicament, laying it on as smoothly and as thickly as I could. But I couldn't stretch this out much longer.

I explained that my parents had shown up at my door unannounced and now were demanding immediate action. "I think I may need some help," I said. "I'm not sure if it's an alcohol issue or what. I think the jig may be up here."

I'm not sure exactly what I meant by that last part or why I said it. But clearly, that possibility was floating around in my head.

The second Marilyn heard the words "alcohol issue," she knew she couldn't help me.

"Craig," she said, "you need to call a specialist. I'm really not qualified to deal with this."

A specialist in pissed-off parents? I thought to myself.

No. She meant an alcohol specialist, someone who works with alcoholics. That became clear immediately. She was probably predisposed to think that since my drinking was the issue that Jane came in with.

"There is a man I know who has dedicated his life to people who are dealing with addiction issues," she said. "Alcoholics, especially."

That was the first time anyone had ever called me an addict or an alcoholic. I let it pass. I didn't need to argue, and it didn't really bother me since she didn't even know me that well. But to appease my parents, I did need to talk to somebody.

"His name is Arthur Knauert," she said. "Doctor Arthur Knauert. He has top credentials. He went to med school at Cornell and did his residency in psychiatry at Presbyterian Hospital. Addiction is his specialty. He has been having some very encouraging results. You might want to talk to him. His office is on the Upper East Side."

"Sure," I said.

"You have a pen?" she asked. I told her I did. She spelled out the doctor's last name—K-N-A-U-E-R-T. Then she gave me his address: 505 East Eighty-Third Street, apartment A. "It's between First and York Avenues," she said. She then gave me his phone number.

"You should call him and make an appointment," she urged.

I didn't want to lose my momentum. Or my nerve. I called Dr. Knauert as soon as I hung up with Marilyn Minor. I left a message on his machine as I had with Marilyn. He also called back quickly.

"My name is Craig Schmell," I said. "Marilyn Minor referred me to you."

"Uh-huh," he said, not revealing one way or the other whether he knew Marilyn, liked Marilyn, or had any idea who I was talking about. He just waited for me to say more.

I didn't know exactly how to explain the situation since I had never met him. And I didn't really know what my problem was or if I had a problem at all, besides the hysterical parents. But I tried.

"My girlfriend thinks I drink too much," I told the doctor. "My parents think my life is a mess. They are insisting I do something and are threatening all kinds of dire results if I don't."

"I see," he said.

This was not a guy who gave too much, not in early conversation. He did have a couple of questions.

"Do you drink a lot?" he asked.

"I like to drink," I said.

"Do you smoke a lot of pot?"

"Pretty much every day."

I didn't think there was anything wrong with that. So I didn't think I needed to lie.

He didn't answer me or ask any follow-up questions. What was he waiting for?

"Can I come see you?" I asked him.

"I don't want to see you," he told me. "Not yet. Before I can see you, you need to go to rehab. Twenty-eight days is about right."

Rehab.

That should have sounded like an accusation. Like an indictment. A punishment. Actually, it sounded perfect. Really, it did.

It would get me out of my parents' house. I'd get a month-long vacation. Time to relax and chill out. I could clear my head, figure out how to calm my anxious mother and father, then get back to the rest of my life. Depending on how tight the program was, maybe I wouldn't even have to quit drinking entirely.

No program can watch you twenty-four hours a day.

The doctor asked if I had health insurance. I told him I did. I didn't mention that my father was paying the premiums. "Would you like me to give you the names of a few programs?" he asked.

He mentioned four treatment programs, and I started writing them down.

The Betty Ford Center in Rancho Mirage, California. The Hazelden Addiction Treatment Center in Center City, Minnesota. I'd heard of those two. I knew celebrities went there.

Then he gave me the name of a place in Florida I'd never heard of and another one in Minnesota, Adult Chemical-Dependency Program of St. Mary's at Fairview-Riverside Hospital.

"They should all take your insurance," he said in a businesslike way. "Pick one. Go to rehab. Give me a call when you get back."

"Okay," I said. "Sounds like plan."

I made a round of phone calls to the programs. They all had admissions counselors who were happy to get on the phone to describe their program to me. I settled quickly on St. Mary's—not because of the treatment model or the program's reputation or even its nice-sounding facilities. I chose that program for one reason alone: it was coed. That was the total reason. That and the fact that it wasn't in New York. If I was going to go through the motions of detox and rehab, I figured I might as well get a vacation out of it too.

The other programs all said they treated the males and females separately. I'm sure they had a reason for that, but coed sounded way better to me. The people at St. Mary's also mentioned a tennis court, a location on the bank of the Mississippi River, and abundant free time for recreation, all of which sounded like added bonuses. But, since none of these places was offering wine with dinner, it was the coed part that sealed the deal for me.

I was feeling better already. I'd be out of my parents' house. I'd have some time to relax and catch my breath. It probably would hurt, I told myself, if I cut down on the drinking a little. After all, I wouldn't want my drinking to get out of hand or anything. Maybe this wouldn't be such a bad experience after all.

13

A MONTH'S VACATION

St. Mary's was my kind of rehab.

That was obvious the day I strolled in, October 14, 1990, wearing Levi's, a leather jacket, and cowboy boots, my idea of how people dressed in the Midwest. *How did I get here?* I thought to myself. I'd taken a taxi from the Minneapolis–St. Paul Airport to Riverside Avenue in the West Bank neighborhood and was dropped off in front of an older, utilitarian building that housed the Adult Chemical-Dependency Program. I was greeted at the front door by one of the junior counselors, who escorted me and my overstuffed blue duffle bag to my new dorm room. As we made our way down the main hallway and through the combination dining/meeting room, I couldn't help but notice other residents checking out the new guy, the same way people did at parties and nightclub openings in New York.

I flashed the same friendly smile I would have at Area or Limelight.

I had never been inside an addiction-treatment center before, so this was all new to me. The people looked normal enough. Most of them appeared to be in their twenties or thirties. Men *and* women, the reason I was here instead of Betty Ford or Hazelden. No one looked tense or angry or especially unhappy to be there. The large, open, central room could have been the lounge at a grad school where the courses weren't too difficult and the students had a lot of time on their hands. People were talking in twos and threes. Others were reading by themselves. Over in one corner, a dozen residents were sitting in a circle in what looked like a group therapy session, though I couldn't hear what they were talking about. All in all, St. Mary's struck me as a perfectly nice place to spend the next four weeks. I didn't see the tennis court, but I saw on the taxi ride in that the Mighty Mississippi—not quite as mighty in Minneapolis as it is in St. Louis or New Orleans—was a block behind us, and the neighborhood was fairly upscale. I'd rather have been out drinking with my friends in Manhattan, but if I had to be in a program, I felt like I had probably chosen right.

During my orientation, my counselor, Diane Lundquist, asked me a bunch of questions, which I answered distractedly, half thinking about what I was saying, half not. This whole process felt like a game to me.

"When was the last time you used alcohol or drugs?" she asked.

"Yesterday," I answered honestly.

"How much?"

"I had one joint and seven or eight triple drinks."

"In the past year, would you say you've had a problem with drugs?"

"Maybe a slight one."

"Do you drink and drive?"

"I live in the city now, but sometimes. I've had a few accidents over the years, running into other cars."

"Do you sleep well?"

"Not so well."

"Do you eat well?"

"I wouldn't say that."

"How would you describe your social life?"

"I would call myself extroverted. I don't like to be alone."

"Do you date? If so, how many times in a typical month?"

"Maybe seven to ten women a month. But that's just an average."

"Are you open to the program?"

"Sure."

"Is someone requiring you to be here?"

"Requiring me? No. But I am getting pressure from my parents and my ex-girlfriend. I took some money from her bank account. She found out."

Diane wrote all this down, taking careful notes as I answered her questions. She didn't say whether these were good answers or bad answers. She just wrote them down.

Then, she reviewed the program rules with me. No alcohol or drugs. No leaving the premises without permission. No contact with my friends or family until family visiting day, which was two weeks in. No sexual activity of any sort. "You are here to make profound changes in your life," the counselor said. "That will only happen if you really engage. So participate in the activities. Be part of the family. Don't waste your time here. Give yourself the best possible shot. The next twenty-eight days really can save your life."

She said this all very eloquently. She seemed to mean every word of it. And I told her I agreed wholeheartedly, though of course I didn't believe my life needed saving. Except for a couple of hysterical parents and a high-strung girlfriend, my life was okay, thank you very much. I didn't say that, but that's what I was thinking as I nodded along. What I said was: "I am very much looking forward to my time here."

Later, she placed a brief written report in my file.

The patient finds it difficult to socialize without the use of alcohol. He reports that he likes to go to clubs and that he never drinks at home or alone. He likes exotic and fancy discos. He indicates that he is highly extroverted and centers his socializing around using

*friends. The patient reports that he has neglected and embarrassed
his friends by his behavior and lost relationships due to his using.
The patient reports that he used to work out daily and indicates
that he quit going several months ago. The patient reports that he
likes sports such as baseball and football.*

Looking back, I can't really remember how much of that I told her
and how much she just surmised. But I did have to say: amid all the
bureaucratic language and the patient-this and patient-that, some of
what she wrote there wasn't too far from reality.

|||||||||||||||||

The first couple of days were a little rough. I got a name tag with a
blue sticker on it, signifying that I was undergoing detox and the time
it would take for my body to adjust physically to the abrupt removal
of all alcohol and drugs. This explained to anyone who didn't know
that I was a newbie why I might be looking a little pale. After drinking
and getting stoned nearly every day for more than a dozen years,
the center's experts presumed that my body had gotten used to the
constant presence of intoxicating substances and wouldn't want to
give them up without a fight.

I did it. I got through that first week of alcohol and drug detox.
Then it was over and, surprisingly, I felt fine. Next came the process
I was really here for, realigning my life so I could live without booze,
pot, and other drugs.

For the next three and a half weeks, I worked out. I got in some
tennis. In the therapy sessions, I tried to be supportive while people
made comments I wasn't listening to. I said what I thought I had
to in the one-on-ones with the counselors. "It's really great to have
the opportunity to reassess things… Just the time away is useful…

Everyone is so supportive. That's great." I flirted with several of the female patients. As for Ms. Lundquist's admonition not to waste my time there? I bullshitted everyone I came in contact with. I didn't admit any truths at all.

I spent some time with one of the other residents. Nicole was her name. She had short, blonde hair and came from outside Chicago. Back in New York, she might not have been my type. But she was smart and funny and seemed to enjoy my company. Unlike me, she was working hard to get her life back on track. We figured out that, after 10:00 p.m., the staff was mostly gone and no one else was paying much attention. We'd slip back to my room—or to hers—and climb into bed together.

If we'd been caught, the counselors would have kicked both of us out of the program. My parents would have disowned me for sure. That would have been the end of my supposed turnaround. I risked that. I was still pushing the envelope, still dodging personal responsibility, still not giving a shit about anything except what I wanted right at that moment. I wasn't focused on potential consequences. I was still deep into diseased thinking, whether I was drinking that day or not. No rules applied to me.

I gave lip service when I had to. When I got called on to speak in one of the group sessions, I always tried to say something that sounded like I was wrestling with the issues that had brought us all here. "It's important to be honest, even when it's hard," I said with practiced earnestness. "I need to set clear goals for myself, things that are challenging but achievable."

Then, I promptly lied about having passed the bar exam.

As the days rolled by, I felt like I was getting fluent in program-speak, the special lingo of recovery that told the other people, "I'm here, and I get it." I couldn't tell if it was working. By that point, I couldn't even decipher what the truth was. Had I been drinking too much? Was I on a downward spiral to oblivion? *Was* I a total piece of shit? Or was this just a pit stop on a life of high-speed adventure and accomplishment? Was everything going fine? I just kept saying whatever I thought I had to. This was new terrain for me, and I was surviving the best I knew how. Fooling everyone around me was what I did. On that topic, I could have taught my own master class. That part came easily to me. And truthfully, I'd been believing my own stuff for as long as I could remember. Why stop now?

As the month progressed, I got more and more of a sense that the counselors weren't buying any of it. They began confronting me directly. "You seem to think you're perfect," one of them said. At first, it wasn't an accusation. More of an observation.

But then it began to sound a bit disapproving. "Are you happy wasting your life like this?"

Eventually, it was almost mocking. "Everything is always someone else's fault, I guess."

I tried to argue, but I didn't get too far. That last one, delivered with heavy sarcasm, was a little jarring to hear. I thought of myself as a leader, an adventurer, someone crafty enough to beat his own path through a tedious and mundane world. I didn't hide behind others, did I? I made my own way. That's what I'd always told myself, anyway.

"I like my life just fine," I told my counselors when I was pushed hard.

Sometimes my nonchalance took the heat off me. Sometimes, it didn't. But I don't think it convinced anyone, certainly not the staff. These were experienced addiction counselors and intelligent people, intimately familiar with the cons and deceptions—and expert self-justifications—of addicts. I was buying time maybe. But I definitely wasn't fooling anyone.

After I'd been at St. Mary's for two weeks, my parents flew out for a family weekend. The counselors must have poisoned their minds.

Or maybe it was the way I was walking around the place, joking with people and working the room. Whatever it was, my father concluded immediately that I was the same old Craig.

"You getting *anything* out of this?" he asked me.

"Absolutely," I said.

"Really?" he answered as if he hadn't seen a speck of evidence.

My mother still had some hope that my twenty-eight days in Minnesota would open my eyes. Mothers always have hope.

"What an impressive place this is," she said as she and my dad prepared to fly back to New York.

"This is serious business," my father added without missing a beat, though the way he said it sounded more like a last gasp. "Don't blow it here."

By then, everyone could see that I was blowing it.

Maybe even me.

||||||||||||||||

As I entered the final week of residential treatment, the reality was growing clear to everyone: despite my month in Minneapolis, I was still damn near the same person I'd been when my cowboy boots and I had arrived.

Two days before we were scheduled to leave, each of the residents was called for an official exit interview. The idea was to mark the progress that had been achieved already and sketch out a life plan for the future. It would be a shame, everyone agreed, to go through the program, do well, and then fall back into the very same self-destructive habits that had landed all of us here.

One by one, the residents went in for their interviews. Mine was the last on the schedule. I didn't listen in on anyone else's interview, but from what people said when they were finished, I think I got a pretty good idea of how these things went. One by one, I heard, the other residents were congratulated on their hard work and excellent progress. Some were referred to halfway houses—in their home communities or in the rural parts of Minnesota. Some of the residents were told that these halfway houses were an integral part of the treatment. The newly sober St. Mary's graduates were told that these next-step residences would provide structure and support as they eased their way back into their old, but improved, lives. As the other St. Mary residents left their interviews, they exchanged hopeful stories about where they were going and what they expected when they got there.

Senior counselor Bonnie Mulligan took a different approach with me. She called me into her office for my exit interview. She had a somber look on her face.

"Craig," Bonnie told me without wasting any time on pleasantries. "We are not going to send you to a halfway house. You haven't earned it."

I knew I wasn't going to be the valedictorian. But I wasn't expecting this. She wasn't done.

"You have learned nothing here," the senior counselor said decisively. "You're still totally full of yourself and totally full of shit," she said. "You don't get any of this. You won't acknowledge you have a problem. You can't see what a mess you have made of your life. Unless you face the truth, you will never make progress. We can't help you now. You are refusing to help yourself."

I sat there stunned.

"We are sending you back to New York to fail miserably," she said. "The only thing we can hope for is that you will learn something from your next failure. Then, maybe you will come back a second time. You might get it next time."

In our entire group, I was the only one who didn't get a referral.

No referral. No congratulatory certificate. No diploma. Instead, she handed me a written report that was, I thought, only slightly more hopeful than what she had just said to me. I guess she didn't want to appear too negative on paper. But even the written report was pretty downbeat.

The patient needs to remain free from alcohol and drugs. He needs to internalize the disease concept. He has not yet surrendered to the illness and has a problem with a higher power. He needs to listen rather than talk. He needs to practice rigorous honesty. He has difficulty with humility and his self-worth is low. He has family relationships to deal with, as well as his relationships with women.

There were some practical suggestions.

The patient is to attend recovery meetings three times a week. He wants to practice honest communication, as well as having close relationships with his sponsor and sober friends. In the area of recovery barriers, he says he will have some difficulty living one day at a time and lying to himself about using. He also wants to establish open communication with his family. He has had a using lifestyle and will work to establish sober friends, attend sober parties, and participate in the alumni association in his area.

And then this:

PROGNOSIS: Fair.

The report was signed, "Bonnie Mulligan, Senior Counselor, Adult Chemical-Dependency Treatment Unit."

Though I was definitely taken aback by the bleakness of Bonnie's verdict, I told myself I didn't really care. *I don't want to go to a halfway house, anyway,* I said to myself. *What kind of prize is that? I'm in charge of my own life. I don't need a bunch of program people to tell me how to live.*

But as the other residents said "goodbye" and "good luck" and headed off in their separate directions, I felt like all my friends were going off to sleepaway camp, and I was staying home for the summer.

|||||||||||||||||

When I got back to New York, I didn't stop at my parents' house in Rockland County. I went straight back to my loft apartment on East Forty-Sixth Street, the apartment with the pee-stained beige couch, the one that my parents had barged so rudely into. Since I was going along with the program, my dad was still paying the rent there.

I had such a mix of feelings swirling around in my head. I hated the way St. Mary's had ended. I was glad to be back home. I was feeling physically healthy, actually quite energetic. The family turmoil seemed to have eased a little, despite the poor impressions my parents had on visiting day. They understood I wasn't the star resident, but at least I was on path, maybe, sort of. I did seem to have bought myself maneuvering room and some time. But I didn't like being called a failure right to my face. Those treatment counselors didn't seem to know anything about respecting other peoples' sensitivities.

But of all those feelings, the one that hit me hardest and stuck with me was that I had failed rehab.

I fuckin' failed rehab.

This was the bar exam all over again.

And my career wasn't the only thing on the line this time. Hanging in the balance this time was my life.

But then, without any warning, I noticed something. It was a small dash of motivation brewing inside me. Nothing huge at first. Just a tiny thought trickling up from the back of my brain.

It was true I had sloughed off treatment at St. Mary's. I had broken the rules. I had treated their program like a joke. I snuck and conned and lazed my way through, like I had been doing in other parts of my life for years.

But I felt disrespected. I felt underestimated. I felt like the people at St. Mary's didn't get me or what I was truly capable of.

That tiny thought? I wanted to prove them wrong.

14

SEE THE MAN

Free at last!

Back in New York, things were already feeling like they might be returning to normal—my kind of normal. Mainly, it was just a huge relief to be out of the claustrophobia of St. Mary's and breathing New York air again. My time in rehab had been judged a failure by the people in charge. My parents had certainly gotten an earful when they came out for family weekend. But despite the negative reviews, I actually felt like I'd achieved something out there. Not lifelong sobriety. I wasn't even interested in that. But I'd gone for help like my parents had insisted. I'd stuck with the program for the full twenty-eight days. I'd had some interesting conversations with the counselors and my fellow residents. I'd met a cute girl. I'd lived up to my end of the bargain—hadn't I?—even if they didn't slap a shiny gold star on my forehead as I packed my bags and walked out the door for good. But as I settled back in New York City, two conflicting feelings were bouncing around in my head.

The first feeling was pride. I was proud of myself. I felt like I had used my charm and my cunning to dodge another bullet. Damn, I was good at this! I had faced a crisis, not entirely of my own making, a crisis my parents' overreaction had imposed on me. I had found a way to deal with it. My parents didn't know all the details of what the counselor had told me. They didn't fully understand what a flop my brush with treatment had been. But if I were declaring the month a success, who were they to say I had failed? Like any parent would, they were clinging to hope for their son. *Who knows! Maybe Craig is better now!* By going through the motions of treatment, I really had shaken my parents off my back. And now look: I was in my old apartment again, ready to head out onto the town. Job well done!

At the same time, however, another feeling was also rattling inside my head, and that feeling was turning out to be harder than I'd imagined to shake. The words of my counselors, Diane and Bonnie, were unexpectedly still gnawing at me. But they were wrong. I knew that. I wanted to show all of them just how wrong.

Bonnie said I hadn't learned anything from my time in treatment. She said I'd only been wasting my time. She singled me out and treated me differently from everyone else in the group. That was harsh! Maybe she was giving me her honest reaction. But was I really that bad? I wasn't the perfect rehab client. And, yes, maybe I'd done some things that were worthy of criticism. I certainly hadn't taken the program as seriously as I might have, as seriously as some people did. Sleeping with Nicole was a clear violation of the rules. No denying that. But Bonnie didn't even know about those antics. I'd only been there for twenty-eight days. How well did she really know me? Who did she think she was? The New York State Board of Law Examiners? I didn't like such negative, clean-cut judgments, not when they were applied to me.

No chance of success?

Learning nothing?

Last in the class?

The more I reflected, the more certain I was: I'll just show her!

Those two conflicting thoughts were sharing space in my brain when I picked up the telephone on Monday morning and phoned Dr. Arthur Knauert. He'd asked me to call when I got back to New York City, and I was calling him. At the very least, I wanted to get credit for following his directions and going out to Minnesota for a month of rehab and treatment. I wasn't sure what else I wanted or what he would say when I relayed that news to him. I figured it wouldn't be just, "Congratulations. Now you're well." I thought he might want me to come in and have a meeting with him. Once he met me, I knew, he'd see that I had a pretty good grip on things and certainly didn't need to be placed under the care of a psychiatrist.

Just as I had the first time, I left a message on his answering machine. When he called back, I told him I'd just spent a month in Minnesota like he'd urged me to. Then, as expected, he asked if I wanted to come see him.

"Sure," I said, without thinking much about the suggestion. "I can do that." We made an appointment for the following Tuesday, November 20, two days before Thanksgiving, at 7:00 p.m.

As I hung up the phone, I didn't really think I needed Dr. Knauert's professional help. I had followed his previous suggestion—that I go in to rehab—and the only thing that changed for the better, it seemed, was my parents' exaggerated concern. Thankfully, that really did seem to have eased. So I did see one possible advantage to meeting with him. If my parents started asking questions again, I'd have something else to throw back at them. They weren't insisting that I continue with treatment. Nothing was said explicitly. But I was sure they would like the sound of my sticking with this. To me, it was like an insurance policy. As long as I was continuing my treatment, how could they stop paying my rent or take some other hostile swipe at me? I didn't want any more unannounced visits, that's for sure.

IIIIIIIIIIIIIIIIII

Dr. Knauert's office was in an unimpressive, five-story, beige-brick apartment building at 505 East Eighty-Third Street between York and East End Avenues in the Yorkville section of Manhattan's Upper East Side. There was a metal fire escape across the front of the building, four steps up to a modest lobby and, off to the left, three steps down to a basement level. That's where the psychiatrist's office was. At the bottom of the stairs, I stepped into a small vestibule, where I pressed a doorbell and waited for someone to buzz me in. A tall, serious-looking man greeted me. He had a pleasant, noncommittal demeanor, bright eyes, and a droopy mustache. He looked like he was probably in his middle forties.

"Are you Craig?" he asked. "I'm Dr. Knauert."

He wasn't unfriendly, but I certainly wouldn't call him gregarious. Very matter-of-fact. He didn't reach out his hand to shake, but he invited me inside.

The basement apartment was set up like an office with a waiting room in front and a room to the rear that had a small desk, a couch, and a couple of leather chairs. The doctor invited me into the inner sanctum to sit down.

The whole thing seemed a little awkward. He didn't have the sunny disposition of Marilyn Minor, the couples' therapist on Park Avenue South that Jane Lewis and I had consulted. Without hardly any preliminary chitchat, he jumped right in.

"So," he asked, "how was rehab?"

The question didn't surprise me, and I knew how to handle it. I had decided that I would not be spilling all the details of what the counselors had told me—that I had wasted the month, that I wouldn't be referred to outpatient care, that I should return to New York to fail. Why get into all that?

"It was okay," I answered.

He nodded.

"How does it feel to be back home?"

"Good," I said.

He asked some basic questions about my past. I told him I had been lying to my parents. I had been lying to my girlfriends. I had been lying to my employers. For most of my life, I had underachieved. And at this point, I hadn't really accomplished very much.

The doctor wasn't giving much and neither was I. "So you like to smoke pot and drink alcohol?" he asked me.

I didn't see any reason to equivocate. "Sure," I said.

"Do you have a problem?" he asked.

"I don't think so," I said. "Everybody smokes and drinks."

"How long have you been drinking?"

"Since I was about sixteen," I said.

"And you're twenty-eight now?"

I nodded. I was five days away from my twenty-ninth birthday.

"How often do you drink?" he asked.

"Four or five times a week. Sometimes more."

"Do you get drunk?"

"Yes."

"Blackouts?"

"Sure."

"Wake up in strange places?"

"Of course."

"Do you think it's a problem?"

"No, everybody does."

"Craig, the behavior you describe makes me believe you are an alcoholic. I have little doubt about that. You also smoke pot? Since when?"

"Since I was sixteen."

"How often?"

"Pretty much every day."

"Pretty much every day for thirteen years? Do you think it's a problem?"

"No, everybody does it."

"Prescription pills?"

"No. Never."

"Anything else?"

"No, drinking and smoking pot, pretty much all the time. That's about it."

"About it?"

"No, that's it."

And it was.

"Do you need to drink and smoke pot?" he asked.

"Need to?" I repeated. "No. I like to, but I don't need to. I choose to. I enjoy doing it. But I wouldn't say I *need to*."

He stopped there and let the silence settle on top of us. I knew that this was a trick some shrinks tried to use. Just saying nothing and waiting for you to fill the silence. I had heard people talk about that or seen it in a movie. I am not sure how I knew about that, maybe even from TV, but I did. And maybe it worked. It didn't make me talk, but it did give our back-and-forth time to sink into my brain.

That short exchange, it turned out, was sufficient for Dr. Knauert to express something that either he was guessing at or had gotten some very fast insight into.

"You probably cannot drink successfully," he said. "Could you make a commitment to me?" he asked.

"What kind of commitment?"

"Make a commitment about how long you'll go without a drink or any kind of drugs," he said.

"How long do you want me to go?" I asked him.

"It's up to you," he said.

This conversation was getting weird. I couldn't drink *successfully*? *I* should choose how long I'd stop drinking or smoking pot?

"How about two weeks?" I suggested.

"Whatever you say, that's the commitment you're making."

"Okay," I said, quickly reconsidering. "Let's do a week."

He nodded. "You're going to make a commitment not to drink or smoke pot or use any other drugs for the week," he said.

"Yes," I told him.

"One week."

"Yes."

I had just spent a month in rehab. I could do a week.

"See you back here in a week? Same time next Tuesday?"

"See you then, Dr. K," I said as I got up from the chair.

He didn't invite me to call him that. But if a second visit was in the offing, I didn't want us to get off to too formal a start. Nicknames tend to bring people closer together. With its silent K and its colliding vowels, "Knauert" was a bit of tongue twister. He wasn't addressing me as "Mr. Schmell." The minute I said it, I liked the sound of Dr. K. It was just respectful enough. I wasn't calling him Arthur or Art or Artie or whatever his personal friends might call him. I was acknowledging that he wasn't my buddy. He was my psychiatrist. But I thought the looser, more casual nickname put us on more of a level playing field, and that could only be to my advantage. Isn't that what I did every time I inserted myself into a concert or a celebrity event? Equalizing my relationship with people who were supposedly above my station? He didn't object. So as of then, I started calling him Dr. K, and I never stopped.

||||||||||||||||

I was never one of those drinkers or drug users who was constantly promising to quit. I never promised to quit, not even for one afternoon, until I went out to Minnesota. But since I didn't think I had a drinking or drug problem, I didn't think I'd have any difficulty spending seven more days clean and sober in New York. It didn't seem like that big a deal. In fact, I got through the first five days without much issue. There were a couple of times I felt like having a cocktail, but not too many since I spent most of those nights watching TV by myself at home.

That changed on Saturday night when I got together with my friend Barry. We went to a club called Tattoo on Fiftieth Street off Third Avenue. Barry knew I was just back from a month in rehab. Being a good friend, he didn't push me to drink. But he did offer to share a joint with me in the Tattoo men's room, and I immediately agreed.

Ah, that felt nice.

I didn't give the night another thought until the following Tuesday, when I was sitting in Dr. Knauert's office for my second visit.

After a brief hello, he got right down to business.

"So how did you do with the commitment you made?" he asked me.

"Pretty well," I said. "I didn't have anything to drink all week, no alcohol." I took a breath, stalling as much as I could. "But I got high. On Saturday night, I was out at a club with my friend Barry, and I smoked half a joint. No big deal. Not a lot. Just half a joint."

Dr. K looked up at me like I'd just told him I had a terminal disease.

"Hmm," he said sharply. He nodded his head, as if he understood. "Are you a man of your word?" he asked.

"I try to be," I answered.

"Are you a man who lives up to his commitments?"

Oh, so that's how it was going to be.

"Just half a joint," I pleaded.

He was obviously taking this a whole lot more seriously than I expected him to. In my mind, I hadn't done anything all that terrible. I had stayed drug- and alcohol-free for six of the seven days. On my way to completing this very successful assignment, I had slipped a little. Talk about focusing on the negative!

"You made a commitment," he said. "You chose what that commitment would be, didn't you?"

"Yeah," I said.

"I didn't tell you what commitment to make, did I?"

"No."

"You chose the commitment," he continued. "You said you would live up to that commitment. And you didn't keep your word. So I suppose your commitment doesn't mean that much."

I wasn't used to being talked to like this. My parents didn't talk to me that way, even when my father was really pissed off. The people at the program in Minnesota, even in their negative assessment, didn't talk to me like that. This guy hardly knew me, and he was turning high and mighty on me.

"You seem like a nice person, Craig," he said. "But," he paused, "I wouldn't say you're a man of your word."

"Well," I said without finishing the sentence because I couldn't think of what else to say.

"Would you like to make another commitment?" Dr. K asked.

That question, I didn't expect. For a moment, I was sure he'd already written me off. Now, he was offering me a do-over? Sitting there in the office, the right answer seemed to be yes.

"Okay," I said.

"What commitment would you like to make?"

I didn't know what to say so I said the same thing I had said before. "I won't drink or get stoned for a week."

"No alcohol or marijuana for a week," Dr. K repeated.

As I walked out of his office, I really meant to do what I had told him I would. And I did it, for the first four days. No booze. No pot.

No nothing. But I had a date on Friday night with a girl I had met at the gym. She was a very successful designer. She drove a Ferrari. We went out to dinner at a sushi restaurant. She ordered sake with dinner. She drank a lot and got pretty drunk. I drank some and just felt blah. We left the restaurant and went back to her apartment, which was in Trump Tower. She climbed onto her bed and pulled me toward her. In the past, this was how I hoped every date would go. I can't say if it was her, if it was me, if it was the sake, or if it was knowing that Dr. K was going to grill me on Tuesday about the commitment I had made to him and to myself. But the whole thing wasn't sexy at all. I didn't want to be there, and I was totally turned off.

As I left her well-appointed apartment and stepped into the shiny gold Trump Tower elevator, I wasn't thinking about her. It was a Friday night in the greatest city in the world. I'd been on a date with a pretty and well-off woman. And I had just turned down sex with her. I was thinking about my psychiatrist instead. That had to be progress, right?

I was eager to tell Dr. K that I had made a breakthrough, that I was finally starting to understand what he was driving at. I couldn't wait to get to his office on Tuesday night. But when I settled back onto his worn leather chair, ready to share the good news, Dr. K stomped on the mood almost immediately.

"How did you do with your commitment?" he asked.

"I didn't smoke any pot," I told him, "but I had a little sake. No heavy drinking. Just sake at a Japanese restaurant."

He frowned. He sighed. He looked really sad. He looked at me like he was looking into my future, and he saw something tragic there. "Isn't sake alcohol?" he asked me.

Before I could answer, before I could tell him that I didn't even enjoy it, he was back talking about commitment and my word and what I thought those things meant.

"Making a commitment is your word," he said. "When you make a commitment and you don't keep your word, you may hurt other people a little bit. And you've certainly done plenty of that. But you always hurt yourself more. You always hurt yourself more."

||||||||||||||||

Major changes rarely happen in an instant. I know that now. It can take years or decades to change your thinking or your attitudes. No one ever becomes a totally different person in an hour or two. But the seeds can be planted in a single reflection or a few short words. As I sat in Dr. K's basement office that evening, a realization began to settle in. My word was important. And to my astonishment, I was open to the idea of being something different. Something better. Something more reflective of the potential I had inside me.

Like many great teachers before him, Dr. K opened my mind to his lesson by sharing an analogy. And things, from that point on, actually began to change in my life.

The next half hour in his office would stay with me for the rest of my life.

"You see that man across the street?" he asked me, pointing out the basement window and toward the sidewalk on the far side of East Eighty-Third Street.

"Yeah, I see him," I said.

"Do you see him?" he asked again. "I want you to see him. Really see him. You see that man, right?"

"I see him," I said again.

"What would you say if I told you that he lies, that he cheats, and that he constantly manipulates people? What if I said that that man makes commitments he doesn't live up to? He underachieved in school, and now he frequently underachieves as an adult. He wastes his time at work and never gives his best effort. He lacks ambition and doesn't even care if he does a good job. What if I said he could have been a better son, could have been a better brother, certainly could have been a better friend, a better boyfriend, better to all the people who came into his life? If all that were true, what would you think about that guy?"

I answered truthfully. "I don't think I'd like him very much."

"*That* man is you, Craig. That man is you."

Ugh! I hadn't seen that coming.

"The way that man treats people?" Dr. K said. "That's exactly the way you treat people, isn't it? People you've just met and also the most important people in your life. At the same time, you treat yourself so poorly. Everything you have done, you have underachieved at. You have lied. You have cheated. You have manipulated. You've stolen from people who trusted you. When you were working, you stole from your employer. You came in late. You left early. Everything you did, you didn't do right."

Dr. K had somehow remembered every little thing I'd barely touched on when I'd first called him from my childhood bedroom and everything I had told him in our few sessions. Now, he was drawing a close parallel between me and that man out the window, that man who symbolized everything that was terrible with me. I got that, even if it was painfully uncomfortable. But the way the doctor was speaking, I wasn't entirely clear which one of us he was referring to. Even as I recognized things about myself, I didn't think it was possible Dr. K could think I was as terrible as the man he was pointing at. Or did he? In his rendering, both of us kind of blended together. I guess that was the point Dr. K was making. I wasn't that man but, then again, maybe I was. It was hard to tell us apart.

"Would you like that man across the street? Would you like that man?"

"Absolutely not," I said, relieved he was talking about the other guy again. "I wouldn't like him at all."

"Well, then," he said. "How could you possibly like yourself?"

And there it was. No hedging. We *were* the same. I didn't like that man across the street. I didn't like myself. Talk about a punch in the gut!

That's when the emotion, which had begun to drizzle over me, came crashing down onto my head. I started crying hysterically. Twenty-nine years old. Sitting in a stranger's office, I was breathing hard and shaking. Tears were streaming down my face. I had never been a big crier, but this was a waterfall. What Dr. K was saying actually made sense to me. And it wasn't what I'd gone there for. It wasn't just the drinking or the smoking. It was all these things I was doing in my life—the stunts, the deceptions, all the getting over people—a lot of it was hurting other people. Russia, the summer in Los Angeles, the Grammy Awards, sneaking into various parties and sporting events— all of it defined me as a liar, a cheat, and a thief. He didn't even know all those details, all those adventures. But somehow Dr. K already understood who I was and what I was. And so did I.

I waited until my sobs subsided. Then, I said to him: "What do I do?"

He spoke calmly and clearly, but there was no equivocation in his voice. "In order to build self-esteem, you have to do esteemable acts."

My face was wet. My eyes stinging. But I tried to understand. Esteemable acts? I knew the word "esteem," like self-esteem, feeling good about yourself. But I had never heard it used that way: esteemable acts. Dr. K must have seen on my face that I needed more of an explanation.

"You do an esteemable act," he said, "by being honest, kind, and a hard worker, by being a good son, a good friend, a good brother."

I let that sink in. "Something you can feel good about," I said, as much a question as an answer.

He nodded.

"Every time you do something kind," he said, "something generous, something to help someone else instead of considering only your own desires—that's an esteemable act.

"Every time you think before you make a decision, every time you display a sober attitude, every time you pause before you leap, you are setting yourself up to perform esteemable acts."

I guess I was starting to get it. I was trying. Dr. K pressed on.

"Every time you do something esteemable, you build your own self-esteem. It's the opposite of what's been happening. Your self-esteem keeps getting damaged by thousands of selfish, thoughtless, cruel, unesteemable acts. Every time you lie, cheat, or steal, you lower self-esteem."

The way he described my situation, it was like I had an account filled with bad acts that I could only work off with good ones.

"It's going to take some time to rebuild yourself," Dr. K warned. "But you might as well get going, start doing some esteemable acts. And none of this is possible if you keep drinking, if you keep getting stoned."

I wasn't sure what one thing had to do with the other, but he explained. "You've used those substances to disconnect you from your actions. They've given you permission and solace, as you've torn down your own self-esteem."

I was so far down this road of self-destruction, I had very little room for error, it seemed. "Be aware," he emphasized. "If you tell one lie here or commit one manipulation there, it knocks you right back down to where you have been, and you've been knocked down too many times.

"That's why you feel the way you do, so disconnected, because you've been doing so many unesteemable things for so long."

That was December 11, 1990. I was twenty-nine years old. I hadn't had a drink for a grand total of four days. As I walked out of the office that night, it wasn't like I was a totally different person than the one who had walked in forty-five minutes earlier. But truly my life never would be the same again.

15

GETTING TO WORK

My visits with Dr. K became a regular and vital part of my life, like stopping every so often at a service station on a cross-country trip.

Fill 'er up, please!

No one made me go, but I couldn't risk what would happen if I didn't. So starting that cold December, each Tuesday night at seven, there I was, sitting in his modest basement office, confronting uncomfortable truths about myself, things I'd been ignoring for the previous twenty-nine years. Each session lasted forty-five minutes, never more, never less.

I found our conversations interesting. Sometimes they were excoriatingly difficult, like when he started pushing me about my professional aimlessness or my insatiable need to date new women. I also found our talks immensely revealing and helpful. His questions clarified things in my mind, things I knew deep down but certainly hadn't been facing. I'd been hiding from stuff for so long, all of it felt urgent and profound. I had a lot of ground to cover. There was no denying that. I had no time to waste.

At the same time, I followed the directions of my St. Mary's counselors. Several times a week, I attended recovery meetings at a place called the Seventy-Ninth Street Workshop. Those meetings gave me a small sense of community, the idea that I wasn't the only one trying to stay away from bad habits and get on with my life. Those meetings also helped to bridge the days between my weekly sessions with Dr. K. But the key for me was my probing discussions with Dr. K. They were truly what propelled me forward.

He asked questions—many, many questions. I answered them as well as I could. He jotted down an occasional note in a spiral notebook. Sometimes, he summarized what I had said and asked if he was understanding correctly. He rarely told me directly what to do or how to deal with my issues. But I had the strong feeling that he was leading me somewhere, urging me, nudging me, encouraging me in a more productive direction.

"We don't ask why," he said to me. "We ask, 'How do we make things better?'"

Dr. K was definitely judgmental. He wasn't one of those shrinks who believed that one choice is just as valuable as another, that any life direction is fine. He pointed. He prodded. He looked sad and hurt when I threatened to slip back into self-destructive habits. But the forward progress was always my responsibility. He made that clear. He couldn't do this for me, whatever *this* was. I had to do it for myself. He'd made that point during our very first session when he'd invited *me* to make a specific commitment about my drinking. Every step I took in his presence was a step I had to make. He considered it my job—not his—to deliver.

Dr. K didn't talk much about himself. But I was curious about how he got interested in the whole issue of alcohol and drugs and how people used them. From what Marilyn Minor had said to me on the phone, addiction had become the focus of his professional life.

So as I sat in the office across from him, I asked straight out: "How did you get into this?"

I half expected him to say that, back in his younger days, he too had battled addiction. But that didn't seem to be what sparked Dr. K's interest. Being in the military did. He told me he had grown up in Queens and had gone into the army during the Vietnam War. In the army at that time, he said, he was around a lot of heavy drinkers and quite a few people who used drugs. But not all of those people suffered severe consequences.

"I wondered why that was," he said. "Why do some people who drink become terrible alcoholics and go on to wreck their lives while others who drink just as much seem to have no lasting effects at all."

I had wondered the same thing, I told him.

"I wanted an explanation," he continued. "What was the difference between these people? Why could some of them drink successfully— or use drugs successfully—and others couldn't?"

There was that word "successfully" again. Dr. K had suspected at our very first session that I wasn't able to indulge in alcohol successfully.

"If I could answer that," he went on, "I thought maybe I could develop some insights into what should be done to help those people who were having problems. Why were those addictions creating such messes in some peoples' lives? It seems to me that you may be one of those people I have spent the past two decades thinking about."

||||||||||||||||

"Tell me about your childhood," Dr. K said to me the week after my weepy office meltdown over esteemable and unesteemable acts. "What was it like for you growing up?"

"I had a fairly happy childhood, I'd say," I answered reflexively. "I had two younger brothers. Our parents loved us all very much. My father was a lawyer who made a nice living. My mother stayed at home with the kids. I would describe us as an upper-middle-class, suburban, Jewish family. When people looked at us, they thought, 'Oh, they're doing well.' That was important to my parents, having people think that."

"And what were you like?" Dr. K asked.

"I was a very outgoing kid," I said. "Very active. Very athletic. Always getting into things. I had plenty of friends. I had challenges like anyone, but overall I would have to say I was very fortunate to grow up the way I did."

Dr. K nodded, but he didn't seem satisfied.

"I am less interested in broad conclusions," he said. "Tell me about some specific experiences that stick in your mind, things that happened that you still remember."

I told him about the day I fell off a slide at the playground and broke my collarbone. I also told him about the time I was jumping on my bed and hit my forehead on the corner of my dresser, which left a scar as deep as the optic nerve. "Look," I said, leaning forward, "you can still see the scar right next to my eye."

I told him about the night my appendix burst and I had to be rushed to the hospital for emergency surgery. I lifted my shirt and showed Dr. K the scar from the operation. "As a kid," I said, "I hated having so many scars on my body. I thought they were ugly, like I'd been all sliced up."

I'm not sure why I focused on my youthful accidents and mishaps, but those were the first things that came to mind. I could have tried to remember birthday parties or celebrating the holidays, but I didn't. Instead, I told Dr. K the story of the afternoon when I was seven years old and I fell from the upper branches of a tree.

"We used to go upstate in the summers," I said. "My family had a bungalow in Monroe, New York. We had woods and lakes and a lot of nature up there. I loved climbing trees. We had one tree near our house, a red oak, just perfect for climbing. The branches formed a natural ladder, and there were lots of spots on the way up to sit and look out at the world."

One day, I explained, we had a couple of friends over. My brother Douglas was also there. "I was high in that tree," I said, "up in the thin, wobbly branches near the top. Only this time, the branch broke, and I went tumbling all the way to the ground."

"Were you hurt?" Dr. K asked.

"I was banged up pretty bad," I said. "But the main thing was that I broke my femur. That's the bone that comes down your thigh. It's the largest and hardest bone in the body."

"I know about the femur," Dr. K said.

"My mother and my father came running," I said. "My friends didn't know what to do. No one wanted to move me. I was moaning on the ground while we waited for the ambulance to come. They kept me in Arden Hill Hospital for six weeks. I was in traction. They wouldn't let me move."

"That sounds very painful," Dr. K said.

"I'd never felt anything like it before," I assured him.

I had told that story many times before. But as I told it to Dr. K, the details were more vivid than ever. It was like I was reliving the whole experience all over again.

I remembered the pain of the broken bone and fear of not knowing what was going to happen and sense of isolation that settled over me as soon as my parents left me at the hospital and went back home.

"My mother had two children at home," I said. "My youngest brother was an infant. My father was building a law practice in the city. He only came up on the weekends. I was there by myself most of the time."

As I got to that part of the story, I could feel an old, familiar sadness settling over me.

"The nights were the hardest," I told Dr. K. "I felt so alone in that hospital. I had no one to talk to and no idea how to fill the time. I made a paper clock in my hospital bed. I set the hands on the clock so they would tell how much longer it would be until my parents came back to see me. It seemed like forever. I was seven years old."

Dr. K seemed to consider that story helpful and revealing. He definitely hung on every word of it, as if it might contain clues to my current situation.

I told him that after I finally got out of the hospital, I had to wear a body cast for the next two months. I missed a lot of school that year and struggled to catch up with my third-grade classmates.

"I probably should have been held back in school and repeated the grade," I admitted. "But my parents didn't want to do that. In their eyes, that would have been some kind of admission of failure. It wouldn't look right. Their attitude has always been, 'If it looks good on the outside, how broken can the inside be?'"

"So you stayed with your class?" Dr. K asked, focusing in on this one point in my childhood recollection. He seemed to think this was an important detail, even though it was more than two decades old.

"Yeah, they just pushed me forward," I said with a shrug. "I never looked back. And I never caught up on the work that I missed, and I never felt good in school after that. I always felt like I didn't know what I was doing. Compared to the other kids, I felt like I was dumb."

It was so strange to be opening up like this to Dr. K, this psychiatrist I had come to see about my drinking and mainly because I felt pressured to. We were still just getting to know each other. I worried I might be sounding like I was whining or blaming my parents for what had happened. That wasn't what I meant to do. It was so long ago and I was just a kid who fell out of a tree. But I realized I also felt a sense of relief saying out loud something that previously I had only pondered in silence.

Only when I had finished describing my tree tumble and its painful aftermath did Dr. K finally speak directly to me. He began by summarizing in his own way what he had just heard. He didn't mince words.

"So you were an active child," he said. "You had some incidents, which left scars. In one case, when you were seven years old, you fell out of a tree, broke your leg, and had a long, traumatic recovery. You were left alone in the hospital, which you hated, and you missed a couple of months of school, while your classmates were moving ahead. And your parents didn't or couldn't protect you from any of that. Is that about right?"

"Yeah," I said. "That's about right. Being a kid isn't easy."

"Childhood can be a challenge," Dr. K agreed. But he wasn't going to let me off the hook with a shrug and an oh-well-that's-life. "What I'm hearing you say is that when you were a child, you sometimes felt ugly, lonely, and stupid. That must have been difficult for you."

I sat back, silent, and thought about the words he used. Ugly. Lonely. Stupid. I had never heard anyone summarize my childhood that way. It wasn't a very cheerful rendering. But I had to admit it was part of how I felt. Not about everything. We'd only talked about a very few childhood remembrances. I also had good memories. But those insecure feelings were definitely a huge part of my childhood.

By my silence, Dr. K could tell that his words were sinking in. He wanted to make sure I wasn't misinterpreting them.

"Feelings aren't facts," he cautioned. "You felt ugly because of the scars. But you aren't ugly. You felt dumb because you missed so much school. But you aren't dumb at all. You are obviously a sharp guy. You felt lonely but in fact you had family and friends all around you. It doesn't mean those feelings weren't real to you. That was how you felt."

There's a reason, he went on, that the facts and feelings of childhood often stick with us as we grow older and become adults. "From the ages of zero to eight," he explained, "children need consistency. They need to feel safe. When there is inconsistent nurturing, children often feel insecure with themselves. Children need two loving parents. They need a safe and quiet home. Whatever disrupts that can feel like a threat."

Dr. K explained: "When a family moves frequently, the children can feel disconnected. When the parents fight a lot, the children hear that, and they blame themselves. Children need to be fed at the same time and put to bed at the same time. That makes them feel secure. A lack of consistency isn't an automatic disaster, but it undermines the nurturing that children receive. Children need consistency to feel safe. When they receive inconsistent nurturing, they feel like they can't trust the world."

"Inconsistent nurturing?" I muttered, repeating the phrase.

"It doesn't mean that the parents were bad or that they didn't love their children or anything like that. It's just a reality in some families."

I needed to reflect on all this. I knew my parents loved us. I grew up in good home. I wasn't abused in any way. But as I turned his words over in my mind, I felt he'd seen in me what I'd never dared to see in myself. And it wasn't just what I remembered from being a child. If I was being totally honest, didn't I still see myself as ugly, lonely, and stupid? Maybe Dr. K was onto something with his theory about why.

"Feelings like that can linger all the way through adulthood," he said, as if he was reading my mind. "And in my work, I have discovered something else."

I could start to see where this was leading. How he believed those things in my past may have put me on the path to today. How those feelings of insecurity and self-loathing had stayed with me into my twenties. I could see how he'd come to these conclusions after studying the lives of people who shared some of the issues I had.

"Inconsistent nurturing is the common denominator for people who abuse drugs and alcohol," he said. "People drink to ease those painful anxieties and feelings of low self-esteem. They often take drugs for the same reason. They overeat, or they gamble, or they engage in other self-destructive behaviors. They feel relief. They feel confident. They like the way it feels. They keep doing it until they reach the point where they have trouble stopping, even as it gradually destroys their lives. It's a pattern we keep seeing over and over again."

|||||||||||||||||

Dr. K, I was learning, had a lot of insights and approaches. He also had a lot of different ways of describing his basic principles for living a decent, honest, productive life. But without my even realizing it, as our sessions rolled on, he was beginning to teach me the concepts and help me put some of them into practice in my life. "Inconsistent nurturing" and "esteemable acts" were always at the core.

These weren't just fairy-tale notions or philosophical concepts. And we weren't just working on the obvious issues of drinking and smoking pot. Wasn't the point of all this to start cleaning up some of my messes and getting my life back on track? Of course it was. And one of the biggest messes, I knew, was the wretched state of my professional career. I didn't really have one. Despite twenty years of schooling—kindergarten through law school—and three missed swings at the bar exam, I still wasn't prepared to do much of anything. I hadn't worked in more than a year and a half. I had never held a job for more than a few months. I sucked as a bartender, a waiter, a law clerk, a lawyer, a business broker, and anything else I had been hired to do. I arrived late, left early, gave minimal effort, and focused primarily on what I could take from the job, not what I could give. Between my many bouts of unemployment, the only question was, "Would I quit before I got fired?" In the seven and a half years since I had gotten out of college, the only thing I had never experienced was actually hanging onto a job. I hadn't built a resume. I'd stacked up resignation letters and pink slips. There was no visible demand for my services. I had no obvious marketable skills. Whatever talents I had were so clouded by my rotten attitude and abysmal work habits, it was hard to imagine any employer taking another chance on me.

But as depressing and hopeless as it sometimes made me feel, I knew I had to tackle this, and so did Dr. K.

"Everyone," he said to me, "needs an answer to the question, 'What do you do?' What's your answer?"

"I don't really have one" was my candid reply.

The what-do-you-do question, he said, was especially true in a super-competitive and high-priced city like New York, where, sometimes it seems, the only thing more important than what you do for a living is how much money you make.

Even my ready line of bullshit—"Um, I'm not doing too much right now"—didn't truly make me feel comfortable. It was an answer, but I knew it was a hollow response that could easily be blown apart with follow-up questions. "That whole subject is inexorably connected to feelings of self-worth," Dr. K said.

So I really needed a job.

The first thing I had to recognize was that being a lawyer wasn't in the cards for me. This, I knew, would be as, if not more, difficult for my parents to accept. But how many more times could I take the bar exam? Even though the state bar exam board would let me keep coming, I was doing worse rather than better on the test, as my faint recollections of law school faded even further into the past. It was a shame that I'd wasted all those years pretending to pursue a legal career. Now, I would have to come up with something other than that.

|||||||||||||||||

I had friends working on Wall Street. Some of them were doing extremely well. One of my roommates at Syracuse, Todd Engelson, was a rising star at Lehman Brothers, the global financial-services firm, one of the oldest and best-established players on Wall Street. In college, I'd always been nice to Todd. He was smart and likeable but shy. I got him into the good parties. I introduced him to girls. We stayed in touch after graduation, and it never escaped my notice how well he seemed to be doing.

In my first year of law school, when I was struggling for Bs and Cs, Todd was bringing home $100,000. In my second year of law school, he was making $200,000 at Lehman Brothers. In my third year of law school, while I was struggling to make Cs and Ds, he was earning $300,000. I didn't know exactly what he was making now, but it had to be north of half a million dollars a year. He'd bought an apartment on First Avenue. He drove a Mercedes-Benz. He had said to me quite a few times over the years: "Craig, if you ever came to Wall Street, you could be very, very good at this."

When Dr. K started talking about my getting a job, Todd and Wall Street were what came immediately to mind.

I collected myself, pulled on a conservative suit, and interviewed with two large Wall Street firms, Prudential Securities and Todd's employer, Lehman Brothers. If I didn't have Dr. K pulling for me, I don't know if I would have had the courage to even walk through those doors. I'd done plenty of audacious things over the years— bullshitting my way into all kinds of places—but somehow this felt different to me.

Frankly, I was surprised how much interest both companies expressed in me. They seemed to think I might be a good fit for them, partly for my gregarious personality and partly because of my law degree. It couldn't have been my work history, since I really didn't have one! Even though I hadn't passed the bar exam, they still thought my legal training was a valuable asset. Whatever. On the job hunt, I'd take any boost I could get. Both firms were proposing to put me through a six-month training program, where I would learn the ins and outs of trading, investing, advising, and whatever else stockbrokers did. After that, I would sit for the Series 7 exam, also known as the General Securities Representative Exam, the basic test that people on Wall Street are required to pass before they can trade securities.

That gave me pause. Naturally, I was a little nervous about the six-hour exam, given my history with the New York State Bar Association. But my friends on Wall Street saw me differently, and they all assured me I'd do just fine. Assuming they weren't lying to me and I passed that thing, I would then be brought on as a junior associate at whichever company I went to. I could be very happy. There was really only one catch: While I was training and testing, I wouldn't earn a full Wall Street salary. It would be just a small stipend, a couple of hundred dollars a week. Who was that going to impress? And what kind of social life could I have on a salary like that?

Around the same time I was talking to Lehman and Prudential, I also answered an ad in a newspaper about another job. During the interview, I was offered a job selling awnings to apartment buildings, restaurants, and other structures. The job paid $50,000 a year plus commissions. It came with a company car. It came with an expense account. And here was the best thing as far as I was concerned: the salary and benefits started on day one. No training program. No licensing exams. Just go to work and start getting paid.

"I think I should take the awning job," I told Dr. K.

It really did sound perfect to me.

Fifty K a year. Bennies and a company car. I could pay my rent, join the gym, and have money in my pocket again.

But Dr. K wasn't impressed.

"Craig," he said, "you have your choice. Take a job or begin a career."

Talk about a thrill kill! He made selling awnings sound like something a law school grad should be ashamed of. I argued with him a bit: "If I take one of the Wall Street jobs, I won't be making a decent salary for six months to a year." Here I was, trying to do something that would solve my immediate problems and maybe get my parents off my back. I wouldn't be hurting anyone. And yet all I could hear was disapproval in his voice. Why didn't he get it? "Isn't it time for me to support myself?" I asked. "I live in New York City!"

But when I got home and thought about it, I had to admit that Dr. K might have a point. If the goal was to build a long-term future, grabbing instant money maybe wasn't the best approach. Or as he put it, the awning salesman position "wasn't the sober choice" for me. The bigger picture, that's what he wanted me to see. It was a fine job offer but not something I could envision as a long-term career, certainly not the equivalent of taking a position on Wall Street. It was a very good job if you didn't understand what I truly needed. Just a few weeks in, Dr. K knew me better than I knew myself. He understood that deep down I *did* want to succeed, in all senses of that word.

As luck would have it, just before I had to make a decision, another option came up. I met a man named Ross Mandell, a seasoned Wall Street veteran who worked for a small brokerage firm called Commonwealth Associates. Commonwealth was tiny compared to Lehman and Prudential, but the employees there all advised clients and brokered stocks—not just the big boys. And their training process was far less bureaucratic. Just as importantly, I wouldn't have to wait forever to bring home a respectable paycheck.

"If you come work with us," Ross told me, "we'll get you licensed as quickly as possible and get you working as soon as you are ready. I have a feeling you'll be very good at this."

16

BLACK HAT BLESSING

Christmas fell on a Tuesday that year. Dr. K shifted our appointment to the following day, December 26.

"You need to find a higher power in your life," he said to me just as our session got underway. I was resistant, I'll admit. I didn't want my shrink turning into my rabbi or my priest. I knew the "higher power" expression. It was right out of recovery literature. And Dr. K was more insistent than usual.

"You mean God?" I asked him.

"It could be God," he answered. "Or not. It's fine to think of it that way. That's up to you. But you should find something, some power, that helps you understand that you are not an all-powerful being. You are not God. Quite the opposite, in fact."

This can be a difficult concept, Dr. K said, especially for people who have turned their lives over to drugs or alcohol or some other life-influencing addiction. "But it's a crucial one," he added.

The way Dr. K explained it, it hardly seemed to matter what that higher power was. "It could be a door knob," he told me. "It could be a swami or an Indian chief or a walk in the woods on a beautiful day—as long as that higher power is not you. But it has to be something," he said, "some force greater than yourself that you are prepared to recognize has genuine power over you. As long as it's not you."

I have to say, I was still a little confused about what he was driving at. But he explained patiently. For all this to make sense, this idea of a "higher power," he told me, I would need to embrace three very basic ideas.

I can't.

He can.

I will let him.

What the first one came down to, as I understood it, was that I had to change my attitude about drinking. I can't. I just can't. There were some things that I just wasn't capable of. I can't fly. I can't get pregnant. I can't breathe underwater. And to that list I would have to add the one more "can't" that had so obviously been wrecking my life.

I can't drink alcohol.

"If you try to breathe underwater, you will drown," Dr. K warned me. "If you keep drinking alcohol, you will die."

With the help of this higher power, he was saying, I had to change not just my actions but the attitudes I held about alcohol.

It wasn't hard to see that this was all true. I couldn't deny it. All the trouble I had ever gotten into—all of it!—was somehow or another connected to my drinking. As far back as high school, all through college and law school, my sorry attempts at keeping jobs and sorrier attempts at relationships—alcohol had been right there with me. After years of turning my head away and refusing to face that reality, I was finally beginning to connect the dots. The suffocating demoralization that I was living in, the hellhole that had gradually become my life—all of it was intimately connected to years and years of drinking and drugging and all the many failings it had brought into my life. What a disappointment! That recurring disappointment—refusing to recognize that "I can't"—was a big part of the reason I felt so bad about myself.

Unless I got on top of it, the "can't"—the *I can't*—part was going to continue to lead to nowhere but dead ends. I had to find some way out of that sucking vortex. The only chance I had was to build self-esteem and the only way to build self-esteem was to do esteemable acts and the only way I was ever going to do any esteemable acts was, first and foremost, to give up alcohol. Completely. I had to start with that.

I can't drink alcohol!

The second part of Dr. K's higher-power equation—"he can"—required me to believe there was someone or something out there that was greater than myself. That concept had always lingered in the background for me. My dad being so religious, belief in a higher power always hung in the Schmell family air. But I wasn't practicing my father's faith. I wasn't religious at all. In fact, I hardly thought about God. I still considered myself Jewish, but only in the vaguest, cultural sense. I had been bar mitzvahed. I had studied Hebrew as a kid. I still remembered a few words of Yiddish, the curse words and the insults. But that didn't amount to much. Growing up in New York, even the Puerto Rican kids knew their *schmucks* from their *schmattas*.

Dr. K gave me a homework assignment. He said: "I want you to make a list for me. Write down twenty-five examples of things that prove to you that a higher power exists in your life—God or however you want to define it."

Later that night, I sat in my apartment thinking long and hard about my homework. At first, I worried that I wasn't even sure what he was driving at. Proof that God, or something higher was already in my life? I'd never studied theology and I'd long ago stopped going to my dad's synagogue. When would I have even crossed paths with God? Then, finally, one thing occurred to me and I wrote it down.

"All the times I drove drunk and I didn't kill anyone."

Before I'd moved into the city and started relying on mass transit, I had driven drunk hundreds of times over the years. Driven so drunk I didn't remember how I got wherever I ended up. I had gotten into a couple accidents. But I never really hurt anyone—not me, not anyone else. That had to be some kind of miracle, right? The odds had to have been against me getting away with all of that unscathed. Had there been a higher power there with me? I couldn't explain it otherwise.

Once I got that one down, others started to flow.

"All the places I snuck into and I was never arrested."

"Getting through high school, college, and law school, even if I did flunk the bar exam."

Pretty soon, I was ticking off all sorts of potential calamities I had somehow avoided, reckless things I had done without suffering the consequences. Stealing. Lying. Cheating. Buying drugs. I could easily have been shot or killed. Even if I'd only been robbed, my picture could have ended up on the front page of the New York Post. "Nice, White, Suburban Boy Scores Pot, Gets Caught, Embarrasses Family." For a Schmell, that might have been worse than prison.

Maybe it was God. Maybe it was God with a little earthbound help from my father. But someone or something was looking out for me, even more than I knew. I got caught a few times, but I certainly never paid the price I could have or deserved to. That's how it felt anyway.

When I went in the next week with my list for Dr. K, he seemed satisfied that I'd come up with a credible list. Next he wanted to know if I was ready to "let him."

"Once you accept the idea of this higher power, you have to really accept it into your life," Dr. K said. "That is what we are challenged to do every day of our lives. Submit. But now we are submitting to something positive, not a power like alcohol that is tearing us apart."

"Okay…" I ventured tentatively. Submitting—to temptation— was part of my usual repertoire.

But Dr. K wasn't backing down. "The people who are able to hand their issues off to God, the people who are able to just let go," he asked, "don't they live much happier lives? Isn't it a huge burden trying to control the world around you and fix people and make them behave according to your preference? Those people are never happy."

This was deeper than anything I'd ever considered. I wasn't quite sure it was true. But I also couldn't disagree. "I guess," I said.

Dr. K asked me to consider it. "You can't control the weather. You can't control the traffic. You can't control your parents. You can't control your kids. You can't control your spouse or your ex-spouses or whoever it is that is driving you crazy now. People don't call you back at work. Someone leaves her shoes on the floor. Maybe you can have some influence, but you really can't control the actions of anyone else. The only person you can control is you. But you'll have help from what some people like to call 'God moments.' Life is so much easier, Craig, when you are able to let go and accept them."

"God moments?" I asked, clearly needing more explanation.

Dr. K nodded. "If you look around," he said, "you will see these special 'God moments' showing up in your life. They often arrive just when you need them most. If you let it, that higher power has a way of reaching out. Protecting you from danger. Encouraging you to do good. Helping you gain access to an insight you didn't have before. 'God moments.' Be on the lookout for them."

||||||||||||||||

I didn't have to wait long.

The very next Sunday morning, I got a call from my friend Steven Weiss. I wouldn't have called Steve a close, close friend. But he and I had been running mates in the bars and clubs of New York City, doing stupid things together on and off for a couple of years. He was a good-looking guy, friendly and trim. Like me, he was from a Jewish family in the northern suburbs. I would say he'd been no more or less self-centered and aimless than I had been over the past few years, though Steve did have more of a religious streak. That might sound strange, given some of the nights we'd spent together. But along with the drinking and late-night carousing, he managed to wake up early on Saturdays to attend temple with his family. More than that, even in the chaos of his young-adult life, he occasionally got up early in the morning to lay *tefillin*, just like my dad did. Steve told me that he believed it brought him good luck.

"Craig, you want to go see the *rebbe* today?" he asked that morning when I picked up the phone.

"The *rebbe*?" From my old *yeshiva* days, I knew that *rebbe* was a Yiddish word derived from the Hebrew word for rabbi. But I had no idea who or what Steve was talking about.

"The *grand rebbe*. Rabbi Schneerson."

"Rabbi who?" I asked.

"Rabbi Schneerson," Steve repeated. "You've never heard of Menachem Schneerson? He's the head Hasidic, like the pope of the rabbis."

"I guess I have," I lied.

I think I heard him sigh in disbelief. "People travel for thousands of miles to meet him. He's in Brooklyn, in Crown Heights. Sunday's the big day for getting in to see him. So do you want to go?"

Despite Steve enthusiasm, this didn't sound like a rousing good time to me, going deep into Brooklyn to see a rabbi. But now I had Dr. K in my head and his "higher powers" and his "God moments," and—who could say?—maybe this would be one of those. I didn't know.

"I'll go," I said finally. "I'll go."

Barely an hour later, Steve and I were walking up a chilly Brooklyn sidewalk to a three-story, red-brick, Gothic Revival mansion at 770

Eastern Parkway, world headquarters of the ultra-Orthodox Chabad-Lubavitch movement. Somewhere inside that massive house, Steve assured me, was the eighty-eight-year-old, Russian-born Schneerson, one of the most influential Jewish leaders of the twentieth century.

Steve was certainly sold. "He's like the messiah, sitting at the right hand of God," Steve said in awe. "We gotta meet him."

I couldn't tell what Steve admired more, the rabbi's religiosity or his celebrity. Was this Steve's idea of a boldface name? "You're starting to sound like me," I said. "The old me."

We were not alone on Eastern Parkway. Far from it. On the sidewalk and in the street in front of 770 were hundreds of men—it could have been thousands—dressed in the latest style of nineteenth-century Eastern Europe: long, black coats and black hats pinched into a triangle at the top. Whatever their ages, all of these men seemed to have long beards and sidelocks that I knew were called *peyes*.

I was wearing jeans and a blue sweatshirt-jacket. Steve was dressed just as casually. A couple of shaggy-haired twenty-nine-year-olds in this sea of black coats and hats, we did not exactly blend in. As far as I could see, Steve and I were the only people on the block who were dressed for the late twentieth century. As a lifelong New Yorker, I'd seen Hasidic men dressed like this, but never so many all in one place. So many of them, all packed in this relatively small section of Eastern Parkway, waiting expectantly. A couple dozen of them were huddled in the courtyard at the bottom of the mansion steps. Extending off to the right, down the corner and beyond, was a mile-long line of similarly attired men, all just waiting, it seemed, to get inside. God only knows how long they'd been standing there.

"Well," I said to Steve. "I guess we won't be seeing the rabbi today. I'm not waiting in *that* line."

It didn't elude my consciousness that just a few weeks earlier a simple thing like a line wouldn't have been an obstacle. It would have been an invitation. The old me, I'm sure, would have already been scanning the scene for a velvet rope and a bouncer with a clipboard I could extract a name from. That was, I guess, the pre-Dr. K me. But something had changed. Somehow, I was struck with a sense of propriety I'd rarely experienced before. This wasn't a nightclub we were standing in front of. It was an Old World religious facility. I couldn't imagine too many supermodels hanging out in there. This was, as they say, a House of God.

Dr. K had told me I needed a spiritual dimension to my life, a higher power I could embrace and even submit to. Dr. K said this was imperative if I was going to leave the booze behind me and start living a happy, productive, esteemable life. Maybe with Steve encouragement I had just stumbled onto one of those "God moments" Dr. K had been touting. If only the crowd weren't so huge! Craig Schmell didn't wait on lines. Even God knew that. But could it really be a coincidence, my having that discussion with Dr. K and then Steve phoning out of the blue about a world-famous rabbi?

It didn't feel coincidental to me.

As Steve and I were standing there, trying to figure out what to do, one of the black-hat men came over to us.

"Would you like to meet the *rebbe*?" he asked.

We nodded eagerly.

"What if I could get you in quickly?" the man offered. "Would you be willing to make a fifty-dollar donation?"

Steve and I didn't even look at each other, and I'm not sure which of us spoke first. We both answered immediately, "Sure!" I was the one, however, who reached into his wallet and pulled out two twenties and a ten. I wasn't really used to paying my way in to anything. But fifty dollars for skipping a mile-long line—the *rebbe* line—sounded like the bargain of the week to me. I'd heard the Lord works in mysterious ways!

"We'll even videotape it for you," he said. "A memory to last a lifetime."

The friendly Hasid took the cash and, without any further delay, whisked us up the front steps of the *rebbe's* headquarters and in the front door. For a moment I had that old familiar feeling. I'd gotten in front of all those men waiting outside. But this was different than my earlier incursions. This time, I'd made a donation, and I hadn't scammed anyone.

"Do you know how to lay *tefillin*?" the man asked once he got us inside.

I mumbled something, recalling my father's morning ritual. Steve offered an unequivocal yes. Our escort handed us two sets of *tefillin*— the head and the arm straps—and a *yarmulke* and thankfully did not watch us closely while Steve executed the ritual and, trying to keep up with every practiced movement, I pretended to.

When we were done, he slipped us into the line, which at that point was at the bottom of a steep, winding, wood-paneled stairway up to the second floor, where I gathered Rabbi Schneerson was. There were still probably thirty people in front of us. But the line was moving quickly. It had to, I guess, with so many people waiting outside. When we got to the top of the stairs, I could see a large, wooden desk. I couldn't see who was sitting behind the desk, but someone was and I assumed it had to be the man.

As we got closer, there he was: an old man with a large, grey beard hunched behind the desk. On the desk in front of him was a pile of money. Even from where I was standing, I could tell the bills were clean and crisp and neatly stacked. They looked perfect, really, like they'd never seen the inside of a cash register or even been touched by human hands.

Suddenly, I felt nervous. I had no idea what I was supposed to do or say once I got to meet the *rebbe*. Then, the man who brought us upstairs gave us a quick rundown of what to expect and a little of the theology behind it, the CliffsNotes version, you could say.

"The rabbi will ask if there is anything you would like him to pray for," the man explained. "For each blessing that you make, he is going to give you a dollar bill. When you leave, you can give that much and more to others so your meeting with the rabbi will be a blessing to others as well."

Pass it on! I think that's what he was trying to say.

Steve might have known all this already, but every word of it was new to me. I wasn't sure if this was the "God moment" Dr. K had been driving at, but I was definitely outside my secular comfort zone.

Even standing there, the metaphor struck me. For years, I had been sneaking into clubs and parties and sold-out shows. I didn't have to sneak this time. For the first time ever, someone else had snuck me in. And now I was about to meet one of the most spiritual men on earth, even if I had never heard of him two hours before.

Suddenly, it didn't seem so far-fetched that my higher power might be speaking to me. After a long, winding journey, I found myself standing just a few feet away from a person so much better than I had ever been. Had I reached a point in my life where at least I was trying to do the right thing? Yes, I thought. This feels right.

As Steve and I stood there, the first thing that struck me was the rabbi's piercing blue eyes. They were as bright as laser beams and a deep, almost pulsating blue. It was mesmerizing. Looking into those eyes, I really did feel like God was behind that oversized desk.

I struggled to take it all in.

The hat. The beard. The stack of dollar bills. The sharp blue eyes. The endless line of black hats behind us. This was definitely not my typical Sunday afternoon.

Rabbi Schneerson spoke quietly, so quietly I could hardly make out what he was saying. Steve leaned forward. The rabbi reached over and slid two crisp dollar bills off the perfect stack. I heard "blessing," which I took to mean that the rabbi was ready for Steve to specify what exactly he'd like sent up to God.

"That I can make a lot of money and meet a hot wife."

A lot of money? A hot wife? Steve. . . no!

The second I heard what he told the *rebbe*, I felt the air rushing out of me. For all of Steve's supposed religiosity, he had totally blown it! That was, I was sure, the worst possible answer. Even I recognized that. So, apparently, did Rabbi Schneerson. He mumbled something I couldn't decipher. Hardly looking up, he slid the two bills across the desk into Steve's general direction.

I was mortified.

Then, it was my turn. I knew I needed a better answer than that, a plea to the Almighty that was at least vaguely spiritual. Clearly, I was no paragon of lifelong devotion. But I knew better than to ask this holiest of holy men for a red Maserati, a juicy steak dinner, or a sexy wife.

The rabbi looked up at me, and I was ready for him.

"That I should find some guidance in my life," I said, "and that my family should only know peace."

I'm not sure where that came from, but it came just in time. And the rabbi's composure entirely changed. He sat up straighter. His blue eyes twinkled again. The faintest little smile slid across his lips.

"Yes," he said, no louder but clearer than before. Then, in Yiddish, he said a short prayer that I couldn't understand.

And here was the strange part: even though I hadn't planned it—when my answer came out, I actually meant what I said.

I did want guidance in my life. I was getting some now from Dr. K and definitely needed more of it. I also wanted peace for my family. After all they'd been through with me, they certainly deserved it.

After five forty-five-minute sessions, Dr. K already had me thinking in some brand-new ways.

The rabbi slid two more dollars off his stack, and he handed them to me. He didn't slide them across the desk in my direction. He reached out and he handed them to me.

When Steve and I got to the sidewalk, I didn't say anything to him about the blessing he'd asked for. Truly, that was between him and the man upstairs, *both* men upstairs, the *rebbe* and his boss, the real Almighty.

In the light of that Sunday afternoon, I looked closely at my two dollar bills. I was right. They must have been hot off the presses from the United States Mint, untouched by human hands. The serial numbers on the bills were in perfect sequence. B64470679A and B64470680A.

I folded them carefully and put them in my wallet, where they have remained ever since and will remain for the rest of my life.

I have friends who believe that all the good fortune I have experienced since that day can be attributed to blessings I sought from Rabbi Schneerson and those two special one-dollar bills.

I think they may be right.

17

TREADMILL GIRL

I started at Commonwealth Associates on January 30, after I'd been seeing Dr. K for not quite two and a half months.

It was a better fit for me than Lehman or Prudential, even if it wasn't quite the instant-money-in-my-pocket solution I had hoped for. I was doing everything right. I'd taken a job with real possibilities for future success. But New York City wasn't any cheaper to live in and even with Commonwealth's quicker timeline, I still needed a way to support myself until I got my own clients and started bringing in my own fees.

Together, Dr. K and I came up with a plan. One last time, I would ask my father for help. Not for a handout but for a short-term loan. Just enough to pay my rent and keep me afloat while I completed my training and passed the Series 7 licensing exam. If my dad would lend me the money, Dr. K and I decided, I would take account of every dollar and pay back every last cent. Of course, I'd made that same promise hundreds of times before. But this time, I would really do it.

"You are learning about commitment and self-esteem," Dr. K said to me.

I went to see my dad. I told him about the job. It wasn't in law, but it was a respectable field where I could really do well. My father noticed my new attitude. He definitely liked the sound of it, though I'm not sure how confident he was about my follow-through. But he agreed to my terms. The total loan would amount to about $3,000 a month.

I'd made promises to my father, to Dr. K, and, most importantly, to myself. Now, it was up to me to follow through. And so I went to work in a way I had never gone to work before. I went to work like I meant it.

At seven o'clock every weekday morning, I hailed a cab outside my apartment on East Forty-Sixth Street and Second Avenue. I would swing by Thirty-Fifth and Lexington and pick up Ross Mandell, then head down FDR Drive to the Commonwealth office on Exchange Place in the Financial District.

From the start, I treated this opportunity differently than any job I'd ever had. I wasn't ducking into empty offices, making excuses and avoiding unpleasant tasks. Here, I tried to learn from the best producers in the office. Several times a day, I pulled my chair over to the desk of someone who was servicing a long-time client or opening a new account. It wasn't that I wanted to look like I cared. I actually did care. I'd sit there and really listen. What did the broker say to the client? How did he describe a particular stock? How did he respond to objections? How did he make sure the security he was suggesting was suitable to the client's risk tolerance and investment goals? There was an art to this and some learnable techniques. It wasn't school, but it might as well have been. In that office with those more experienced people, I was learning to be a stockbroker on Wall Street.

Given my abysmal bar experience, I was not looking forward to taking the Series 7. But Dr. K and I talked about it. If I wanted to live a decent and productive life, I had to put in the hard work. I didn't just wake up on the day of the test and wing it; I prepped.

In April, I passed on my first try. Just shows what a little studying can do.

I had one more daunting task before I could take on my own clients. I had to open thirty brokerage accounts for Ross. I opened those thirty accounts in twenty-eight days, faster than any new hire in the history of the firm.

"You're going to be very good at this," Ross told me, echoing what my Syracuse friend had said. This time, I think I believed it. I hadn't faked this. I'd put my mind to it, and I'd done a very good job. Maybe I had finally found a career I was good at and wanted to stick with. Too bad I hadn't discovered it before three years of law school and three cracks at the bar exam. Then again, I wouldn't have had the attitude and the focus to succeed before facing my issues and meeting Dr. K.

I really enjoyed helping clients with their investments. I actually had a knack for picking investments. And I realized that in at least one way I'd come into this job with a skill that none of the study guides ever mentioned. From watching Ross and the more experienced brokers, I learned that selling stocks was all about telling stories. No one could deny I'd always been good at that. My first month as a broker, I made somewhere between $15,000 to $20,000. To me, that was incredible! Money, I knew, wasn't the only measure of success. But after so many years of mooching, earning my own way did give me a palpable sense of worth. No doubt about it, I liked what I was doing.

I wasn't sure what came first. Did I like what I was doing because I was good at it, or was I good at it because I liked what I was doing? Both, I'm sure. But this was something I had never felt in my life—as a scam artist maybe, but never on the up-and-up. I had never taken such pride in my job before. For the first time ever, I wasn't watching the clock all day. There were nights I'd excitedly stay at work until eight or nine for a chance to speak with West Coast clients. My own clients.

None of that came without deliberate determination on my part to remain on track. After long days at work, I'd often drop by a late-night meeting on Seventy-Ninth Street. And no matter what my office schedule was, I never missed my Tuesday night appointment with Dr. K. Why would I? Every week, I had a chance to talk with the smartest person I had ever met. He kept me balanced. Every time we met, he taught me more and more about who I was and what I could be.

Slowly, I began to see that my old thoughts and attitudes were upside down and backwards. With Dr. K reminding me, I began looking for positive relationships and esteemable acts to perform. That's where it all started, he kept repeating—with esteemable acts. It was the only way to build the self-esteem I had so sorely been lacking. With some honest introspection and Dr. K's explanations, I came to see that esteem really was at the core of everything.

Sober attitudes, he counseled.

Sober attitudes and thoughts lead to wise choices.

Easy does it.

First things first.

Less is more.

You never make anything better by making it worse.

Dr. K had a seemingly endless supply of expressions he liked to use, phrases that encapsulated his insights about how to live a decent and successful life.

He repeated these phrases frequently until they were imprinted on my brain. And after a while I understood why he did. Those phrases were instructions. Inspirations. Guideposts. Words I'd be able to apply to almost any decision I had to make. Ultimately, I'd be calling up these concepts whenever I needed them and incorporating them into my daily life.

Most of them, it seemed, involved calming down, being thoughtful, and not letting my emotions get the better of me. I knew

I had tendencies in the opposite direction. Those tendencies, I knew, would be something I would have to fight against for the rest of my life. With his expressions, Dr. K was impressing on me the importance of developing more positive and productive attitudes while I confronted the nearly total mess my life had become.

Pause.

Think.

Quiet.

Respond with intellect, don't react with emotion.

Up to that point, I'd been motivated almost entirely by my emotions. It became even clearer to me that most of the poor choices I had made before Dr. K were made with unsober attitudes and thoughts. Attitudes and thoughts like . . .

I want what I want, and I want it now.

More is better.

React to life and worry about the consequences later.

That was the old me. The new me stopped reacting to life and started responding to it. I learned to keep my mouth shut . . . a little. I learned to take the cotton out of my ears and just shove it into my mouth.

Easy does it.

First things first.

Less is more.

Pause.

Think.

Quiet.

I was taking this advice and putting it into practice in my life, and it seemed to be working for me.

I became one of the top producers at Commonwealth Associates. Oh, and I repaid my father just as I had promised to.

I told myself: "I am going to be the man I always wanted to be."

||||||||||||||||

The first time I laid eyes on Lynda, she was running on a treadmill beneath the blaring dance music at the Vertical Club on East Sixty-First Street. I didn't know who she was. All I knew was that she was a dark haired beauty with a trim, fit body who could run like the wind. Unlike a lot of the Vertical Club's female members, this girl didn't look like she'd just spent half an hour in the dressing room applying makeup and hairspray and picking out just the right see-through leotard. She was more natural than the others, more comfortably athletic. She exuded a different kind of confidence.

This was the fall of 1991. The fitness boom had taken full hold in New York City. With its high-energy exercise classes and gleaming Cybex machines, the five-story Vertical Club was packed day and night with young professionals and others on the make, meeting, greeting, moaning, groaning, and maybe getting a little exercise too. A lot of the guys were there at least in part to meet women, many of whom were there at least in part to connect with guys. Eleven months sober, all this was perfect for me. The Vertical Club had all the things I liked about nightclubs—and no booze!

"I don't go to the gym to pick up girls," I told my friends. And that was the truth. But I couldn't help noticing this one young woman on the treadmill.

I nodded hello one day when we passed each other near the free-weight area. Another time, I smiled at her between the locker rooms and the juice bar.

She nodded and smiled back. But that was all she did.

Then, I got lucky. I was talking with my friend Rob Camshay, and she walked up. It turned out she and Rob had gone on a date together. She was coming over to cancel their next date.

He introduced us. I heard her name for the first time. I didn't want to interfere with whatever she and Rob had going on. But I was happy that now at least this girl knew who I was.

"You like my Italian stallion?" he asked me as she walked away.

I told him, yes, I did.

Rob told me she came from Staten Island. She had just graduated from college in Boston and lived with a female roommate in an apartment on East Sixty-Ninth Street. She had a job with News America, a Sunday-newspaper coupon company owned by the Australian media baron Rupert Murdoch. The next couple of times I saw her at the Vertical Club, I was comfortable being a little friendlier.

"How was your weekend?" I asked her casually one Monday afternoon.

"I don't really remember," she said with a laugh.

"Maybe you're hanging with the wrong people," I answered just before I walked away. That was very much an old-Craig maneuver, something I liked to do when I had just met someone. Express interest and then excuse myself. My strategy was never linger too long in conversation. Leave 'em thirsting for more!

I guess you could say I was still a work in progress.

A couple of weeks later, another friend and I went to a Knicks game at Madison Square Garden. No, we didn't have to sneak in. This time I went through the turnstile with my new season tickets. After the game, we stopped at a dive bar in Times Square called Dave's. Even though I wasn't drinking anymore, I still liked bars. The people. The atmosphere. The social possibilities. As soon as we walked in, I saw several people I recognized from the Vertical Club—including dark haired Lynda from the treadmill, standing at a tall table with two or three friends.

I didn't go right over and speak with her. That would have been so uncool, I thought. Instead, I walked past her, not saying a thing but making sure she saw me. If she said hello I figured, she must like me at least a little.

She did.

We talked for a few minutes at her table, I don't even remember about what. Then, I said, "I gotta run." Less is more. Before I left, I said to her: "Lynda, if you're not married, engaged, or in love, tell me your phone number." I didn't slide a napkin and pen toward her.

"Just…" I said with practiced pickup line confidence, "tell it to me."

"Don't you want to write it down?" she asked.

"I'll remember."

Eleven months sober, could I now actually remember a telephone number? Yes! All I had to do was repeat it over and over in my head as I walked away. Then, as soon as I was in the clear, I quickly wrote it down.

I called her a couple of days later. We agreed to meet for dinner and a movie the following Sunday, November 17.

She came up to my apartment at Turtle Bay Towers. Despite agreeing to go out with me, she didn't remember my last name. She told me later she had to glance at the subscription label on a copy of *Sports Illustrated* that was lying on my coffee table. She did it discreetly enough that I didn't notice. We went for Chinese food and then to the Loews 34th Street theater to see the remake of *Cape Fear*. The Martin Scorsese psycho-thriller, which starred Robert De Niro, Nick Nolte, and Jessica Lange, had just opened that week. Creepy Max Cady, the De Niro character, kept dreaming up new ways to torture his former public defender, Nolte's Sam Bowden. But as captivating as his acting was, I kept glancing over at Lynda.

At dinner after the movie, she told me about her family on Staten Island and her excitement at being out of college and in the city as a working adult. For once, I was comfortable just being my honest self. I told her about my new career on Wall Street and my own family.

We talked about sports and music and living in New York City. She was a young college graduate, eight years younger than I was. But she seemed plenty mature and could certainly hold her own in conversation with me.

When it was time to wrap up the evening, we shared a taxi up First Avenue. I told her I'd had a really great time. She said she had too. As the driver stopped to let me out at Forty-Sixth Street, I gave him a $10 bill to cover the fare and got to use another of my corny prefab lines:

"Take good care of her. She's all I have."

Only this time, it didn't sound quite as much like a line.

||||||||||||||||

Lynda had met the new Craig. Let me amend that. Lynda had met an early version of the developing new Craig. After almost exactly one year talking with Dr. K, I still retained some aspects of the old me. I was still smooth talking. Clearly, I hadn't shaken the pickup lines. But I was living a much more productive life by then. Buoyed by Dr. K's encouragement, I was doing many more esteemable acts. I liked the person I was becoming. I was attempting to be a man of honor, integrity, and commitment. I wasn't masking my discomfort and anxiety with alcohol and drugs. For ten months, I'd been working at Commonwealth Associates. I had outgrown the need to live off the strained generosity of my folks. In fact, doing that now would have felt like an embarrassing failure. I was making a living, paying my bills, and—look—I'd actually met a young woman who wasn't just attractive. She seemed to like me, and she definitely seemed to have something on the ball.

From the moment I started dating Lynda, I didn't cheat on her. That alone was monumental. I had never been faithful to anyone before. I didn't steal her ATM card. There was something different not just about me but also about us. I took her to a business function. She met the chairman of my company. She made a good impression. I really felt like I was coming into my own.

That's not what Lynda was hearing on the street.

Many of the people who knew me—not my closest friends but many of my casual acquaintances—had no idea how I had changed. My gym buddies. My nightlife pals. Guys I knew from college, law school, and being young in Manhattan. The only me they knew was the old one.

Lynda asked me one night: "Why do so many of your friends keep telling me to stay the hell away from you? I keep hearing from people, 'He is bad news.'"

Ouch! I hated hearing that. I explained as well as I could.

"They know the old Craig," I said to her. "All I can tell you is that, through my actions, I am not that guy anymore."

I opened up, in far greater detail than I expected to—about everything. About my growing up and how I thought it had affected me. About the way I had skated through so much of life, never rising to my real potential, never being willing to do the hard work. About the crazy stunts I thought would make me seem bigger and more important. About the many deceits and disappointments I had left in my wake. And I told her all about Dr. K. How he had confronted me directly and forced me to truly see the person I had become. How he challenged me to stay sober and do esteemable acts. How the path he put in front of me was difficult but already rewarding. How I had made real progress, I thought, but wasn't close to done.

"Since I met Dr. K," I told her, "my life is completely different than it used to be. Honesty, integrity—that's what's important to me. Through esteemable acts, I am able to build my self-esteem."

I held back nothing.

She didn't run like hell.

Actually, she seemed to really care about me.

I couldn't believe my luck, though I knew it wasn't luck at all. A grown-up relationship was one of the benefits of living like a grown-up.

No relationship is perfect. No two people are exactly the same. Lynda and I had different backgrounds. We came from families that practiced different religions. We didn't care. Her family didn't care. But my family, especially my father, was another matter. He did not like the idea of my having a serious relationship with someone who wasn't Jewish. For a long time, he even refused to meet her.

Let me tell you what Lynda was like. She invited me to her apartment for dinner on Valentine's Day, a Friday night. She lit Shabbat candles and from memory recited the Sabbath prayer. She'd been studying Hebrew. Her Jewish friends taught her the prayer. Even though I wasn't very religious, she knew this was part of my background, and she wanted to be a part of it.

"You're a keeper," I told her, and I meant it.

18

ONE MORE TIME

My life felt like it was finally coming together, far more than I expected. I was staying clean and sober. I was getting more and more serious with Lynda. I wasn't cheating on her or dipping into her checking account—not even once. I was doing well on Wall Street, well enough to buy a six-bedroom beach house in the Hamptons with a tennis court and a pool.

As good as I felt though, I knew from the rehab counselors and from Dr. K that progress for people with diseased attitudes does not always come in a perfectly straight line. Backsliding was always a possibility, and I was definitely concerned about that. I didn't want to be doing fine—and then, at the first bump in the road, start drinking again, start getting stoned again, or start running around on Lynda. That wasn't what honorable men do.

Still, my friends were constantly asking me: "When are you going out again?"... "Can we come along next time?... "Won't you sneak us in somewhere?" My first thought was—um, I don't think so! I was through defining myself as a manipulator and a liar and scam artist, all the reasons I'd ended up where I ended up. That was the old Craig. I was the new Craig now.

But then I thought about it some more. Was I overreacting here? What was the big deal? I was still a social creature. I still loved my friends and spending time with them. I wasn't drinking, but I still liked to go out and have a good time. And finding my way into amazing places, let's be honest: that was something I had gotten a lot of pleasure from and shown a world-class talent for. Why hide my light under a bushel? Being a better person didn't have to mean staying home alone every night and watching TV, did it? I didn't think so.

So on a handful of special occasions, I headed back out. I rounded up a small posse of friends. Using one technique or another—I had dozens by then—I got everyone inside some major New York City events and made sure we were all treated quite well once we got there. I had my moves down so well, this was hardly even a challenge anymore. I didn't do it often. It wasn't remotely like the frantic pace of my pre-Dr. K years. But even as I was pulling my life together and performing my esteemable acts, I did grab for a few uninvited thrills. I was back at Radio City Music Hall for the Grammy Awards—twice. I was there again for the MTV Video Music Awards. Radio City was starting to feel like my second home, I knew the place so well.

I brought four or five or six friends to each of those events. Lynda even came along to the MTV Awards. We sat third-row center *in front* of Bruce Springsteen and John F. Kennedy Jr., who was wearing a pink polka-dot tie and, I was happy to hear, had finally passed the New York State Bar Exam—on his third try. I swear I wasn't jealous at all. After terrific performances by the Stones and Snoop Dogg and a painfully awkward kiss between Michael Jackson and his wife, Lisa Marie Presley, the whole mob of us traipsed over to the postshow supper at the Four Seasons Hotel. It's amazing what you can learn about if you keep your ears open. Lynda and I spent a good part of the after-party hanging with Aerosmith's Steven Tyler. Not once did we hear his famous scream. He was soft-spoken and could not have been friendlier or more relaxed.

||||||||||||||||

The big event, the one that really felt like my grand finale, wasn't at Radio City. It was seventeen blocks to the south at Madison Square Garden, home to the New York Knicks and the New York Rangers—I had season tickets to both—and "the world's most famous arena." As a lifelong sports fan with a special love for hockey, I could hardly imagine a more fitting swan song than this.

The Rangers had a magical 1993–1994 season, finishing with the best record in the National Hockey League, 52-24-8. In those eighty-four regular-season games, the Blueshirts were not shut out once. General manager Neil Smith and head coach Mike Keenan had assembled and nurtured a truly dangerous lineup. Two years earlier, they'd picked up center Mark Messier from the powerhouse Edmonton Oilers. He was the captain and undisputed leader of the team. Brian Leetch and Sergei Zubov were a brick wall on defense. Zubov even led the team in scoring that season. Add Adam Graves and Kevin Lowe and Steve Larmer and the amazing Mike Richter in goal—on this team, it was hard to know where to stop naming names.

So expectations were in the stratosphere when the Rangers faced the New Jersey Devils in the Eastern Conference Finals. The series went to a full seven games, at the end of which the Rangers finally put the Devils away in a pulse-racing, home ice, overtime win. Stéphane Matteau's wraparound goal had the ecstatic home crowd, including me, chanting. "Matteau! Matteau! Matteau!" It must have been amazing for him to hear that. He'd only been a Ranger for three months. Then, it was time to face the Vancouver Canucks for the

NHL championship, as symbolized by the pinnacle of professional hockey glory, a mammoth trophy of silver and nickel alloy known as the historic Stanley Cup.

So much was on the line now. The Rangers hadn't won it all in fifty-four years. Frustrated fans had been grumbling for most of that time about the Curse of 1940, offering crazy theories about why their team didn't bring home a Cup since then. Fans of opposing teams, the New York Islanders especially, had spent years taunting the Rangers mercilessly with singsongy chants of "1940! 1940!"

This time, the Rangers got off to an encouraging start, winning three of the first four games. Game 5, promising to end everything, was back at the Garden. "TONIGHT'S THE NIGHT," the *New York Post*'s front page screamed. I could have sold my two game 5 tickets for $4,000 each, even though my seats were only so-so. That's how many New Yorkers wanted to be there in person to see the Rangers put the hated Canucks away. But the Rangers lost that game, which sent the series back to Vancouver, where the Canucks won again, evening the series at a nail-biting 3-3. Everything would be decided in game 7, at Madison Square Garden, Tuesday, June 14, 1994, only the second time since 1971 that the finals had gone to seven games.

Did I mention that game 7 fell on a Tuesday? Well, it did. Dr. K was understanding when I asked if we could do Monday that week. He knew what a Rangers fan I was.

I was kicking myself for not selling my tickets to game 5. I could have made a bundle and probably found some other way to get in. I was the master of that, wasn't I?

Then, I got cute. I gave one of my game 7 tickets to my buddy Michael Chuback and sold the other one. I didn't get $4,000, but I did get $2,500. The market had faded a bit. Too many Rangers fans felt like they'd paid too much to watch the team lose game 5. But I was happy with what the ticket fetched and I told Michael I still had every intention of maneuvering inside and sitting next to him. There was no way I was missing the biggest night in Rangers history. Even Dr. K said I could go. When Michael and I got to the Garden that night, I bought the cheapest ticket I could find, a seat way up in the nosebleed section that cost me $400. We headed inside together.

After Michael got settled in my old seat, he stepped away long enough to slip his ticket stub to me, which gave me access to the section. I stood behind the rail until I spotted an empty seat behind Michael—there are always empty seats—the thrill made all the sweeter by the $2,100 ticket-swapping bonus I had earned.

The Garden was positively buzzing as the Rangers leaped out to a 2-0 lead. I could taste a victory. I could see the Cup in my mind. All Rangers' fans could. But Canucks captain Trevor Linden sent a giant groan through the home crowd with a shorthanded goal early in the second period. Now, it was 2-1. Our captain, Mark Messier, answered theirs with another Rangers goal. It was 3-1, but there was another full period to play. When the players came back on the ice, Linden seemed determined to bring the Cup back to Canada. He tightened things again with a goal early in the third. It was 3-2. My heart was racing, and it would not stop. I don't think anyone sitting near us was breathing at all. I know Michael and I weren't.

With five minutes left, Canucks center Nathan LaFayette wobbled a loose puck off the post behind Rangers goalie Mike Richter. Michael and I couldn't stand the tension anymore. This was it, do or die. Protect the one-goal lead or lose the championship. Michael and I snaked our way down to the edge of the ice. It was bedlam down there. But we didn't care. We had to be as close as we could.

In the final thirty-eight seconds of play, there would be three heart-stopping face-offs, all at the Rangers' end of the ice. Messier won the first two. The crowd was on its feet. The win was right within grasp.

When the ref dropped the puck and Steve Larmer cleared it out of our zone, Rangers fans, Michael and I very much included, were certain the curse had finally been broken, only to be stunned by what I swear was a totally unjustified icing call. The wild celebration, just then erupting on and off the ice, was halted abruptly. And the Ghosts of 1940 got one last chance to haunt.

One-point-six seconds were left on the clock.

The face-off was to Richter's right, just a few feet from the goal. Craig MacTavish took the draw against Canucks' center Pavel Bure, with Rangers Messier, Larmer, Leetch, and Doug Lidster on the ice. This time, every one of them was playing defense. MacTavish won the face-off, sending the puck careening into the corner. One last time, Larmer pinned his man into the boards. The horn sounded. The fireworks blasted off. The crowd screamed with unbridled joy.

The Rangers had finally done it. The curse was no more.

No one wanted to leave. Fresh waves of fans pinned Michael and me against the glass. The real celebration began on the ice. I didn't know where to look first. Then, I caught sight of our hero captain. No one looked more thrilled than Mark Messier. He momentarily suspended the laws of gravity with a frenzied, hopping dance move. From where I stood, it didn't even look possible. Men his size in ice skates are not supposed to levitate that way!

As the ticker tape fell and the roar inside the Garden refused to subside, Messier accepted the Stanley Cup from NHL commissioner Gary Bettman. As the Rangers captain held the massive trophy over his head, it looked at least the size of a small automobile, even with the added heft of number 11's heavy pads. But this wasn't one man's victory. It belonged to all of us, players and fans. So each of the Rangers took a turn with the cup, holding it and hugging it and carrying it across the ice. Many of them hoisted it high above their heads and leaned into the crowd so the fans could touch the sacred trophy.

Michael and I didn't get to touch it, not yet. But our overwhelming feelings were perfectly articulated by a fan's sign a few rows behind us—"Now I Can Die in Peace."

||||||||||||||||||

It took a while, but the players slowly began exiting the ice, and the fans started to file out of the Garden. The fans were heading home or going out to celebrate on Seventh Avenue. The players, I knew, were on their way to the home-team locker room, where they would hold a press conference for the reporters and then have a quieter celebration of their own. Or maybe it wouldn't be so quiet. I didn't know.

But as Michael and I stood there, not wanting to call it a night, it suddenly hit me: what I had in my inside jacket pocket. I hadn't given it a single thought all night. But now it was occurring to me just in time.

Before I left the apartment, I had grabbed two Madison Square Garden all-access VIP passes, just in case. Barry had given them to me. They were from some long-ago concert or event neither one of us could remember. The passes were laminated in plastic and attached to metal chains. I believe that one was real and the other was a clever copy, but the fake was good enough that I couldn't tell which one was which. Whatever. I had them, and Michael and I definitely weren't ready to go home.

It had been a while since I had tried something like this, and I wasn't sure how I felt about it. I didn't even know if the passes would carry any weight at all. Maybe a Garden security guard would take one look at them and laugh. The passes didn't have a date or an event name. They said nothing about the Rangers or the Stanley Cup. But I pulled the passes out of my jacket pocket and showed them to Michael. His eyes brightened, and I asked: "You wanna try?"

I didn't have to ask twice.

"Sure," he said. "Why not?"

Without another word, Michael and I slipped those passes around our necks and made our way through the exiting throngs to the lower level of The Garden and the door to the Rangers' locker room.

There were two guards at the door and half a dozen New York police officers standing nearby. As Michael and I approached, I was leading the way. I held up my pass and nodded at one of the guards. Michael did the same. The guard nodded back and let us through the door. It couldn't have been easier.

Under Dr. K's influence, I was all but retired from the scam business. But clearly I hadn't lost my touch.

As we got inside, the locker room was packed. Team officials. Television camera crews. Cops and politicians. New York mayor Rudy Giuliani was grinning and high-fiving like he just might have scored the winning goal himself. Messier and a few other players were answering questions to a big crowd of reporters. Everyone seemed positively thrilled.

That's when I got my first up-close view of the Cup.

It looked about like I thought it would—a shiny fat cylinder with an oddly proportioned small bowl on top—just really, really big. You don't get a sense of that on television and even from the stands. There was writing on the trophy, the etched names of NHL's greatest champions. Someone pointed out the spot where this year's Rangers team would go. Several players were standing around the trophy. Others were pouring champagne into the bowl, then taking large, celebratory swigs. All of them were smiling and laughing and hugging each other.

Michael pulled a camera out of his pocket just as Messier was coming out of the press conference.

"Hey, Mark," I said. "Take a picture, please."

Damn, where did that come from? Was the old Craig really back?

Messier posed cheerfully while Michael got off a few quick shots.

Then, I asked Brian Leetch.

And Mike Richter.

And Neil Smith.

And Mike Keenan.

By the time Michael stopped shooting, I got pictures with almost half the team.

I noticed then that the mob around the trophy was finally thinning out. That's when Michael and I made our move. He went first, lifting the cup to his lips just like so many of the players already had and took a celebratory gulp of champagne.

Then, it was my turn.

I stepped forward.

I lifted the trophy. It weighed a good thirty-five pounds. I placed my lips near the edge of the bowl, never quite touching. Even in this crazed, frenzied moment, my sobriety was that important to me.

Did I drink champagne from the Stanley Cup? Not quite but close enough.

|||||||||||||||||

So why did I have a hangover in the morning? Not a hangover in the usual sense. I hadn't taken a sip of alcohol. I'd had an exhilarating night at The Garden. The curse was lifted. My beloved Rangers had finally brought the Cup home. I celebrated in the most dramatic way imaginable. I drank—in my way—from the damn cup. I even made a couple of thousand dollars off the night.

So why did I feel shitty the next day?

I knew exactly why. I didn't want to be that person anymore, even if I possessed an unbeatable technique. I had worked too hard to get where I was going. I dreaded next Tuesday when I'd be talking about this with Dr. K.

Of all the uninvited incursions I had launched, this one felt kind of dirty to me. I didn't do anything particularly egregious. I didn't exchange a single word with the guard at the locker room. But we arrived on false pretenses. We rode in on phony passes. And I wasn't that guy anymore. I wasn't perfect yet. I wasn't sure if I would ever be. But I'd been making such progress changing my life around. I knew I wasn't supposed to be pulling off schemes like this.

Did I feel guilty? I suppose I did.

I was trying to be a man of honor and integrity. This didn't feel like that.

"What the fuck are you doing," I said to myself.

"Who gives a shit about photos with jocks and celebrities?"

"You don't need to be backstage anymore."

It was an exciting weekend. On Friday, the Rangers held a ticker-tape parade up Broadway. A few hours later, I was in my basketball seats at the Garden watching the Knicks win game 5 of their championship series against the Houston Rockets. On one trip to a concession stand, I saw a crowd gathered, all eyes transfixed on a small TV. That's where I watched O. J. Simpson's surreal white Bronco chase.

By the time I saw Dr. K on Tuesday, the shots I had taken at myself were far more aggressive than the ones he unloaded.

I told him what I had done and what I had learned from the experience. I admitted that ego and excitement and deception still called to me.

"I'm a work in progress," I said. "I'm not entirely there yet. I'm not sure I'll ever be. But I am definitely making progress."

"Craig," he said to me, not sounding angry or even sad. "It's about progress, not perfection. We're all works in progress. Just keep progressing. That's all anyone can ask."

"I know that rush is still inside me," I told Dr. K. "The urge to manipulate. The challenge of maneuvering. The thrill of getting inside somewhere I don't belong. The pleasure of getting away with it." I paused, but just for a moment. "I don't define myself that way anymore. I don't justify the deception. But I hate to tell you, Doctor, it's still in there somewhere."

Dr. K absorbed what I said to him. I'd admitted that in some small way after so much progress, I might still be broken, some parts at least. I thought he was going to be upset or disappointed. He didn't seem to be either.

"I hate to tell you, Craig," he said. "But it's true. You'll always have to manage that. It will never fully go away. That feeling you describe, it will stay with you forever."

19

REAPING THE BENEFITS

All I had to do from here was live my life with honor and integrity. How hard could that be? Did I have to burn my backstage passes too?

I knew the principles. Dr. K had been hammering them home with me every Tuesday night. I knew what I needed to do. Pause. Quiet. Respond, don't react. You never make anything better by making it worse. Let sober attitudes lead my thinking and produce wise choices. Keep doing esteemable acts.

There was no doubt I was seeing results. I could see them at work, where my career was really taking off. I could see them in love, where the best girl I'd ever met was hinting that she might like to spend her life with me and start a family together. Even with one or two high-profile slipups along the way, the results of my time working with Dr. K were clear in many parts of my life. I wasn't chasing self-destructive behaviors, not often at least. I wasn't my own worst enemy like I used to be. I didn't need booze or pot to escape. I was setting higher standards for myself and mostly living up to them.

I moved from Commonwealth Associates to the investment banking firm Whale Securities, where I provided similar advice to clients but on a slightly larger scale. Who needed a law license? I was doing great on Wall Street, making what to me felt like excellent money and really coming into my own.

I had no doubt how I felt about Lynda. She was the best. I always got the sense that she appreciated me for the same reasons I was starting to appreciate in myself. She wanted a man she could trust. But as she kept dropping the marriage hints, I wasn't sure how to respond. Yes, I liked being with her. She had moved into my loft on East Forty-Sixth Street. I had stayed totally faithful to her. But after the kind of life that I'd led—so many years of being out of control and running around—was I really cut out for a death-do-us-part exclusive commitment with anyone? Could I say "I do" and really live up to that forever? I needed to talk with Dr. K.

"I love her," I said as we began our next session. "I can definitely see spending my life with her. But marriage? That sounds so final. If we got married, if I made that commitment, I could never be with anyone else ever again. It's not that I want to. But forever sounds like an awfully long time."

"Forever is forever," Dr. K said.

"If I am going to be a man of honor and integrity," I continued, "I have to be sure I don't make promises I can't live up to."

"I hear you," Dr. K said. "That's exactly right."

I was really struggling with this.

I'd been seeing Dr. K for almost five years by then. We'd talked about nearly everything. My drinking, my scams, my family, my jobs, my friends, Debbie, Jane, and all the other girls. But this was different. Lynda was different. And I hoped I was different too. Dr. K, as he often did, managed to focus me and put my mind at ease.

"Easy does it," he said. "One step at a time. If you get engaged and decide it's not right for you, you don't have to proceed. You understand, right?"

I told him I did.

"But just the fact that you are asking the question this way, that's a very good sign," he said. "I think you may be ready for this. Everything you've said about Lynda, you do seem committed to her."

"I am," I agreed. "I am. I've never felt this way before."

With Dr. K's encouragement, I put my jitters aside and moved forward.

One Friday early that summer, when Lynda was coming out to the beach house in the Hamptons, I bought four hundred red roses. Yes, I still liked grand gestures. Before she arrived, I placed the roses everywhere. In the living room, in the dining room, and even in the kitchen. I didn't know if the house looked more like a floral shop or a funeral home. Surely, some of my friends would have a snappy answer to that. But those four hundred roses made quite a visual statement.

When I finished placing the roses around the front of the house, there wasn't any place you could glance without seeing flowers. My hands were also bleeding from all those thorns. The place really did look like a scene out of a romance movie. Now, I just had to wait for Lynda's response. I don't care how long you've been dating. There is always a hint of fear.

When Lynda walked in the door and saw all those roses, her first question was: "Is this for me?" That's when I climbed down on one knee and finally got to ask her: "Will you marry me?"

She still looked shocked—maybe more because of the roses than the question. She had been waiting long enough for me to ask. I do think she understood where the extravagance of the proposal came from. That I loved her. That I was ready. And that I was promising to be the kind of man who lived up to his commitments, yes, 'til death do us part.

And she said yes.

||||||||||||||||

Lynda and I got married on August 17, 1996, at Tamcrest Country Club in Alpine, New Jersey. As with any big wedding, there were a couple of rough spots along the way. My father insisted on a kosher reception. My mother wore a dress that was partially white. "The bride is supposed to be the only one in white," Lynda said to me. My parents also invited most of the guests. But we had a beautiful ceremony. The alcohol flowed for those who were drinking. People danced into the night. And even though the food was kosher, everyone agreed it tasted great. We even had a special guest.

I knew that Dr. K always liked to keep his professional life and his social life completely apart. He was adamant about that. When I invited him to the wedding, I really didn't think he would come. But I looked over at one point during the cocktail hour and there he was, standing by himself in a grey suit and red tie. I grabbed Lynda's hand and rushed over. He offered his very best wishes to her and said congratulations to me. Frankly, I was shocked to see him there and deeply gratified that he chose to come.

Then, Lynda and I began a life together as husband and wife.

Our first daughter, Brittany, arrived January 23, 1999. Our second, Carly, came barely thirteen months later, on March 3, 2000. I loved being a husband, and I couldn't believe how amazing it felt to be a dad. And good things just kept happening to me.

Up until then, I had worked for two relatively small Wall Street firms, Commonwealth Associates and Whale Securities. I had begun to wonder how I would do at one of the bigger, better known firms.

Given my results so far and my growing list of clients, it turned out the big boys were also interested in me.

Just after Carly was born, I was recruited hard by a large, global brokerage firm, one of the largest asset managers in the world, serving individual and institutional investors on six continents. I met with the firm's president and CEO, two highly impressive executives. They were sufficiently eager for me to come over that they offered a seven-figure signing bonus. The deal worked like this: I could take $1 million in cash or $1.2 million in company stock. I discussed the choice with Dr. K.

"I'm thinking about taking the cash," I told Dr. K. That might have been the old Craig talking: I want what I want and I want it now.

That's certainly how Dr. K read it. He looked at me as if to ask: You still haven't shaken all your unsober attitudes, have you? Then, he led me through a comparison of the pros and cons of each choice.

"The cash is a sure thing. And you'll get it right away," he said. "But if you take the cash, it will also be taxed immediately. So the million dollars will become six hundred thousand overnight."

"That's about right," I agreed.

"On the other hand," Dr. K continued, "if you take the second option, you will get a twenty percent bonus, an extra two hundred thousand dollars, and you won't have to pay taxes on the transaction until you sell your shares."

Who knew Dr. K wasn't just a psychiatrist? He was also an amateur accountant.

"And there's something else to consider," he went on. "Taking the stock connects you more closely with the firm you are going to work for. You told me last week how much you love—is it the president and the CEO? 'They are such great men.'"

"That's right," I said.

"If you truly believe in the great men who run the firm, wouldn't you want to be their partner and have your future aligned with theirs?" Dr. K asked. "If they do well, you do well."

Every other broker hired my year took the cash. I took the stock. Once I'd thought about Dr. K's comparison and followed up with my own analysis, the decision seemed like a no-brainer. And I'm so glad I passed on the immediate gratification of the cash. At that point, the firm's stock was trading at $25 a share. When I left five years later—hired away by another investment bank, an even larger and more powerful firm—the company was trading at $125 a share. Taking the stock turned out to be a very wise choice. I wish all my stock picks appreciated so well.

It was funny, wasn't it? I was discussing a million-dollar offer while sitting in the same basement office where I'd once been jobless, flat broke, and with no obvious path up. With Dr. K's guidance, I hoped to keep making decisions like these.

By then Lynda, the girls, and I had moved into a two-bedroom, thirty-ninth-floor co-op apartment on First Avenue and Fifty-Sixth Street. But with two active children, we knew we needed more room. Yet we also loved the building, and we didn't want to move. So I asked myself: What's the wise thing to do here? Should we move? Should we wait for a larger apartment to hit the market? Was there a third option? I knocked on our immediate neighbor's door and inquired politely: If we could settle on a fair price, did he have any interest in selling his apartment? He did, absolutely, he said. He sounded as if he'd been waiting for me to knock.

We settled on terms in a hurry. He was happy and so were we. Combined, the two co-ops made a spacious family apartment, nearly 2,600 square feet with views that went on forever, perfect for Lynda, Brittany, little Carly, and me. Again, the choice turned out to be a wise one. I can't say if all this was luck, wisdom, or the rising Manhattan real-estate market—probably a combination of all three. But when we finally got ready to move to a large suburban house in Rumson, New Jersey, we sold that combined city apartment for $1.5 million more than we had in it.

Even Dr. K was impressed.

‖‖‖‖‖‖‖‖‖‖‖‖‖‖‖

It wasn't always easy living up to Dr. K's dictums. His notions of honesty and personal responsibility extended to all parts of life. Major things and minor things. Trivial comments and deep commitments. When you tell someone, "I'll call you tomorrow," you should always make the call. When you promise to help a friend in trouble, you should absolutely be there. When you say, "I'll meet you at nine thirty," don't stroll in at ten. When you say, "My children are the most important thing in the world to me," you must live like they are. You should be available. You should stay healthy. You should do everything you can to provide everything they need. As I often discovered, Dr. K's standards could be brutal.

One day, one of my cousins came by for a visit. As we spoke, he told me he was having financial difficulties. He said he was feeling pretty squeezed.

"How much do you need?" I asked. "I'll lend it to you."

"About fifty thousand dollars," he answered.

Why did I make the offer? To show off to my cousin? To toot my own horn? Maybe. I'd also like to think I was trying to be kind. But my timing couldn't have been worse. It so happened that I didn't have many liquid assets at the moment. Most of my money was tied up in the stock market and in real estate. Truthfully, I never thought he would take me up on my comment or my offer or whatever it was.

I breathed a sigh of relief when he handed me some wiggle room. "Craig, that's very nice of you," he said. "But I don't know. Let me give it some thought."

The rest of the week, I didn't give our conversation much thought. Then the following Saturday, the phone rang at home.

"Is that offer to lend me the fifty thousand still available?" my cousin asked.

I didn't know what to say. Now, I was the one who needed some time. I stalled. "Give me a couple of days," I told him. "I'll get back to you."

I really wanted no part of this, and I started thinking of reasons why I didn't have to be. He and I weren't that close, really. My own funds were tight right then. But this was a situation of my own making. I had offered, hadn't I?

Tuesday night, I was there for my usual appointment with Dr. K. I hadn't yet called my cousin back. "My ego got the better of me," I admitted to Dr. K. "I was feeling braggadocios and I said something I didn't really mean. What do I do now?"

I could feel another lesson coming on, and I wasn't sure I was going to like it. It was from the same font of wisdom I'd been tapping since I first laid eyes on Dr. K.

"You know you have two choices, right?" he said. "Either give him the money or not."

Damn, he was always so literal!

He presented the options to me like he always did. Starkly. I knew when he was finished, I would have a choice to make. "You don't have to give him the money," Dr. K said. "But if you don't, you will define yourself as someone who is unreliable. You will define yourself as a liar, someone who doesn't live up to his commitments. On the other hand, if you give him the money, you will live up to your word and be a man of honor and commitment."

I hated to hear that. "Oh, Jesus, Doc," I groaned. "You gotta put it that way?"

He nodded at me and said: "You have to ask yourself one very basic question." I remember this like it was yesterday. "You have to ask yourself, 'Is my self-esteem worth fifty thousand dollars?'"

"Really?" I asked.

"It's that simple," Dr. K declared. "Give the money and live up to your commitment or don't give the money and define yourself as a liar. You have to make the choice because only you will have to live with whatever choice you make."

I went home that night and thought about it long and hard. I'd been blessed. Despite my own tight cash flow, I knew I could raise the funds. Being a man of honor and integrity had paid plenty of dividends for me. If the price of keeping my self-esteem intact was $50,000, maybe I'd have to pay.

I called my cousin. I told him I'd have the money for him whenever he was ready. With great relief and appreciation, he came by that afternoon.

I did the right thing. I know I did. Even though I never got a nickel of the money back from my cousin, Dr. K had taught me: my self-esteem was worth a whole lot more.

||||||||||||||||||

Over the years, as my circumstances kept improving and I improved too, I grew more and more grateful to Dr. K. He was more than a talented teacher and therapist. I genuinely liked him. I really came to grasp how unique and brilliant he was. Kind. Smart. Humble. What wasn't to like? Every day, he was saving people's lives just as he had saved mine. He knew exactly what he believed in: that the problem was almost never the alcohol or the drugs or any other addiction. The problem was inside the person who reached for those self-destructive escapes. It all went back to inconsistent nurturing, Dr. K was convinced. Those substances, whatever they were, were easing and masking and compensating for damaged self-esteem. And in their very addictive nature, they made things so much worse.

"Why aren't more people in your profession focused on this?" I asked Dr. K one day.

This perplexed me. Low self-esteem seemed damn near universal. The consequences of addiction were everywhere. Almost everyone I knew doubted themselves, often without good reason. Many reached for self-destructive behaviors.

Many psychiatrists and psychologists, he explained, are reluctant to work with addicted patients. They consider therapy for addicts more or less a waste of time. "The patients relapse," Dr. K said. "They lie. They seem to get better and then they get worse. That's a common view in my profession. My colleagues tell me, 'You don't want to work with these patients. They will always disappoint you.' But I just haven't found that to be true."

I didn't like hearing about such defeatism from people who should know better. It sounded counterproductive to me and also cruel. But Dr. K clearly hadn't bought into it.

"I believe many of my colleagues are treating these patients wrong," he said. "They don't understand what causes the problem so they can't effectively treat it."

I had no doubt that Dr. K was onto something, something important, something profound. I was walking proof of that. So were his other patients, several of whom I had referred to him. After all he'd done for me, I wanted Dr. K to spread his insights and his methods everywhere.

At the end of January every year, I knew, he flew out to Colorado Springs for something called the International Winter Symposium on Addictive Disorders, a conference for mental-health professionals who dealt with addiction issues. He gave lectures and participated in seminars. From what he told me, it wasn't a massive convention. But the participants were extremely dedicated and passionate, he said, and their numbers had been growing over the years. The annual gathering seemed to mean a lot to him. But as far as I could tell, that group and their meetings were the full extent of how far Dr. K went to share his insights with the world.

"You should take your message to the masses," I pleaded with him. "You need to spread this around. Do you have any idea how many people could benefit?"

"I appreciate that," he said. But I wouldn't say he sounded convinced.

"You should write a book," I told him. "You should make tapes and videos. People need to hear this message. I can help you get your message out there."

I reminded him that I knew people in finance and in the media. We could create a whole campaign, I told him. "You know how inventive I can be."

He laughed at that. But still he didn't budge.

He said he was very happy with his little practice in his little office down the stairs and the thirty to thirty-five patients he saw every week. He was the most humble and sober man I had ever met.

"I know I help people," he said with quiet confidence. "I am very happy with that. I share my insights. My patients achieve results. I know what I am good at. This is exactly what I want to do with my life."

20

READY OR NOT

One Tuesday night in April of 2003, I received disturbing news. "I have some health issues," Dr. K said to me at the end of our session. "I am not going to be able to see you for a while—or see any of my other patients."

I knew a few of them, friends or acquaintances I had referred to him. He told everyone the same thing.

I was rattled.

I wanted to know more.

I couldn't accept his short explanation.

I was scared.

I didn't like missing our sessions, even for a few weeks. I had been seeing him for more than twelve years by then. He had taken vacations. He had attended his addiction symposiums in Colorado. But nothing open-ended like this. Not once since our very earliest meetings in his office, when I'd fumbled my first two commitments and he asked me, "Do you see that man?" As far as I could recall, Dr. K had never cancelled an appointment on account of being sick.

He deflected when I asked what was wrong. "It's a medical issue," he said.

I had heard the term "separation anxiety." I was pretty sure it applied to me. Dr. K gave no indication about how long he might be absent. He left a whole lot up in the air.

I'd spent hundreds of hours in his small basement office, and I'd revealed so much to him, hardly ever holding anything back. Despite that, I knew only the basics about Dr. K's family and personal life. He never offered much, and I mostly didn't pry. "Let's focus on you," he would say whenever I wandered too close for comfort. I knew he had a wife named Carol. I knew they had a son who was very bright and attended a select public school in New York City. I knew they lived not far from the office on the Upper East Side. I knew that every New Year's Eve, they liked to order a dish of take-out food from each of their favorite restaurants, regardless of cuisine or ethnicity, then sit down together as a family for an at-home, best-of, end-of-the-year feast. I thought that was a cool ritual, but that was about all I knew.

The first week or two, I tried not to dwell on the fact that my Tuesday nights were suddenly free. I was busy at work. My wife and two daughters were waiting at home. My life was plenty busy. But when I didn't hear anything for three or four weeks, I called a couple of the other patients I knew. They had no more information than I did, and they weren't enjoying his absence any more than I was.

I started imagining things, none of them cheerful. Whatever was wrong with him, I hoped he would get better soon. He had patients counting on him. I worried for him. I worried for me.

When I still hadn't heard anything after seven long weeks, I decided to take matters into my own hands. Dr. K had taught many lessons in all our time together. Sitting around passively and accepting what happens was not one of them. Was he in the hospital? Was he at home? God only knows! Anything was possible. Was he in a coma?

Was he being kept somewhere that phones and email and communication weren't allowed? I didn't like any of the options, and I didn't understand why he couldn't just send word to us.

I left a message on the answering machine in the office. Then, I left another three. He didn't call back. I didn't have his home number. But I knew people and I had skills, the same skills that had gotten me into the Kremlin, the president's motorcade, the Stanley Cup locker room, Radio City Music Hall, and on and on and on. I put those skills to work again. By asking around and phoning some friends and calling in a couple of favors, I was finally able to track him down. Dr. K was in Columbia Presbyterian Hospital, the same institution in Upper Manhattan where he had completed his psychiatry residency. For a moment, I thought about the line between doctor and patient. Then, I decided to cross it. I would call him. I had no idea how he might respond.

I phoned the hospital switchboard and asked for Arthur Knauert's room. The operator put me through right away.

The voice that said "hello" sounded slightly hoarse but was alert and alive and instantly recognizable.

"Hi, Dr. K," I said. "It's Craig Schmell. What's going on?"

I was hugely relieved that he didn't hang up the phone. He didn't sound irritated or angry that I had called. He actually sounded happy to hear from me.

"Hey, Craig," he said, as if we'd just spoken the previous Tuesday.

"How are you?" I asked.

Then, he got more somber.

"Craig," he said, "I am very sick."

He told me he had cancer, advanced pancreatic cancer, and the doctors were not offering much encouragement. "It's moving quickly," he said, "and I don't have too much time."

"Really?" I said, not knowing what to say.

If I'd known what to say, I couldn't have gotten the words out. I started to cry. Cry like I hadn't cried since that day he'd pointed through his office window at a stranger standing on the sidewalk, who turned out to be me. The tears were trailing down my face and onto my shirt collar. I was just sobbing into the phone.

He was calm. He sounded at peace. He recognized his higher power had a plan for him.

The feelings were washing over me so quickly, I didn't know how or what to say. I tried to explain how much he meant to me. I told him how much I was going to miss him and how blessed I felt that he had entered my life. I told him that I realized I wasn't the only person he had helped, and I said I knew he knew that. Then, the shock and sorrow turned in to something far more toxic. Terror.

"What do I do?" I asked him. "I don't know what to do."

"Listen to me, Craig," he said, his voice several notches firmer than at the beginning of the call. "You know exactly what to do."

Then, he repeated himself. "You know exactly what to do."

When he said that, I found his answer jarring. "What do you mean?" I asked, though even as I asked the question I thought to myself that maybe I did know what to do.

I had spent twelve and a half years of Tuesdays sitting in his office. He had explained a lot to me in that time. He had made me a better person. His ideas had literally saved my life.

So, yes, I heard him. He didn't have to spell it out all over again. He knew it, and I knew it too.

Easy does it.

First things first.

Pause.

Quiet.

Respond, don't react,

You never make anything better by making it worse.

We'd been sharing those concepts and applying them to my life since November of 1990. I was such a different person than I was back then.

"I have given you everything you need," Dr. K said, calming me from his hospital bed. "You know how to use it. You know. You are one of my prize students. You will be just fine."

And you know what? I actually believed him.

||||||||||||||||||

Dr. K died in his hospital bed on July 15, 2003.

His family held a private funeral. That was the way he wanted it. I spoke with his wife on the phone a couple of days after. "I want to organize a memorial service for his patients and other people whose lives he touched," I said.

She said she thought that was a fine idea. "He'd appreciate it, even though he would never ask you to do it," she told me. But she cautioned she wouldn't be able to share her husband's patient list with me. "He had a strong belief in protecting people's privacy," she said. "You understand." I did. I would have to find the other patients on my own.

Finding his other patients turned out to be easier than it might have been. The ones I had referred to Dr. K had been calling me constantly during his illness, and many of them were connected to others, once or twice removed. In a matter of a day or two, we had reached out to just about everyone.

We held the service at the Town and Village Synagogue on East Fourteenth Street. Dr. K's wife, their son, and her sister came. So did almost every one of his current patients and many of his former ones. I wasn't surprised by the turnout. I couldn't imagine anyone voluntarily staying away.

The memorial was difficult at times and inspiring at others. One by one, people stood and shared their stories. In often painful detail, they described the shape they were in before meeting Dr. K—how poorly they felt about themselves and how that began to change. They shared remembrances of how tough and how rigid he could sometimes be. And they quoted their favorite Dr. K principles. One young woman said that by following his call for "pause" and "quiet," she had saved her troubled marriage. An older gentleman said that by "responding, not reacting," he had reestablished relations with his grown children after years of being estranged.

And so it went for two solid hours. There were tears and hugs and a few glum silences. Everyone had Dr. K stories, and many got to share them. It was clearly cathartic for the patients. It was uplifting, I hoped, for the family. I felt proud to have gathered the clan.

I had so much in common with these people, even beyond being patients of Dr. K. We had traveled similar roads, it seemed, to destinations so much better than where we had begun. Dr. K had been our guide, our teacher, and our friend. All our lives had been changed by his wisdom and love.

When the memorial service was over, no one was ready to leave. We lingered as long as we could, asking each other, "So what are you going to do now?"

Some people expressed nervousness about the future. Others said they were ready for whatever might be next, knowing they'd been armed and were feeling confident. Several times, I shared the words that Dr. K had expressed to me: "You know exactly what to do."

Each and every time I repeated that phrase to someone new, I got a similar response. *Yes. I'm ready. Thanks to Dr. K and his teachings, I think I know what to do.*

He was gone but he still lived inside all of us. He had changed our lives greatly and forever. He had made us better human beings, and we knew it.

Before we left, I suggested getting together for a weekly "Dr. K meeting" to keep his principles and teachings alive. Of course, it wouldn't be the equivalent of seeing Dr. K again. Everyone understood that. It would be more like a gathering for people who were dealing with similar issues and experiences.

This one incredible man had taught us all so beautifully. We knew how to keep each other honest and intact. The clear-eyed principles that had gotten us this far were embedded in each of us. We really did know what to do.

The synagogue on East Fourteenth Street offered space to us, and the meetings began. For many of Dr. K's patients, it was a valuable transition. It didn't last forever. After a year or two, people began to drift away. But for as long as we needed each other, Dr. Arthur Knauert kept us going.

|||||||||||||||||

A thousand times, I have thought about what the rest of my life would have been like if Dr. K had lived. So much richer, I'm sure—and not just financially. I have asked myself at challenging moments: What would Dr. K say? We'd spent enough time together that I had learned most of the lessons he had to teach. I usually knew what was right. I usually knew what to do. I didn't succeed spectacularly at everything, but I always tried. Many of the issues that had dogged my younger years were gone or vastly diminished, thank God. I never drifted back to alcohol or marijuana. I didn't surrender my core values to a sick and desperate quest for self-esteem. I knew not to define myself by the gossip-page VIPs I could hang out with. I truly didn't give a shit about standing with a bunch of rock stars in front of a stack of Marshall amps.

I missed Dr. K terribly, that was for sure. But I still had everything he had taught me, and I still relied on that nearly every day. I never forgot what Dr. K said about my children being my top priority. Lynda and I were so proud of our daughters. Brittany and Carly were growing up beautifully. My Wall Street career kept soaring. It was an honor going to work every day. I picked my stocks. I rode the market. I liked my colleagues. My clients were making money. I kept going up, up, up.

Until someone slammed the brakes on that.

And then things started going down.

It wasn't just me. It was almost everyone on Wall Street—companies and individuals, large firms and small. Bear Stearns, savvy and aggressive, collapsed first. That was March of 2008. Then came Lehman Brothers, after 158 years in business, the fourth-largest investment bank in America—suddenly vaporized! It was crash time on Wall Street, and no one was immune. Experts were calling it the Great Recession, the steepest downturn since the Great Depression of 1929. Stock prices were nose-diving. The derivatives market was in free fall. Home mortgage foreclosures were shooting into the stratosphere. Real people were getting slammed. Maybe some of them should have known better. Maybe too many people made unwise choices and took out mortgages they couldn't afford to repay. But that didn't excuse the runaway greed on some corners of Wall Street. What kind of integrity had those so-called professionals shown?

With hardly any warning, I felt like I was in a fog. My clients were calling, understandably frantic. I was trying to calm them down. "We're hanging tight," I said. "The worst thing to do in a panic is to sell."

I stepped into the office of one of my friends at work. "What does a heart attack feel like?" I asked him. He could see I wasn't joking. "I think I'm having a heart attack."

"You're not having a heart attack," he assured me. "Something very bad is happening, and you're scared."

I tried to collect myself. "I just watched my personal stock account drop $1.5 million in two months," I told him. "A heart attack might be more fun." I think I meant it.

Thankfully, I still had Dr. K in my head, and he was talking to me. It was my voice, but they were his words. I'd been riddled with fear and anxiety but now I had the tools to respond. I knew how to change my thinking. I could adjust my attitude. I could pause and be quiet and respond with wise choices.

"Easy does it," I said to myself. "First things first." I knew that 99 percent of my negative projections never came true. This too shall pass.

In the middle of the night, I was still waking up sweating. Then, I would calm myself down. Yesterday, I told myself, I couldn't do anything about. Tomorrow, I may not even be alive. Today is all I have. I have a family that loves me. We have meals on the table and a roof over our heads. The girls are healthy, and so I am.

I was gaining control of my emotions, responding, not just reacting. I swear Dr. K was there with me.

I had an insight, an insight he easily could have shared with me. It went like this: My life, I realized, was too connected to forces I couldn't control. I couldn't control the stock market. It goes up. It goes down. I didn't run the US economy. The Federal Reserve wasn't waiting for my call. And too many of my assets were tied to Wall Street. My job. My investments. My entire professional and financial life. Shouldn't I practice what I'd been preaching to my clients? Shouldn't I spread my own risk around?

I heard about a company called Retro Fitness. They owned gyms. Nice quality, moderately priced gyms. The latest equipment, clean facilities, nothing extravagant, but everything you need. For the cost of a couple of McDonald's hamburgers and fountain Cokes, you could join Retro Fitness and work out as much as you wanted for a month.

Now, that sounded like a promising business to me, especially in the depths of a Great Recession. People go to gyms in up and down markets. In down markets, people are likely to go to the gym even more, especially if it doesn't cost them an arm and a leg. They have more time on their hands and feel more stressed. A gym is a place to hang out and do something esteemable. And this business was totally separate from the finance industry, ideal diversification for me.

My friends didn't get it. They told me I was nuts. My dad wondered, "You're really gonna open a gym in the middle of a recession?" But I believed in myself, and I believed in what Dr. K had taught me. I took $1 million from my savings, virtually every nickel I had, and I opened a Retro Fitness franchise in Fairfield, New Jersey. After a year, that gym was doing so well, I went to the bank and borrowed some money. I opened a second gym in Staten Island, New York. Then, I called my father and told him the good news. I was opening a third one, this time in New City, not far from where we'd all lived together on Topaz Court.

Soon enough, my three franchises were three of the top producing gyms in the entire Retro organization. I paid off my bank debt in a hurry. The cash flow was spectacular. I had a talented partner running the day-to-day, and I never had to quit my banking job. The market came back. My own portfolio recovered. My clients were calling happy again. I was comfortable, secure, and diversified while most of my friends and colleagues were still dusting themselves off.

Thanks, Doc.

21

FINALLY GETTING IT RIGHT

Life seemed almost idyllic to me.

The man who went out every night was now perfectly happy staying at home. The guy who couldn't hold a job for more than six months had now been in the same industry for more than a quarter century, only leaving a firm when he chose to. The good-for-nothing bum who once needed his daddy to cover the rent and credit card bills was now living with his beautiful wife and gorgeous daughters in a stately brick home on nearly two acres in upscale Rumson, New Jersey, just a short drive from Bruce Springsteen and Jon Bon Jovi. And he felt no compunction to knock on their doors and ask for photos.

It all looked great on the outside. How broken could the inside be?

Some days I woke up hardly able to believe how far I had come. I hadn't had a drink for nearly three decades. Brittany and Carly were loving high school, becoming mature grown-ups right before my eyes. I had a thriving career on Wall Street and a profitable gym business—five Retros by then. Banks now came to me with loan offers, wondering what new businesses I might like to start. Dr. K's insightful words still echoed in my head, guiding me almost a decade after his tragic passing. But here's the thing with ancient psychological issues and profound personal growth. You're always a work in progress, no matter how far you've come.

Despite the progress I had made, the old Craig still popped up from time to time. Clearly, those demons were still inside me, playing to my ego, laying their diabolical traps for me.

One night on my way home from work, I stopped at Walgreens to pick up a lightbulb. I was tired. I was hungry. I was late for dinner. I found the bulb without any problem and made my way to the store's one open register, where an older woman was ringing up purchases and five people were already standing in line.

I could tell this wasn't going to be quick.

I waited. The cashier was slow. The line hardly moved. I waited some more. After two or three minutes, there were still three people in front of me, and one of them was a woman with a basket filled to the brim with merchandise. I was impatient. Then, I was angry. Then, I was glancing around for a manager and seething to myself: How dare Walgreens not have two or three cashiers on duty at such a busy hour? Don't they know people are trying to get home for dinner? Don't they know who I am?

I'd had enough.

With the $1.79 lightbulb in my hand, I stepped out of line, abandoning the slowpoke cashier and the other customers. I walked out of the store, climbed in my car, and drove directly home.

It was only later that evening that it hit me: that was one of the stupidest things I'd ever done. If I'd been caught shoplifting at Walgreens, I could have been arrested. I could have spent a night in jail. I'd have to tell my family. People could easily find out. I could have my Series 7 license yanked. At the very least, I'd have some uncomfortable explaining to do. The whole thing could end up in the Jersey papers. I could see the headline now: "DIM BULB: Exec Throws It All Away for $1.79."

That's right. For less than $2 and five or ten minutes of my time, I ran the risk of losing nearly everything. What would Dr. K tell me to do to make it right?

The next morning before work, I went back to Walgreens and asked for the manager. I told him I had walked out of the store the night before without paying for a $1.79 lightbulb, and I would like to pay for it now. He seemed a little surprised to hear my story—I may have been the first shoplifter who ever returned to pay for a stolen item. But he understood what I was saying, rang me up at a side register, and thanked me for coming back.

I've had slipups like this one all over the world, things I have done that upon reflection didn't live up to the high standards that Dr. K set for me. Not often, thank God. But often enough. On a family vacation to Paris, I used some trickery to beat the long lines at the Louvre. I'm not proud of it. I shouldn't have done it. But I did. In December of 2012, Lynda, Brittany, Carly, and I took a holiday trip to Italy. On the afternoon of Christmas Eve, we hired a guide who took us on a tour of the Vatican. We visited St. Paul's Cathedral, the Sistine Chapel, and St. Peter's Basilica. We exited the basilica and stood for a moment in St. Peter's Square, watching workers setting up folding chairs for Midnight Mass. We went for a delicious dinner near the Spanish Steps at a Tuscan restaurant owned by a friend of a friend.

As we walked out of the restaurant, I asked Lynda and the girls: "So what do we want to do now?" My daughters said they were tired, but I perked up: "We're in Rome on Christmas Eve. Let's go to Midnight Mass! How can we miss something as amazing as that?"

I'm not saying the girls were excited, but they were good sports.

By the time we returned, St. Peter's Square was totally packed. The folding chairs in front were filled with VIPs who had special tickets. Two giant TV screens were showing the pre-Mass rituals from inside the massive basilica. Being true to form, I didn't want my family stuck all the way in the back. Over the eye rolls of Brittany and Carly, I walked everyone toward the front of the square near the entrance to the basilica, right behind the roped-off folding chairs.

We stood there for at least half an hour, just soaking everything in, catching occasional glimpses of the colorfully dressed Swiss Guards. Suddenly, I noticed four men in white robes leaving their seats in the roped-off section. "Follow me," I whispered, as Carly shot me a look that I interpreted as *uh-oh-here-we-go-again*.

I led Lynda and the girls around the side and back up to the front, where a guard stopped us. "Four empty seats," I said, motioning to the very front row. "Just a second," he said in flawless English. Then, he nodded, pulled back the rope, and let us through.

Once we settled in, even Carly was impressed. Dozens of priests and bishops were on the altar. At the center was Pope Benedict XVI, who looked downright spry for eighty-five. The Holy Father asked a series of profound questions in his homily, including one about the importance of engaging in our outer and inner worlds: "Why should we not also be moved by curiosity to see more closely?"

After the homily and blessing and quite a few hymns and prayers, Pope Benedict handed the hosts to several other clergymen, who came down from the altar to distribute Communion. Half a dozen made their way directly out the basilica doors.

As luck would have it, one of the priests walked directly toward me. He looked ready to give me Communion. The girls glanced at me. Lynda looked at me. I didn't know what to do.

Should I take Communion? Should I not?

Suddenly, Dr. K was in my head again.

"You need a higher power," he was saying again. "Your higher power can be anything." When he'd said it, I wasn't sure what he meant. Now, I had a much clearer idea.

"*Corpo di Cristo,*" the priest said to me, body of Christ in Italian.

"Amen," I knew to answer.

It was Christmas now. I was at the Vatican with my family. I had just received Communion blessed by the Pope, who was praying for all the faithful and asking us all to go forth joyfully. I still had sins that needed forgiving. I was open to all the help I could get. But I liked my odds. Now, I'd been blessed by Rabbi Schneerson in Brooklyn and Pope Benedict in Rome.

IIIIIIIIIIIIIIIII

Here's the thing about life: it keeps throwing stuff at you, no matter how prepared you think you might be. In the summer of 2013, six months after we'd gotten back from Rome, Lynda said something that I was completely unprepared to hear.

"I want a divorce," she said.

After gasping and wondering if I'd heard her correctly, my first response was that this could not possibly be true. I felt like my wife of seventeen years had just taken a giant sledgehammer and smashed our beautiful brick house in New Jersey—then smashed our family too. Why would she want to do that?

I had been a good husband, I thought. I had provided well. I had tamed my serious demons. I had stuck with Dr. K and followed the guidance I received. I had been totally faithful to Lynda. I loved her. I loved our children. I loved our life. Why couldn't she see how wonderful our life was?

I knew I wasn't perfect. I had to control my ego. I slipped up sometimes. Was I too preachy? Was I too demanding? Did too much of the old scamster still linger in me? I didn't know. I just knew the day Lynda told me she wanted a divorce was the worst day of my life, harder than the day my parents banged on my apartment door, tougher than the crash of 2008, more painful than falling out of that tree, though those might well come in as numbers 2, 3, and 4.

Lynda couldn't really explain it in a way that I understood, but she made one thing perfectly clear: She wasn't interested in counseling and wasn't interested in trying to save our marriage. She just wanted out. She had fallen out of love with me and wanted to go her separate way.

I was crushed and confused, but it was completely out of my control. We told the girls when they got back from sleepaway camp. They were obviously upset, though it was hard to gauge how deeply. They were as blindsided as I'd been and probably didn't even know themselves how they felt. Lynda and I both hired lawyers and prepared ourselves for the ugly battle ahead: The never-ending litigation. The super-sized legal bills. Armloads of anger, resentment, and bitterness. We'd both had friends who'd gone through divorces. Maybe it was for the better in the long run, but the experience, as far as I could tell, was always awful. It all sounded unspeakably horrible to me.

What was I supposed to say now? What was I supposed to do? What I really wanted was to slip away to Dr. K's basement office and ask him for guidance. I clearly needed someone to help me sort this out.

After the shock wore off, what I felt next was anger at Lynda. I wanted her to be accountable for her life choices, the way I'd been forced to be accountable for mine. "You want out of this marriage?" I said sharply during one especially tense exchange in our suddenly chilly kitchen. "Fine. We'll sell this beautiful house. You will move into a little apartment. I will get an apartment. The girls will bounce back and forth." I stared at her with contempt. "Is that what you want?

Your lawyer and my lawyer will fight over everything. Our kids will be the biggest losers. The legal fees will eat up half of everything we have, everything we built for the girls. Their security, their future, their home. That's what's going to happen."

That's what happens in most divorces where the people have children and property. There is a whole divorce industry making sure of it.

But I couldn't do it.

I just couldn't do it.

I couldn't allow what had happened to so many others happen to us. It just wasn't right.

As much as I wanted to hurt Lynda for hurting me, as much anger as I had in my heart, Dr. K was inside my head. He was saying the things he always said. Pause. Quiet. Never had I needed those words more. Respond, don't react. You never make anything better by making it worse. Through the blackness, through the resentment, through the heartache—the new me was shoving the old me aside.

I said to myself, "I want to do this with honor and dignity. Right now, I want to be the man I have become, not the man I worked so hard to leave in the past." I vowed that I wouldn't let this challenge— the biggest challenge of my life—drag me back into the hostility and bitterness that I'd worked so hard to climb out of.

As far as I was concerned, there was really only one question that should guide everything: "What is in the best interest of our children?"

I remembered what Dr. K had said to me: "If you say your children are the most important thing in your life, then you should live like they are." I was ready to do that. But what exactly did that mean?

One thing it meant, I knew, was that we had to find a better way to get divorced.

|||||||||||||||

I went to my lawyer and I said, "Let's do this as honorably as possible. Tell Lynda's lawyer we will give her a full and honest accounting of everything we own. She can take half of everything. I won't fight her on any of it. Taking a penny away from Lynda would be stealing from my children. I just won't do that."

I drew up a full financial statement: my salary, my bonuses, my investments, my businesses, my bank accounts, our house, and all our bills—everything. Lynda didn't believe me at first. She thought I must be hiding assets. She insisted on bringing in forensic accountants to see if I was trying to cheat. I was not. I included everything.

Dividing the assets was the easy part. Dividing our lives, I knew, would be much more complicated.

Where would Lynda move to? Where would I live? Would the girls go back and forth between us? Would they stay together? Would they have to change schools and make new friends? And what about Lola, the dog? What would happen to Lola?

Young lives are wrecked in many divorces. I love my daughters more than any other two people on earth. I had an idea.

"Let's not anyone move," I suggested. "Let's keep the house, at least until Brittany and Carly are out of high school. The girls will live in the house—in their house—all the time, just like they've been. They will keep their bedrooms and keep their friends and keep their school and keep their dog. They can live just like they've been living. Lynda and I can rotate in and out."

"A nesting agreement," the lawyers called it. I had never heard the term. We weren't the first, my attorney explained, to ever do this. But in the bitter annals of American divorce, it remained extremely rare.

We wrote up a detailed plan. We the parents agreed to switch on a regular schedule. If Lynda was in the house from Friday to Monday, I would arrive on Monday and stay until Wednesday. Lynda would come back on Wednesday and stay until Friday. I would arrive Friday, and then it was my weekend. And on and on it would go.

Even with the general outline agreed upon, it still took the lawyers more than a year to get us in front of a judge. This seemed ridiculously long to me, but everyone told me it was lightning speed for a New Jersey divorce. On January 7, 2015, we had a hearing in the Family Division of Superior Court in Monmouth County, Judge Angela White Dalton presiding.

I'd learned she was a new judge, but I sensed she was a no-nonsense person. As we waited for our case to be called, a downbeat parade of sad-looking men and women came and went from the courtroom.

Finally, it was our turn. After the judge said good morning to us and our lawyers, she told us that she had reviewed our agreement. I didn't know what she was going to say. "I see you are going to nest with these children," she said, pausing just long enough to let me wonder. "I think that's amazing."

Our no-nonsense jurist sounded quite emotional as she pressed on.

"I want to applaud you," she said. "It makes me well up, and I don't even know you. I think it's wonderful."

She cautioned that our approach might not be easy. "To the extent that you can continue, I hope it works," she said. "I really do. It shows that you were able to put your children above everyone."

That was the point, wasn't it?

"Your kids are going to grow up. They are going to get married. They're going to have graduations. They're going to have all kinds of things that you're both going to have to be a part of. It seems to the court that your efforts right now demonstrate you're looking forward to the future while being able to move forward with your lives."

It wasn't her job, Judge Dalton said, to pass judgment on whether our approach was fair or reasonable or downright crazy. But everything that happened in court that morning told me she was genuinely moved that we were willing to try. "I do want to thank you for the way you've conducted yourselves, and I wish more people would follow your example."

The judge took out a pen. She signed the judgment of divorce.

"Good luck to everyone," she said. Then, she reached for a tissue and dabbed the tears from her eyes.

|||||||||||||||||

The judge cried.

I'd never heard of a judge crying on the bench during a divorce case, but Judge Dalton cried.

Then, Lynda and I got busy making our nesting agreement and our unique divorce succeed for our family.

It wasn't always easy. I rented an apartment where I stayed when it wasn't my time to be with the girls. Lynda made arrangements of her own. From the beginning we tried not to be too rigid, accommodating each other's schedules and last-minutes emergencies. And we still did a lot as a family.

We went out together for birthday dinners. Lynda and I went together to school events and parent-teacher conferences. When Brittany started looking at colleges, we traveled together with her. And I am so proud to say, the girls really thrived.

Their lives after the divorce were really not so different from before. It's as if they have parents who go on business trips. Dad's away, Mom's at home—or vice versa. They have their friends. They have their school. They have their bedrooms. They have their dog. They have a family as close to intact as the realities of our lives can possibly allow.

I am proud to have been able to do that. I never could have done it alone.

AFTERWORD

PASSING IT ON

Life rolls on, as thrilling and as meaningful as it has ever been.

In the fall of 2016, my older daughter, Brittany, was applying to colleges. Brittany is a terrific student, like her younger sister Carly, and several excellent schools had already expressed interest in her. As part of the application process, she was asked to write essays on a variety of topics, academic and personal.

All the schools had an open-ended assignment, inviting the applicants to tell any story "that is so meaningful your application would be incomplete without it." Brittany went somewhere I'll bet few of the other applicants did. She opened her essay with *The Three Little Pigs* and the famous threat of their nemesis, the Big Bad Wolf: "I'll huff, and I'll puff, and I'll blow your house down!"

"I never sought to be compared to a pig from a fable," Brittany wrote. "It is not the most glamorous second identity. I guess the comparison isn't that far of a stretch, though, given that I have grown up in a brick house that has withstood many attempts to be 'blown down.' Over the years, my brick house has remained intact through events as severe as a hurricane and the demise of a relationship; it continues to shelter values, such as religions and people, that don't necessarily belong together.

"The greatest threat occurred during my freshman year of high school when my parents got divorced," she continued. "It was a fairly 'normal' divorce, other than that my sister and I, and my now divorced parents, have remained in the same brick house, making the divorce completely unconventional and somewhat defeating the entire purpose of separating in the first place. Although these terms did not necessarily make sense, I did not question their consequences, satisfied that I wouldn't have to leave the comfort of my own room and start fresh in a new home that contained none of my childhood memories.

"Even though my parents were no longer married, I did not expect much to change since our living standards remained completely the same. However, by living through this unique situation and witnessing my parents' selfless behavior, I have been impacted more than I would have been if my parents had followed the conventional style of divorce by moving us to two separate houses. My parents have constantly modeled a life of loyalty, commitment, responsibility, and above all stability, which has made our brick house so secure. Through their actions, I now recognize my own ability to put others before myself and to express commitment through my own actions, as well as the value of loyalty.

"As my parents continue to live together under one roof, even post-divorce, forming and maintaining relationships is an increasingly significant value that has been symbolized in my brick house. Just as my parents did not physically split up our home, I am loyal to my friends and family because strong relationships are important to me. Although my parents are divorced and our house can become bedlam at times, they still maintain an amiable relationship that has shown me how important strong bonds are in life, whether it be with family, friends, or those in my school community.

"Despite what might look like disruption in my life, I have always been able to remain focused and dedicated to my responsibilities and relationships. Just as the third little pig took the time to build a strong house that could withstand the wolf, my family and I have done the same.

Signed, Brittany Schmell."

IIIIIIIIIIIIIIII

We have come so far, all of us have, but I feel like I have only begun. Over time, my memories have shifted and grown sharper. I can still vividly recall the stunts that used to thrill and define me, as I used my cunning and my charm to insert myself into places I was never invited or supposed to be. I had amazing adventures, and I have proof. I see the reactions I still receive when I tell these stories. I got an early glimpse of where our world was heading—the rising celebrity culture, the excessively extravagant gesture, the carefully crafted media event. In some ways, I even helped to propel it.

Looking back, I can see that I really was the Forrest Gump, the Leonard Zelig, of my generation, the unknown person who turned up unexpectedly wherever the action was: Live Aid, the Grammys, Donald Trump's yacht, the Kremlin, the president's motorcade, the World Series, the Stanley Cup, and a nearly endless lineup of other era-defining locales and events.

I wouldn't give up those experiences for anything. I saw so much and so directly. I experienced things few civilians ever do. I had personal contact with some of the greatest figures of my time. And eventually I came to recognize how hollow and pointless so much of that was. It wasn't until I looked deep inside myself that I could clearly see the world.

That didn't happen by accident. And it never would have happened on its own. As my stunts got more extravagant and my deceptive talent continued to grow, my life was spiraling out of control. But I was blessed. Call it a higher power if you want to. Thanks to a fed-up woman and two loving parents, I was forced to confront reality. Then, some caring and competent professionals stepped in, led by the brilliant and humble Dr. Arthur Knauert.

Dr. K never got the public acclaim he deserved. He certainly didn't seek it. But his knowledge and his insights can still help to change the world. Spreading his understanding is one of the primary reasons, more than a quarter century after I first stepped into his modest basement office, that I felt compelled to write this book.

I'd have been happy letting my youthful adventures fade into the mists of memories. I could have shared my stories with a few close friends and the occasional shocked acquaintances and left it at that. Frankly, I wasn't eager to reveal the details of my own persistent cluelessness and my sputtering, slow-motion journey to maturity and adulthood. But something larger was at stake. I had knowledge that needed sharing. Thanks to Dr. K, I had arrived at important truths about the larger human condition and the ailments and limitations that dog millions, not just me. Inconsistent nurturing. Low self-esteem. The gentle hiding places that alcohol, drugs, and other addictions often provide. The self-destructive traps they leave for us. I learned all this from Dr. K. As the years rolled by, I felt a growing responsibility to share it with the world, even if that meant revealing uncomfortable secrets about myself.

I don't care so much about money anymore. Professional triumphs are satisfying, but they are not how I measure myself. I know what's important to me now. I love my friends and my family more than ever. I believe in kindness and empathy. And I want to spread these life-saving insights as widely as I possibly can. I think I showed great ingenuity when I was crashing the world's most exclusive venues. *The Uninvited* is a first but crucial step on the journey I am taking next. I want to help people who are fighting the battles I did—against insecurity, against insatiable ego, against diseased thinking, against low self-worth. I want to share my valuable tools.

These days, I devote many of my waking hours to what I increasingly see as my true life's work. Counseling others who are struggling. Talking to interested audiences and groups. Amplifying the life-saving principles that Dr. K revealed to me.

This is what I tell people: "My life is defined by the choices that I make. And the choices that I make are influenced by the attitudes and thinking that I keep. Unsober attitudes and thinking lead to poor choices. Sober attitudes and thinking lead to wise choices." That really sums up everything. There is a huge thirst out there for greater understanding. These insights keep saving lives wherever they go.

I don't have Dr. K to guide me anymore, not in the way I once did. But I have his eternal principles. Now you do too.

IIIIIIIIIIIIIII

Dr. K's fingerprints are all over everything I do now. He gave me the courage to go into the gym business when the stock market was tanking. He gave me the clarity necessary for handling my divorce. He gave me the knowledge I needed to carry on after he died. "You know exactly what to do," he told me, and he was right. I did. It's amazing, isn't it? The three toughest days of my life—when my parents turned up at my apartment, when the stock market crashed, when Lynda told me she wanted a divorce—also turned out to be three of the best days ever. My confusion turned into motivation. My pain turned into growth. I finally got ahold of myself. I gained deeper understanding, and I achieved things I never knew I could. All of that is inside me now.

Today, I keep a picture of Dr. K inside my wallet. It lives right next to Rabbi Schneerson's one-dollar bills. Both remind me of the journey I have taken and the new responsibility that I have: to do whatever I can to spread this message around.

When Brittany showed me her college essay, I was touched, of course. Every parent loves warm words from a child. Her words confirmed to me what Lynda and I had hoped to achieve, even at that deeply difficult time. I knew we had the power inside ourselves. We could do what was right. We could put aside the bitterness. We could accept the challenge Dr. K laid out for us and really put our children first. We could live up to the best of who we were. I wasn't expecting gratitude from my children. That wasn't the point. But I got teary all over again at Brittany's recognition.

I had to share it with someone.

I sent an email to Judge Dalton. In her line of work, I assumed she didn't get too many thank-you notes. I wanted her to know what together we had achieved.

In the subject line, I put "My daughter's college entrance essay." I attached what Brittany had produced.

Then I wrote: "Dear Judge Dalton, you may not remember me, but my name is Craig Schmell, and on 1/7/15 I appeared in front of your courtroom to finalize my divorce. At that time, you had tears in your eyes when you told the court how wonderfully my ex-wife and I handled a very difficult process, even commenting on the nesting agreement we established.

"I write to you today to show you how the fruits of our hard work and dedication—doing the right thing—has paid dividends beyond our wildest dreams. Attached is my daughter's college entrance essay, which she showed me last night for the very first time.

"I thought you would love reading it because you sit in a very difficult chair, having to watch such chaos and destruction in so many families. I hope this email and my daughter's essay confirm that it is possible to terminate a marriage with dignity and class, and I hope this gives you hope. As someone told me once: 'You never make anything better by making it worse.'"

"With respect, Craig Schmell."